Women and Irish diaspora identities

MANCHESTER
1824

Manchester University Press

Women and Irish diaspora identities

Theories, concepts and new perspectives

Edited by D. A. J. MacPherson and Mary J. Hickman

Manchester University Press
Manchester and New York
distributed exclusively in the USA by Palgrave Macmillan

Published by Manchester University Press
Oxford Road, Manchester M13 9NR, UK
and Room 400, 175 Fifth Avenue, New York, NY 10010, USA
www.manchesteruniversitypress.co.uk

Distributed exclusively in the USA by
Palgrave Macmillan, 175 Fifth Avenue, New York,
NY 10010, USA

Distributed exclusively in Canada by
UBC Press, University of British Columbia, 2029 West Mall,
Vancouver, BC, Canada V6T 1Z2

British Library Cataloguing-in-Publication Data
A catalogue record for this book is available from the British Library

Library of Congress Cataloging-in-Publication Data applied for

ISBN 978 07190 8947 3 hardback

First published 2014

The publisher has no responsibility for the persistence or accuracy of URLs for external or any third-party internet websites referred to in this book, and does not gurantee that any content on such websites is, or will remain, accurate or appropriate.

Typeset
by Helen Skelton, Brighton, UK
Printed in Great Britain
by CPI Group (UK) Ltd, Croydon, CR0 4YY

Contents

Part III: Irish women and the diaspora in the British world

Figures and tables

Abbreviations

ANIA	Americans for a New Irish Agenda
AOH	Ancient Order of Hibernians
BUF	British Union of Fascists
CICA	Council of Irish Counties Associations
CWL	Catholic Women's League
FLOL	Female Loyal Orange Lodge
GLA	Greater London Authority
GLC	Greater London Council
ILGO	Irish Lesbian and Gay Organisation
INO	Irish Nurses Organisation
IRA	Irish Republican Army
LOBA	Ladies' Orange Benevolent Association
LOL	Loyal Orange Lodge
NGO	non-governmental organisation
PFI	Pregnant from Ireland
STDF	Stepney Tenants' Defence League
UCM	Union of Catholic Mothers
UCW	Union of Catholic Women

Notes on contributors

Mary E. Daly is Professor of History and Principal of UCD College of Arts and Celtic Studies. She is the author of many books and articles on the history of nineteenth- and twentieth-century Ireland, including *Women and Work in Ireland* (1997); *The Slow Failure: Population Decline and Independent Ireland, 1920–1973* (2006); *The Irish State and the Diaspora* (2010).

Breda Gray is Senior Lecturer and Director of the MA in Gender, Culture and Society at the Department of Sociology, University of Limerick, Ireland. She has published widely on themes of gender, migration and diaspora including *Women and the Irish Diaspora* (Routledge, 2004). She is Principal Investigator for the IRCHSS-funded project 'The Irish Catholic Church and the politics of migration' (www.ul.ie/icctmp) and Co-Principal Investigator on the Government of Ireland, Irish Social Science Platform project 'Nomadic Work/Life and the Knowledge Economy' (http://nwl.ul.ie).

Mary J. Hickman is Professorial Research Fellow at the Centre for Irish Studies, St Mary's University, Twickenham, London, and Emeritus Professor of Sociology and Irish Studies at London Metropolitan University. She established the Irish Studies Centre at London Metropolitan University in 1986, where she was also Director of the Institute for the Study of European Transformations from 2002–2012. Her publications include *Migration and Social Cohesion in the UK* (co-authored with N. Mai and H. Crowley, Palgrave, 2012). She has been Visiting Professor at: New York University, Columbia University, the New School for Social Research, Victoria University, Melbourne, and University College Dublin. She is Chair of the campaign Votes for Irish Citizens Abroad (VICA) based in London.

S. Karly Kehoe is Lecturer in History at Glasgow Caledonian University. Her research focuses on gender, diaspora, religiosity and ethnicity in nineteenth and twentieth-century Scotland, Ireland and Canada. Her first book, *Creating a Scottish Church: Catholicism, Gender and Ethnicity in Nineteenth-Century Scotland* was published by Manchester University Press in June 2010.

D. A. J. MacPherson is Lecturer at the Centre for History, University of the Highlands and Islands and, prior to that, was most recently a Research Fellow at the John Hume Institute for Global Irish Studies, University College Dublin. He is currently researching women's associational culture within the Irish diaspora, with a particular focus on women in the Orange Order in Britain and Canada. He has published articles on Irish women's history and the Irish in Britain in *Irish Historical Studies*, *Women's History Review* and *Immigrants and Minorities*. His first book, entitled *Women and the Irish Nation*, was published by Palgrave Macmillan in 2012.

Jennifer Redmond is currently CLIR Postdoctoral Fellow and Project Director, The Albert M. Greenfield Digital Center for the History of Women's Education at Bryn Mawr College, Pennsylvania and was previously Irish Research Council for the Humanities and Social Sciences (IRCHSS) Postdoctoral Research Fellow (2009-2011) at the Department of History, NUI Maynooth. Her doctoral research on Irish women's emigration to Britain in the Free State period was completed at the School of Histories and Humanities, Trinity College Dublin in 2008 and her book on this subject, *Moving Histories*, is forthcoming. Her current postdoctoral research focuses on citizenship issues and Irish emigrants in Britain during World War Two.

Louise Ryan is Professor of Sociology and Co-Director of the Social Policy Research Centre at Middlesex University. Originally from Cork, she has a PhD in Sociology from University College Cork. She has published widely on varied aspects of migration and has a particular interest in social networks, transnational families and ethnic identities in the context of migration. Louise has under taken research on Irish migrants, Polish migrants and most recently on Muslim migrants and refugees in Britain. Her work has been published in *Sociology*, *Sociological Review*, *Journal of Ethnic and Migration Studies*, *Journal of Ethnic and Racial Studies* and *International Migration*. Her most recent book is *Gendering Migration* (co-edited with Wendy Webster, 2008). Louise is a member of the editorial board of *Sociology* and is a member of the ESRC review college.

Bronwen Walter is Professor of Irish Diaspora Studies at Anglia Ruskin University. She is internationally recognised for her research on Irish migration to Britain and the wider experiences of the Irish diaspora. Her academic publi-cations include a monograph *Outsiders Inside: Whiteness, Place and Irish Women*

(Routledge, 2001) and articles and chapters on a wide range of aspects of Irish emigration and settlement abroad. She has also made substantial contributions to policy and co-authored the widely cited report for the Commission for Racial Equality, *Discrimination and the Irish Community in Britain* (1997) (with Mary J. Hickman). Her report *Irish Emigrants and Irish Communities Abroad* was produced for the Irish Government Task Force on Policy Regarding Emigrants (2002). Her current research focuses on multi-generational Irish identities in England, Newfoundland and Australasia, and her particular interests lie in comparing trajectories of whiteness and Irishness, exploring English/Irish hybridities and examining linkages between genealogies and citizenship.

Charlotte Wildman is Lecturer in Modern British History at the University of Manchester, after also holding teaching posts at the University of Nottingham and University of Manchester. She is interested in urban culture in Northern England during the early twentieth century and, in particular, the ways in which women could perform a range of identities through their appropriation of consumer culture. Dr Wildman is currently completing her doctoral research for publication, including a monograph titled 'Soaring Skyward: Spectacular Urban Culture in Liverpool and Manchester, 1918–1939'. The next project looks in greater detail at Irish-Catholic women's experiences of modernity in interwar Liverpool.

INTRODUCTION

Irish diaspora studies and women: theories, concepts and new perspectives

D. A. J. MacPherson and Mary J. Hickman

Popular usage of the term 'Irish diaspora' has grown in parallel with the prolif-eration of academic studies that apply the term to any number of migrant or ethnic groups.[1] In an Irish context, during the 1990s President Mary Robinson was at the forefront of public discussion in which the 'Irish abroad' became the 'Irish diaspora'. Robinson's conception of an Irish diaspora embraced a diverse notion of national identity which, according to one of the contributors to this volume, embraced a re-imagining of 'belonging and identity based on diversity, multiple affiliations and multi-located identifications'.[2] As Robinson's successor as President, Mary McAleese introduced a gender dimension to debate about the Irish diaspora, talking in broad terms about the 'global Irish family'.[3] The aim of this book is to capture how scholars have begun to explore the nature of women's experience of the Irish diaspora and how this relates to recent theoret-ical debate about diaspora.[4]

While no longer one of Donald Akenson's 'great unknowns' of Irish migration history, and despite increasing scholarly attention,[5] women's experi-ences remain marginal in many general accounts of migration and diaspora. To take but one recent study of the Irish abroad, John Belchem's book on Irish-Catholics in Liverpool exemplifies this trend.[6] While briefly mentioning women, Belchem does not engage in a sustained analysis of their communal, social, religious and political activities in the city. Equally, little has been done to integrate women into the emerging scholarship on diaspora, transnationalism and Irish migration, including recent surveys in *Irish Economic and Social History* and *Immigrants and Minorities*.[7] This book aims to redress this scholarly imbalance by comparing Irish women's experience across the globe, setting this research in the context of recent theoretical developments in the study of diaspora. It is an interdisciplinary collection, featuring articles by scholars of Irish women and the diaspora in geography, history and sociology from across Britain and Ireland.

This book demonstrates the important role played by women in the construction of Irish diasporic identities, comparing Irish women's experience in Britain, Canada, New Zealand and the United States. It represents an important reassessment of historians' periodisation of the Irish diaspora, with a number of contributors assessing Irish women's experience during the early-mid and late part of the twentieth century.[8] This book builds on the engagement of women social scientists with the Irish diaspora and brings a significant collection of historical writings about women's experiences and identifications into this cross-disciplinary conversation. Importantly, it shifts discussion about women and the Irish diaspora away from the United States, and reasserts the importance of Britain for Irish women's migration, especially in the twentieth century.[9] Moreover, a number of contributors to this book consider how Irish women engage in the public life of the migrant community and thereby help to construct a diasporic identity, a significantly under-researched aspect in Irish diaspora studies.[10] We hope that this book will stimulate more interest in a conversation between other locations of the Irish diaspora and the dominant story about the USA and in the process bring into view the complexity and heterogeneity of Irish diasporan locations and experiences. Given its empirical and theoretical scope, then, this volume makes a significant contribution to the historical and contemporary analysis of Irish women and the diaspora. In addition to advancing theoretical considerations of Irish women and the diaspora, this book also contributes to the broader field of Irish feminist studies in the contributors' examination of identity, subjectivity and women's engagement with Irish public life in the diaspora. This introduction surveys the development of Irish diaspora studies, placing it in the context of recent work on gender, migration and Irish women and providing an indication of how the contributors to this book deepen our understanding of diaspora, boundaries and hybridity.

Historians and social scientists' use of the term 'diaspora' in Irish studies

In 2003, Kevin Kenny outlined some of the problems with the adoption of the term 'diaspora' in Irish ethnic and migration studies.[11] Surveying the broadening out of its definition from classical dispersion and exile from homeland to encompass any type of migration or ethnic identity, Kenny called for a more precise usage of the term that focused on exploring the transnational connections between migrants and the 'home' country and placing this in a comparative framework with other ethnic groups.[12] Kenny attached particular analytical value to exploring the notion of an Irish 'diasporic sensibility', in which the Irish abroad considered themselves to be connected through some measure of common, shared identity, providing examples of Irish nationalist political and trade union activity which demonstrated such a relationship between migrant community and home.[13] Kenny's critique of the term 'diaspora' is largely based on the recent broadening of the traditional usage of the concept by one school of thought within diaspora studies (see Breda Grey's chapter in this book) and he largely ignores the diasporic research and theories that have stemmed from cultural studies and anthropology.[14]

Other historians have echoed Kenny's skeptical and cautious use of the term 'diaspora'. Drawing together three leading historians of Irish migration, a 'symposium' in the journal *Irish Economic and Social History* examined how Irish emigration could be explored through the analytical framework of diaspora. Don MacRaild echoed many of Kenny's concerns, arguing that historians should concentrate on finding evidence to demonstrate the existence of networks of communication that facilitated and maintained a diasporic consciousness among Irish migrants.[15] Enda Delaney discussed the need to avoid any labelling of the Irish diaspora as a unitary identity, emphasising the necessity in recognising the diversity of Irishness abroad and its complex, 'ambiguous' relationship with the notion of homeland.[16]

Such an approach, focused on mentalities and a multiplicity of Irish identities indicates ways in which historians can engage with broader theoretical discussions of diaspora. Cultural anthropologists have argued since the 1990s that the term diaspora captures the way in which people can live their lives in many different locations, be they physical or imagined, and in doing so experience a sense of identity and subjectivity that is also multiple and hybrid. In their recent book *Diaspora and Hybridity*, Virinder Kalra, Raminder Kaur and John Hutnyk argue that it is more helpful to think of diaspora less as a group of people and more as a process through which migrants can connect places of residence to 'intimate or material connections to other places'.[17] They demonstrate how the work of Stuart Hall and Paul Gilroy are important to an understanding of diaspora that stresses the multiple belongings of identity, where it is possible to be *from* one place but *of* many others.[18] Avtar Brah's concept of 'diaspora space' captures the hybrid nature of diasporic identity that connects these multiple locations. Brah suggests that in the process of the encounter and mixing of different migrant identities with those of the long-term settled, a place of settlement such as Britain becomes a diaspora space in which 'the genealogies of dispersion' are intertwined with 'those of "staying put"'.[19]

In an Irish context, Mary Hickman has called for the more traditional comparative migration studies advocated by some of the historians discussed above to be integrated with the theoretical approaches of sociology, cultural studies and anthropology, which have produced what she describes as the 'post-modern concept of diaspora'.[20] Marc Scully has taken up such an approach, using empirical research on Irish identities in England to explore how theories of diaspora and transnationalism can be used to explain the constitution of individual identities.[21] Hickman has also advocated the salience of diaspora space as a concept for the revisitng of national (re)formations. This entails a re-examination of national (re)formations in order to scrutinise the impact of the presence of particular diasporas, and the confluence of many diasporas, on formatory moments or processes in the (re)configuration of specific nation states. The lens of diaspora space can access the ways in which the discourses, practices, hierarchies and identities of present day societies are layered on those of previous immigrations, prior encounters and the new social relations they inaugurated.[22]

This book aims to explore the place of Irish women in the diaspora using both theoretical and empirical perspectives. In particular, it reflects on the gendered nature of diasporic identity and how Irish women are situated in the complex nexus of identities between Ireland and the diasporan Irish.

Gender, migration and diaspora: theoretical approaches

Research on women, diaspora and diasporic identity is, though, still relatively underdeveloped. Much scholarly literature has appeared in the last thirty years exploring women's experience of migration and settlement.[23] Few, however, have focused on the gendered nature of diaspora or the experience women have had in developing a sense of diasporic identity. Instead, many valuable studies have examined how women's migration has been shaped by work and family. In particular, much research has concentrated on how women have become migratory in order to exploit the gendered nature of various labour markets, working in 'feminised domains' such as domestic and care work and aspects of the service industries.[24] Other studies argue that women's migration was largely shaped by family and family networks, further limiting the study of migrant women to private concerns of the home and to work that was largely considered gendered and unproductive.[25] When the concept of diaspora has been added to these types of study, the focus has tended to remain on a gendered definition of work and family.[26] While an important collection of interdisciplinary essays, edited by Marlou Schrover and Eileen Janes Yeo, has recently demonstrated the need to explore the more public aspects of women's migration, through associational culture, politics, citizenship and other areas, they too recognise the limitations of gendered readings of diaspora.[27] Yeo's essay, especially, captures how, in order to understand women's role in diaspora, it is necessary to focus attention on the family home as a site for the formation of ideas about 'homeland', a key component of some diasporic identities.[28]

Research on Irish women's experience of diaspora stands out, however, as leading the debate about the gendered nature of diaspora. The work of Bronwen Walter and Breda Gray, both contributors to this book, has demonstrated how concepts of diaspora can throw light on Irish women's lives abroad, from work on Irish women's 'invisibility' in Britain, to the gendered narratives of identity experienced by women in the Irish diaspora. In her book *Outsiders Inside* (2001), Walter argues that Avtar Brah's concept of 'diaspora space' is vital to understanding the complex identities and sense of belonging experienced by Irish women living in Britain and the United States, where they 'may be perceived as outsiders in their cultural affiliation as "Irish", and to patriarchal societies as women, but considered insiders as "white" people'.[29] Breda Gray has problematised notions of diaspora, using the concept to explore and subvert ideas about a unified Irish identity, either at home or abroad. She examines the lived experience of Irish women's lives in both Britain and Ireland and concludes that diasporic identities function in both countries. In Ireland, women's identities were shaped by the experience of family and friends in Britain. Echoing Gilroy's notion of 'double consciousness', Gray suggests that those who moved to the UK, through a process of 'displacement and hybridisation', experienced a diasporic identity that shifted constantly between the two countries. Moreover, these women's sense of belonging was shaped by the desire and possibility of returning to the 'homeland', demonstrating their 'roots' in Ireland and the 'routes' travelled between Ireland and Britain.[30] Louise Ryan's research has also been fundamental to expanding our understanding of Irish women's experiences of living in Britain across the length of the twentieth century. Although not engaging directly with concepts of diaspora, Ryan's important work does draw upon a number of theoretical perspectives, such as social network theory.[31]

Walter, Gray and Ryan, then, all indicate ways in which sociological, anthropological and cultural theories can be applied to the experience of Irish women in Britain, providing a necessary comparative framework, which is explored further in this book. Most recently, they have been involved in the first special edition of a journal devoted to Irish women and diaspora. While recognising the continued resonance of Akenson's characterisation of the absence of women in studies of the Irish diaspora, this volume of *Irish Studies Review* took as its point of departure post-'Celtic Tiger' Ireland and the renewed forms of migration that have occurred in recent years.[32] *Women and Irish Diaspora Identities* builds significantly on this research, having grown out of a symposium organised in conjunction with the John Hume Institute for Global Irish Studies at University College Dublin in 2010.[33] This event brought together some of the leading authorities on Irish women and diaspora with emerging historians in this area. The discussions that emerged from this symposium are reflected in this volume, especially the emphasis on how theoretical perspectives can inform our understanding of Irish women's migratory and diasporic experiences.

Overview and organisation of the book

This book is divided into three parts. The first groups together the chapters by Daly and Gray which introduce the key historiographical concepts and theoretical discussions of Irish women and diaspora. The second part explores case studies of Irish women in Britain, focusing on the 'medical diaspora', the role of religion in shaping a diasporic identity, and public displays of Irishness, discussed in chapters by Ryan, Wildman, Redmond and Hickman. The final part examines

Irish women's experience of diaspora in the British world, combining the chapters by Walter, Kehoe and MacPherson in an examination of Canada, Scotland and New Zealand.

Mary Daly opens the volume by surveying Irish female migrants and the Irish female diaspora since the famine. Daly considers the gendered nature of migration and the role women played in the construction of diasporic identities, through their work in the home, in the Catholic Church and in the under-researched arena of ethnic political organisations, suggesting many directions for future research. Focusing in particular on the migrant decision, Daly indicates important ways in which the Irish diaspora can be seen as gendered. Moreover, she argues that women's role in the articulation of diasporic identities could be fruitfully explored if scholars paid greater attention to associational culture, in which women played a key part in creating hybrid identities that connected different Irish diaspora locations.

Following Daly's historical framework, the chapter by Breda Gray provides an important theoretical exploration of the concepts of transnationalism and diaspora, considering how these ideas may be used as conceptual frameworks for the study of Irish women's migration. Gray makes a key distinction between the two terms, arguing that transnationalism may be used as a lens through which to frame questions about networks that transcend a national level, while diaspora, in the three approaches she identifies, is always about the politics of belonging, in particular diasporic notions of homeland. Drawing on Brubaker's recent theoretical work, Gray argues that diasporas are more a 'category of practice' than bounded groups. This chapter places her earlier research on Irish women in Britain and the Republic of Ireland during the 1990s in the context of the more recent theories of diaspora articulated by Sudesh Mishra that emphasise the de-territorialised and de-centered nature of diasporic subjectivities.[34] Gray explores how transnationalism and diaspora may be gendered, examining the heteronormative and nationalist framing of diaspora and how this may be challenged. To demonstrate the centrality of gender in diaspora as a 'category of practice' Gray draws on her own past research to offer examples of how nationalist heterosexual norms act on Irish women's aspirations and shape their lives in the diaspora. She also points to how the theoretical potential offered by diaspora can be identified in practice by focusing on where boundary erosion and hybridity occurs across the scales of nation-state, women's bodies and women's lives.

In Part 2, Louise Ryan develops this book's theoretical engagement and applies it to a case study of interviews with Irish nurses who arrived in Britain between the 1940s and 1980s, exploring in particular these women's relationship with Catholicism and how this shaped a diasporic Irishness. Ryan examines the sociological concept of boundaries and how it may be applied to Irish women's experience of religion in postwar Britain. She argues that religion was a key site on which Irish women in Britain negotiated their identity, functioning as a 'bright' and 'blurry' boundary which both helped their integration in their new home and differentiated them from Protestant Britain. In hospitals, Irish nurses were often drawn closer together by their shared Catholicism but their religion could also function as a source of tension with non-Catholic colleagues, who often disapproved of and obstructed mass attendance and other religious practices. In the wider Irish community, the church continued to function as a focal point for group identity. However, institutions like schools and the Irish Chaplaincy could also serve to exclude those who did not conform to certain expectations of morality and behaviour.

Charlotte Wildman's chapter also considers how the Catholic Church could be a focal point for women's Irish identity in Britain. Wildman examines the experience of Irish-Catholic women in interwar Liverpool, arguing that, contrary to much scholarship, their identity was shaped by modernity. During the late 1920s and early 1930s, the Catholic hierarchy in Liverpool became increasingly more relaxed about women's engagement with modernity and began to promote a specifically Catholic consumer culture. Moreover, this could be a public role for women, as demonstrated by the programme of 'Catholic Action' during the 1930s in Liverpool. Women were seen as the moral foundation of the Irish-Catholic community in the city and were given prominence in organisations such as the Union of Catholic Mothers and their campaign for Catholic education. Irish-Catholic women in Liverpool were encouraged by the Church to engage in specific types of paid work, such as nursing and teaching, and this, in turn, gave rise to a new mass consumer culture driven by women's waged labour. Wildman focuses in particular on the fascinating examples of the campaign to build a Catholic cathedral. Women were at the forefront of a very modern form of consumer culture that aimed to raise funds for Lutyens' grand design, while emphasising a particular form of gendered diasporic Irishness through the consumption of 'Cathedral Tea' and other products. This chapter, in its examination of fashion, shopping and household consumption, makes a significant contribution to scholarly understanding of the interaction between Catholicism, consumption and modernity in interwar Britain. Moreover, Wildman argues that it is important to consider the ways in which Irish women's diasporic identification was not just the product of late-twentieth-century modernity but was, instead, something produced by Irish-Catholic women living in interwar Liverpool.

Irish women's experiences during the mid-part of the twentieth century are taken up by Jennifer Redmond in her innovative use of new archival material, World War Two travel permits issued by the British and Irish governments. Redmond demonstrates the importance of individual level data in shaping our interpretation of Irish women's experience in Britain, exploring the diversity of their work in the medical profession in wartime. This 'medical diaspora' was a key part of Irish women's migration to Britain and indicates the economic and personal agency that these women had. Moreover, Redmond illustrates how Irish women who came to Britain as nurses, midwives or doctors, maintained diasporic ties to Ireland through the return visits that required these travel permit applications. Most of these women were single and returned to Ireland temporarily on holiday, illustrating the continuing importance of family networks in shaping a diasporic Irishness.

Mary Hickman's chapter concludes the section on the Irish diaspora in Britain with an examination of the layers of belonging and diasporic identities revealed by recent St Patrick's Day celebrations in London. Focusing on the concept of hybridity, and what produces points of communion and axes of dissonance across social divisions in an institutional setting, Hickman argues that the St Patrick's Day Festival in London demonstrates the multiple and disparate nature of the Irish diaspora in Britain. From 2002, the St Patrick's Day Festival encapsulated a 'diasporic dynamic' that was based largely on generational tension. While Irish women were prominent, both organising and participating in the events, gender did not emerge as a prominent basis of social divisions. The momentous symbolic importance of the restoration of Trafalgar Square to use by Irish organisations and the public claiming of the streets of central London that the parade represented produced no gender differentiations amongst the women and men on the Advisory Forum which organised the events. Instead, disagreement over the nature of the celebrations centred on generational differences, in which the dominance of a group of 1980s or more recent middle-class emigrants sometimes produced tensions with the second generation and the 1950s emigrants. Hickman, therefore, problematises our understanding of the place of Irish women in the diaspora and stresses the importance of being aware that gender difference is not always a prominent aspect in the formation and articulation of diasporic identities, and that specific gendered practices can be the basis of coalescence rather than division.

The final section of the book begins with a chapter by Bronwen Walter which explores themes of global and local interconnection in her analysis of the relationship between Irish women and other diasporic groups. Walter uses a comparative framework to consider the notion of 'placing' in the experience of Irish women abroad, comparing Irish women in Britain with other diasporic groups in Britain, examining Irish women's experience throughout the British world and contrasting Irish women with women of other diasporas. Walter argues that different scales of specific places are essential in understanding how identities are shaped, 'operationalising' Brah's concept of 'diaspora space' to examine the interactions between different diasporic groups. Walter analyses the experience of Irish women in Britain, Newfoundland and New Zealand, concluding with a comparison between the position of women in the Irish diaspora with that of Zainichi Korean women in Japan.[35] She begins by exploring the 'shared group spaces' that intersect the experiences of Irish and Jewish women settling in London from the late nineteenth century onwards, examining both their shared positioning and co-operation, as well as their competition and conflicts. Walter's comparison of different diasporic women demonstrates the importance of examining the Irish diaspora in a global context. She argues that identifying similarities and differences in the experiences of these apparently different groups highlights significant common factors and specificities which may otherwise go unremarked, and this chapter draws Irish women into global frameworks or multi-generational diasporic identities.

Karly Kehoe's chapter further addresses the experience of Irish women in the context of the British world, providing a comparative and multi-located study of the Irish diaspora.[36] Kehoe compares the contrasting experiences of Irish female religious in Canada and Scotland, demonstrating women's role in the construction of Irish diasporic identities in these different locations, connecting the global and the local. From her analysis of nineteenth-century convent archives, Kehoe argues that, while Irish nuns played a significant role in the promotion of an Irish-Catholic identity in Toronto, those in Scotland were marginalised and under-represented within the Scottish church. It highlights variations in diasporic experiences and reveals the importance of local circumstances and preoccupations in determining the extent to which the Irishness of the migrants was accepted or contested abroad. *Being* Irish in Scotland meant something very different to *being* Irish in Canada, despite the fact that there were many shared experiences that existed to help shape the global Irish diaspora.

The final chapter in this book considers the experiences of one of the most invisible groups in the Irish diaspora: Protestant women.[37] Jim MacPherson focuses on the experience of Irish Protestant women in the formation of diasporic communities through a case study of women's participation in the Orange Order in Canada during the first half of the twentieth century. Women's Orange lodges were established in Canada in 1889 and, by the mid-twentieth century, the Ladies' Orange Benevolent Association (LOBA) could claim over 30,000 members in almost all of Canada's provinces and territories. While the Orange Order across Canada became a pan-Protestant organisation over the course of the twentieth century, attracting members from Scottish and English backgrounds, the Orange Order retained a strong Irish element in many parts of Ontario, including Toronto, Hamilton and London. This chapter examines how members of the LOBA maintained a sense of Irish Protestant identity, focused on their associational life in female Orange lodges. While much theoretical literature has begun to recognise the gendered nature of diaspora formation, it does so largely within a framework dominated by considerations of family or personal networks that emphasise women's gendered role within the private sphere. Instead, by examining associational culture we can begin to explore how women could engage in the public life of the migrant community and thereby help to construct a diasporic identity.[38] Analysing the female Orange Order in Canada brings an important historical perspective to bear on diaspora strategies by considering how diasporas can be constructed through migrant women's associational networks. Drawing on Avtar Brah's concept of 'diaspora space', this chapter examines communication between migrants and their 'home' lodges in

Scotland which were published in the *Belfast Weekly News* and the Toronto *Sentinel*. These newspapers, together with the physical process of migration and return, helped to create a diasporic consciousness among both the Orangewomen in Canada and those who remained in Scotland and Ireland, demonstrating how diaspora strategies can incorporate a dynamic interaction between 'home' and migrant destination. Much as Mary Hickman's chapter demonstrates that gender is important for coalescence rather than difference in the context of the London St Patrick's Day parades, this final chapter also emphasises the varying ways in which gender features in the articulation of social relations within the Irish diaspora.

The essays in this collection consolidate a number of key areas in the field of Irish diaspora studies, demonstrating how the complexity of Irish diasporic identities is both gendered and must be explored through women's experiences as well as through men's and, in specific circumstances, more so. By engaging with current interdisciplinary theoretical debate, this book confirms the importance of Irish women and diaspora as a vibrant area of research which continues to lead broader discussions about the gendered nature of migration, diaspora, transnationalism, hybridity, identity and belonging. It breaks new ground in its theorisation of gender and diaspora and, through the various empirical case studies presented here, provides a number of possible directions for future research. This book demonstrates the need for greater research on the experiences of Irish women in Britain and throughout the British world, while also reassessing the dominant periodisation of the Irish diaspora through many contributors' focus on women's experience throughout the twentieth century. Moreover, the essays in this volume indicate the importance of comparative studies to future research on diaspora. Women's lived experience in the Irish diaspora was, and is, diverse and varied, and theories of diaspora help us to understand the gendered nature of diasporic lives and identities.

Notes

1 R. Brubaker, 'The "diaspora" diaspora', *Ethnic and Racial Studies*, 28 (2005), 1–19.
2 B. Gray, *Women and the Irish Diaspora* (London: Routledge, 2004), p. 35. See also D. N. Doyle, 'Cohesion and diversity in the Irish diaspora', *Irish Historical Studies*, 31:123 (1999), 411.
3 Gray, *Women and the Irish Diaspora,* pp. 150–8.
4 While all the contributors in this volume engage with theoretical discussions of the term 'diaspora', the aim of this book is not to provide an overarching, agreed definition of the term. For a useful recent survey of different approaches to use of the term, see K. Tölölyan, 'Diaspora studies: past, present and promise', Working Paper 55, April 2012, *Oxford Diasporas Programme* (Oxford: International Migration Institute, University of Oxford, 2012), available at www.imi.ox.ac.uk/pdfs/imi-working-papers/wp-55-2012-diaspora-studies-past-present-and-promise, accessed 12 May 2012.
5 The work of Louise Ryan, Breda Gray and Bronwen Walter, all contributors to this

volume, has been instrumental in developing our understanding of Irish women and the diaspora.

6 J. Belchem, *Irish, Catholic and Scouse: The History of the Liverpool Irish, 1800–1939* (Liverpool: Liverpool University Press, 2007).

7 'Symposium: perspectives on the Irish diaspora', *Irish Economic and Social History*, 33 (2006), 35–58; Special Issue on 'Irish migration, networks and ethnic identities since 1750', *Immigrants and Minorities*, 23 (2005). As Roger Swift and Sheridan Gilley have written, the lack of scholarly attention given to women remains one of the 'failures of the historiography of the Irish in Britain'. R. Swift and S. Gilley, 'Irish identities in Victorian Britain', *Immigrants and Minorities*, 27 (2009), 131–2. In a welcome recent development, Don MacRaild's second edition of his survey of the Irish in Britain does include a chapter on 'Gender and Ethnicity', which draws in particular on the work of Louise Ryan. See D. M. MacRaild, *The Irish Diaspora in Britain, 1750–1939* (Basingstoke: Palgrave Macmillan, 2011), pp. 141–57.

8 For an example of the focus on nineteenth-century Irish migration, see the Special Issue on 'Irish identities in Victorian Britain', *Immigrants and Minorities*, 27 (2009).

9 See, for example, J. Nolan, 'Women's place in the history of the Irish diaspora: a snapshot', *Journal of American Ethnic History*, 28 (2009), 76–81.

10 For a recent example of research that seeks to explore more public aspects of gender, migration and diaspora, see M. Schrover and E. J. Yeo (eds), *Gender, Migration and the Public Sphere, 1850–2005* (London: Routledge, 2010).

11 K. Kenny, 'Diaspora and comparison: the global Irish as a case study', *Journal of American History*, 90 (2003), 134–62.

12 *Ibid.*, 150. For a useful overview of different definitions and typologies of diaspora, see R. Cohen, *Global Diasporas: An Introduction*, 2nd edn (London: Routledge, 2008), especially pp. 159–74, where Cohen discusses the complex and multiple 'strands' that constitute a diaspora.

13 Kenny, 'Diaspora and comparison', p. 143.

14 For a further example of how an historian has applied a limited theoretical under-standing of 'diaspora' to the study migrant groups, see S. Constantine, 'British emigration to the empire-commonwealth since 1880: from overseas settlement to diaspora?', *Journal of Imperial and Commonwealth History*, 31 (2003), 16–35 and for a critique of his approach, see D. A J. MacPherson, 'Migration and the female Orange Order: Irish Protestant identity, diaspora and empire in Scotland, 1909–1940', *Journal of Imperial and Commonwealth History*, 40:4 (2012), 619–42.

15 D. M. MacRaild, '"Diaspora" and "transnationalism": theory and evidence in expla-nation of the Irish world-wide', *Irish Economic and Social History*, 33 (2006), 51–8.

16 E. Delaney, 'The Irish diaspora', *Irish Economic and Social History*, 33 (2006), 45.

17 V. S. Kalra, R. Kaur and J. Hutnyk, *Diaspora and Hybridity* (London: Sage, 2005), p. 29.

18 *Ibid.* S. Hall, 'Cultural identity and diaspora', in J. Rutherford (ed.), *Identity: Community, Culture, Difference* (London: Lawrence and Wishart, 1990), pp. 222–38; P. Gilroy, '"It ain't where you're from; it's where you're at…": the dialectics of diasporic identification', *Third Text*, 5 (1991), 3–16.

19 A. Brah, *Cartographies of Diaspora: Contesting Identities* (London: Routledge, 1996), p. 209.

20 M. J. Hickman, '"Locating" the Irish diaspora', *Irish Journal of Sociology*, 11 (2002), 16.

21 M. Scully, 'The tyranny of transnational discourse: "authenticity" and Irish diasporic identity in Ireland and England', *Nations and Nationalism*, 18 (2012), 122.

22 M. J. Hickman, 'Diaspora space and national (re)formations', *Éire-Ireland*, 47:1 & 2 (2012), 19–44.

23 See, for example, K. M. Donato, D. Gabaccia, J. Holdaway, M. Manalansan, P. R. Pessar, 'A glass half full? Gender in migration studies', *International Migration Review*, 40 (2006), 3–26; S. M. Sinke, 'Gender and migration: historical perspectives', *International Migration Review*, 40 (2006), 82–103; H. Lutz, 'Gender in the migratory process', *Journal of Ethnic and Migration Studies*, 36 (2010), 1647–63; D. Gabaccia, *From the Other Side: Women, Gender, and Immigrant Life in the U. S., 1820–1990* (Bloomington: Indiana University Press, 1994); F. Anthias and G. Lazaridis, *Gender and Migration in Southern Europe: Women on the Move* (Oxford: Berg, 2000).

24 For an overview of this, see Lutz, 'Gender in the migratory process', p. 1652; J. Andall, *Gender, Migration and Domestic Service: The Politics of Black Women in Italy* (Aldershot: Ashgate, 2000); H. Lutz (ed.), *Migration and Domestic Work: A European Perspective on a Global Theme* (Aldershot: Ashgate, 2008); J. M. Moya, 'Domestic service in a global perspective: gender, migration and ethnic niches', *Journal of Ethnic and Migration Studies*, 33 (2007), 529–40.

25 M. Boyd, 'Family and personal networks in international migration: recent developments and new agendas', *International Migration Review*, 23 (1989), 638–70. Hannah Lutz discusses how areas of women's labour, such as domestic work, have become defined as non-productive, drawing on the work of Carolyn Steedman in her book *Labour Lost: Domestic Service and the Making of Modern England* (Oxford: Oxford University Press, 2009). See Lutz, 'Gender in the migration process', 1649 and P. Hondagneu-Sotelo, 'Feminism and migration', *Annals of the America Academy of Political and Social Science*, 571 (2000), 107–20.

26 See, for example, the chapter on 'Gender and diasporas' in J. E. Braziel, *Diaspora: An Introduction* (Oxford: Blackwell, 2008), pp. 66–84. Louise Ryan's work on family networks in migration has been instrumental in problematising the domestic focus of much research in this area. In particular, she has demonstrated how the very breadth of such family networks, incorporating siblings, aunts, cousins and other relatives, was central to migrant women's access to work and social activity outside of the home. See, for example, L. Ryan, 'Family matters: (e)migration, familial networks and Irish women in Britain', *Sociological Review*, 52:3 (2004), 360.

27 Schrover and Yeo (eds), *Gender, Migration and the Public Sphere*.

28 E. J. Yeo, 'Gender and homeland in the Irish and Jewish diasporas, 1850-1930', in Schrover and Yeo (eds), *Gender, Migration and the Public Sphere*, p. 15, 17.

29 B. Walter, *Outsiders Inside: Whiteness, Place and Irish Women* (London: Routledge, 2001), p. 14.

30 B. Gray, 'Gendering the Irish diaspora: questions of enrichment, hybridisation and return', *Women's Studies International Forum*, 23 (2000), 167–85. Here, Gray refers to the influential work of anthropologist James Clifford. See J. Clifford, 'Diasporas', *Cultural Anthropology*, 9 (1994), 302–38. See also Gray, *Women and the Irish Diaspora*.

31 For examples of Ryan's work which engages with social network theory in exploring the experience of Irish women in Britain, see L. Ryan, 'Migrant women, social networks and motherhood: the experiences of Irish nurses in Britain', *Sociology*, 41 (2007), 295–312; L. Ryan, 'How women use family networks to facilitate migration: a comparative study of Irish and Polish women in Britain', *History of the Family*, 14 (2009), 217–31.

32 E. McWilliams and B. Walter, 'New perspectives on women and the Irish diaspora', *Irish Studies Review*, 21:1 (2013), 1–5.

33 The editors would like to thank the John Hume Institute for Global Irish Studies at UCD for hosting this event. In particular, the help and support of Brian Jackson was very much appreciated.

34 See S. Mishra, *Diaspora Criticism* (Edinburgh: Edinburgh University Press, 2006).

35 For the utility of the multi-generational approach, see T. J. Meagher, *Inventing Irish-America: Generation, Class and Ethnic Identity in a New England City, 1880–1928* (Notre Dame: Notre Dame University Press, 2001).

36 D. H. Akenson, *The Irish Diaspora: A Primer* (Belfast: Institute of Irish Studies, Queens University Belfast, 1996).

37 *Ibid.*, pp. 157–88. Recent examples of research on Irish Protestant identities include S. Morgan and B. Walter, '"No, we are not Catholics": intersections of faith and ethnicity among the second-generation Protestant Irish in England', in M. Busteed, F. Neal and J. Tonge (eds), *Irish Protestant Identities* (Manchester: Manchester University Press, 2008), pp. 171–84 and W. Jenkins, 'Ulster transplanted: Irish Protestants, everyday life and constructions of identity in late Victorian Toronto', in Busteed *et al.*, *Irish Protestant Identities*, pp. 200–20.

38 For a limited recognition that women could contribute to the process of diaspora formation through associational life, see M. Schrover and F. Vermeulen, 'Immigrant organisations', *Journal of Ethnic and Migration Studies*, 31 (2005), 823–32.

PART I
Concepts and theories

1

Irish women and the diaspora: why they matter

Mary E. Daly

Resolving to do something to better the circumstances of her family, the young Irish girl leaves her home for America. There she goes into service, or engages in some kind of feminine employment. The object she has in view – the same for which she left her home and ventured to a strange country – protects her from all danger, especially to her character: that object, her dream by day and night, is the welfare of her family, whom she is determined, if possible to again have with her as of old. From the first moment she saves every cent she earns – that is, every cent she can spare from what is absolutely necessary to her decent appearance. She regards everything she has or can make as belonging to those to whom she has unconsciously devoted the flower of her youth, and for whom she is willing to sacrifice her woman's dearest hopes. To keep her place, or retain her employment, what will she not endure? Sneers at her nationality, mockery of her peculiarities, even ridicule of her faith.[1]

The poor Irish emigrant girl may possibly be rude, undisciplined, awkward – just arrived in a strange land, with all the rugged simplicity of her peasant's training: but she is good and honest. Nor, as she rapidly acquires the refinement inseparable from an improved condition of life, and daily association with people of cultivated manners, does she catch the contagion of the vices of the great centres of wealth and luxury. Whatever her position – and it is principally among the humble walks of life the mass of the Irish are still to be found – she maintains this one noble character-istic – purity. In domestic service her merit is fully recognised.[2]

Women have featured, albeit intermittently, in writings about Irish emigration long before historians – inspired by second-wave feminism – began to focus their scholarly efforts in that direction. However in the past Irish women emigrants were commonly found in the records of poorhouses, charities, or in censorious accounts depicting poverty or a lifestyle deemed unacceptable to the norms of respectable womanhood, bare-breasted, drunken, brawling, slatternly women. John Francis Maguire's account, written in 1868, can be seen as an attempt to provide a more positive alternative version. Maguire set out to examine how the Irish emigrants were faring in America, given the conflicting reports that were reaching Ireland; whether Irish–Catholic emigrants were abandoning religious practice, and how the Irish in America regarded the British government. Like many of his successors, he was concerned about the moral and physical dangers associated with city life, especially for young women, and with the consequences of a predominantly Catholic peasantry migrating to a country where Catholicism was a minority religion. Maguire wrote of the moral dangers that emigration presented for Irish women – both on the long sea passage, and when they reached America. He recounted how 'a young and handsome Irish girl who was lately trapped into hiring, in a Western city, with a person of infamous character', was rescued by an older, wiser Irish woman and taken to a refuge run by the Sisters of Mercy.[3] Despite trumpeting the virtue of Irish women – one bishop described them as the 'salt of the earth' – he conceded that 'in some, yet comparatively few, places in America a certain percentage of women of bad repute are necessarily of Irish origin'.[4] However as further proof of their virtue and their contribution to the Catholic Church he wrote at length about the role of Irish religious sisters in founding and running Catholic hospitals, providing expert nursing care – including the care of soldiers during the civil war – and their involvement in Catholic schools and orphanages.

By the mid-twentieth century the locus of most descriptions of Irish emigrants had moved from North America to Britain: Britain was the principal destination for Irish emigrants from the 1880s, and with the introduction of restrictions on US immigration in the 1920s and the onset of the great depression in 1929, emigration to the USA fell sharply. Yet until the 1960s the profile of Irish women emigrating to Britain was not dramatically different to that of Irish emigrant women in the United States almost a century earlier: they continued to be concentrated in domestic service and hotel work (also mentioned by Maguire), though a growing number were migrating in order to train and work as nurses. In the mid-twentieth century Irish parents continued to dispatch daughters in their mid-teens to a foreign country in the expectation that their remittances would help support the family back home, and church and state continued to express fears at the moral dangers facing young Irish women living and working in alien cities. Maguire's 'person of infamous character' was now succeeded by the unmarried Englishman who lured an unsuspecting Irish girl into a job as a children's nurse, in a home that turned out to lack both wife and child.[5] Whereas Maguire wrote of the need for congressional legislation to protect female passengers from sexual advances during the transatlantic crossing,[6] Irish clergy were demanding that the Irish government should ban the emigration of young women under sixteen years of age.[7]

By the middle of the twentieth century, however, there was growing criticism within Ireland directed at the numbers of young single women who were emigrating and their motives for leaving. Insofar as emigrants had been criticised within Ireland in earlier times, the criticism did not specify gender, or it was directed towards men. By the mid-twentieth century however, while the 'angels' described at length by Maguire hadn't entirely disappeared, the category was increasingly reserved for Irish nurses or religious sisters. Politicians, senior officials and clergy regularly expressed concern about the moral dangers to female emigrants, and many of these statements showed little confidence that these young women had the capacity to withstand these temptations.[8] Part of this growing concern reflects a greater awareness of some of the more distressing aspects of emigration: English Catholic charities made Irish politicians and the Irish Catholic hierarchy fully aware of the numbers of single Irish women who travelled to England to give birth in search of anonymity, and these charities also made the Irish authorities fully aware of the costs of caring for these women and their infants.[9] Another source of concern was the sharp fall in the numbers of women in rural Ireland: in 1951 there were 868 women per 1000 men, and the 'flight of the girls' was often blamed for the low rate of marriage.[10] The gratitude that Maguire had expressed for the personal sacrifice made by many female emigrants was increasingly replaced by critical comments as to their motives. There was a growing opinion that Irish female emigrants were leaving for personal fulfilment, career ambitions or perhaps marriage. *The Commission on Emigration* summarised the position as follows:

> Although female emigration, like male, is the result of a variety of causes, the purely economic cause is not always so dominant. For the female emigrant improvement in personal status is of no less importance than the higher wages and better conditions of employment abroad and some of the evidence submitted to us would suggest that the prospect of better marriage opportunities is also an influence of some significance. Large numbers of girls emigrate to domestic service in Great Britain because they consider that the wages, conditions of work and also the status of domestic service in this country are unsatisfactory. Many others emigrate because of the opportunities of obtaining factory or office work are better than here, and in the nursing profession numbers leave the country because the remuneration, facilities for training, pension schemes and hours of work in this country are considered to be unattractive.

This rather academic summary does not reflect the much more forthright views expressed by some members of the Commission during the course of collecting evidence. When members were taking oral evidence from the Irish Housewife's Association, statistician Roy Geary interjected 'it is probably true that large numbers of men are forced through unemployment and poverty to emigrate. In the case of women, emigration is largely just the result of a desire for change'. When Stanley Lyon, another statistician and member of the Commission, visited a dancehall in England frequented by many Irish emigrants, he was horrified to see that many men and some women were under the influence of drink; he described the women as coming from 'very low stratums of life', 'mostly from the west'. At another point during his visit to England he noted that the men were 'all of good type', the girls of 'much lower class'. This stereotyping was not unique to Irishmen: an official of the British Ministry of Labour in Lancashire reported that 'while Irish men gave little trouble, girls were either very good or very bad; there was no middle way'.[11] The impressionistic evidence given above, which straddles two centuries and both sides of the Atlantic, shows that descriptions of Irish female emigrants are replete with gender, religious and racial discourse, and furthermore that women's emigration is viewed somewhat differently to emigration by men. So, one key question that must be addressed is what were/are the differences? And, second, what does this tell us about Irish women's lives, Irish diasporas and perceptions of Irish womanhood?

Emigration is one of the central and enduring realities of modern Ireland. The origins of modern mass emigration can be traced to the early eighteenth century; Ireland, unique among modern nations underwent approximately one century of sustained population decline, which was caused by emigration. In 1881 40 per cent of those born in Ireland were living outside the country; in 1911 the proportion was 33 per cent.[12] Women have accounted for up to half of Irish emigrants since the mid nineteenth century, and they have formed a significant cohort of emigrants irrespective of destination.[13] Donald Akenson has used the term, 'The great unknown' for the title of a chapter on Irish female emigration, where he identified six distinct categories of female emigrants, each reflecting specific strategies of emigration and different stages in a female lifecycle: widows with dependent children; married women emigrating with husband and children; married women with a spouse but no children; young dependent single women emigrating with one or more family members; single adult women of marriageable age; and older single women.[14] Whereas Jewish women – the only other ethnic community with roughly equal numbers of men and women emigrating during the late nineteenth century – generally travelled as part of a family group – as wives, daughters or sisters, and many of them as dependent children[15] – by the 1870s Akenson notes that the majority of Irish female emigrants could be classified as single adult women of marriageable age, generally travelling alone. Between 1855 and 1914 the proportion of emigrants to North America aged 15–24 ranged from one-third to 44 per cent and girls tended to emigrate at a somewhat earlier age than boys.[16] It is arguably this long-established pattern of Irish single women emigrating and commonly leaving their family behind that gives unique significance and colour to their history, and it also opens up considerable scope for analysis of their motivation and the moral hazards which they might face. Yet despite much recent historical research, many aspects of women and the diaspora continue to justify Akenson's description of 'the great unknown'; most specifically the difficulties in tracking second and subsequent generations of Irish women (and indeed men) in Britain, especially the descendants of those who emigrated prior to 1914. This chapter does not claim to make known the unknown; neither does it profess to provide a comprehensive overview of Irish women and the diaspora. Drawing on extant research into Irish female emigration, it attempts to highlight some of the key debates with respect to women's motives for emigrating: were emigrating women making a dash for freedom, or meeting family needs and expectations? Were they seeking economic independence or trying to improve their marriage prospects? And did emigrant women preserve and transit Irish cultural values in their new homes, or were they to the fore in promoting assimilation?

While Maguire and much of the later literature focused on Catholic emigration, most of the earliest Irish women emigrants were Protestant, from Ulster Scots families, and the story of Protestant women emigrants, though less prominent in the literature, is also significant, if perhaps less burdened with religious, national and perhaps even gender stereotypes. Mass emigration from Ireland to North America began in the eighteenth century with the migration of indentured servants, mainly from Ulster, although at this stage women emigrants would have been very much a minority; women accounted for only 20–30 per cent of indentured servants in colonial Pennsylvania. Nevertheless, already in the eighteenth century, women were emigrating to North America, either alone, or as head of a household travelling with young children. Miller *et al.*'s unrivalled study of emigration to colonial America records the story of Ann Dougherty, who in 1754 had transported herself and three small children from Ireland to Pennsylvania, and to cover the cost of the journey was 'obligded' to bind her children as servants to the captain of the ship. He had sold one son to a trader in Virginia – i.e. outside Pennsylvania – without going through the proper legal process; in 1760 she petitioned the court to have him returned.[17] As the cost of emigration fell in the 1830s and 1840s, and the numbers emigrating grew sharply, the proportion of emigrants who were women steadily increased: from one-third of emigrants to North America in the 1820s, to half by 1845, the eve of the famine. Robert Kennedy has suggested that from 1881 until the 1960s women accounted for a majority of emigrants from Ireland, except during periods of war, as when Irish agricultural techniques were undergoing very rapid change as they did in the 1950s, with a severe fall in the number of male workers and therefore higher male emigration.[18]

Chain migration, with a fare being paid by a family member who had already emigrated, and emigrants travelling to a place where family or friends and neighbours had already settled, was common for both women and men. In turn they were expected to finance future emigrants and to offer some initial support when they arrived. Few Irish emigrants were funded by state or landlords, but there were exceptions: Akenson writes of the 'active importation of women' by British colonies in Australia, New Zealand and South Africa.[19] Fifty thousand pauper women inmates of Irish workhouses were assisted in emigrating to north America between 1840 and 1870. Four thousand female (famine) orphans were given subsidised passages from Irish workhouses to Australia. In a colony with an acute shortage of young women, they were seen as potential servants and/or wives and the majority of Irish emigrants on assisted passage to Australia from the 1840s to the 1870s were women.[20]

Many patterns established in the nineteenth century persisted into the second half of the twentieth century. Women continue to account for approximately half of all emigrants from Ireland. From 1926 until 1996 female and male net emigration from independent Ireland was almost identical, though the proportions varied over the decades. For Northern Ireland the post-1921 patterns were somewhat different, with higher male emigration in the years after World War Two, but in the later years of the twentieth century almost equal numbers of women and men were leaving Northern Ireland.[21] Emigrant women continued to be young and single. In the mid-nineteenth century Irish women emigrated to Britain at an earlier age than Irish men because they had fewer prospects of finding paid work, however menial, in rural Ireland; this was also the case a century later.[22] The overwhelming majority settled in cities, where they found work as domestic servants or other forms of personal service, and occasionally as factory workers, although by the 1950s a growing number were finding work in nursing and teaching, often training in these professions after they emigrated because financial and educational barriers to entry were lower in Britain than in Ireland. Women were more likely to remain settled in large cities than men, who might move to take jobs in more remote places, in construction or mining. By 1860, 57 per cent of Irish-born residents of New York City were women.[23] In 1951 one-third of Irish men resident in Britain were in the greater London area, compared with 44 per cent of Irish-born women.[24]

One of the key questions that must be addressed is to what extent the motives and experience of Irish female immigrants differed from men's? The vast numbers of emigrants, and the diversity of religion, education, time of leaving and destination, suggest that sweeping generalisations should be avoided. There is a dramatic difference in life history and motivation between the story of Agnes (later known as Kim) O'Shea, a UCD medical graduate, who emigrated in the 1940s to take up a position in a Lancashire hospital, and Mary Malone from County Waterford, a scrubwoman in nineteenth-century New York, who was poorly paid because she lacked any skills in cookery or laundry and fine ironings.[25] While looking at the bigger aggregate picture, it is vital not to lose sight of these differences.

Nevertheless women earned less than men regardless of whether they lived in Ireland, Britain, or North America. Pregnancy, childbirth, early widowhood, or abandonment by men were all-too-common occurrences in women's lives, regardless of location. Women and children were more likely than men to become dependent on charity and public welfare. In the late eighteenth and early nineteenth centuries two-thirds of those applying to almshouses in Philadelphia were women, as were one-third of Irish applicants (a significantly higher figure than the proportion of Irish in the city who were women).[26] In mid-nineteenth-century Liverpool, women constituted almost two-thirds of those relieved by St Mary's Conference of the Society of St Vincent de Paul, which was run by Irish emigrants and catered for their needs.[27] In New York City the charity of Our Lady of the Rosary cared for 60,000 Irish immigrant women from 1883 until the 1960s. Irish women emigrants appear to have been at greater risk of imprisonment or confinement in a mental hospital than native-born women,[28] though as yet it is unclear whether Irish women emigrants were at greater risk than emigrant Irish males. Yet despite the strong evidence relating to destitute and needy women emigrants, there is a strong current in the histo-riography which suggests that, on balance, emigration was of greater benefit to women than to men, mainly because of the poor opportunities that Ireland offered them.

David Fitzpatrick has described emigration as 'female escapology': 'For those women who left Ireland, the nineteenth century was often a time of triumph rather than subjection'.[29] Kerby Miller has suggested that the status of Irish women, never high, deteriorated after the famine, because the economic value of female labour declined with the collapse of domestic textiles and the shift from tillage – which involved some women's work in the fields – to pasture, where women's role was limited to milking cows and making butter. 'Moreover, as arranged marriages became near universal, women lost even the freedom to choose their own mates, while the dowry system transformed them from independent personalities into a species of closely guarded property'. A declining marriage rate (approximately one-quarter of adults never married) and later marriages meant that a growing number of women married much older husbands in 'loveless "May-December" matches', ending up as 'middle-aged widows who projected frustrated affections on sons and bitter jealousy on dangers and prospective daughters in law'. Miller is one of many historians who suggests, that in such circumstances, emigration had much to offer to Irish women: the prospect of economic independence, marriage without the need for a parental dowry, or flight from moral disgrace and consignment to the unmar-riageable, because she had given birth to a child outside marriage.[30] Miller's overall thesis is that many Irish-Catholic emigrants carried with them to the US a pre-modern, passive value system, which predisposed them to view emigration as exile, and they continued to regard the US and American industrial urban society in an ambivalent manner. However he suggests that the better economic prospects helped those from the most disadvantaged backgrounds to overcome homesickness and adopt a more positive attitude. 'Female emigrants seemed especially prone to make realistic assessments of America's comparative advan-tages, less likely than husbands or sons to cling to old customs or romanticize the society left behind'.[31] Yet in a later article, Miller – writing with David Doyle and Patricia Kelleher – adds significant qualifications to the more general assump-tions given above, specifically the superior status of women in pre-famine Ireland, or that women's status deteriorated after the famine watershed.[32]

If we make the assumption that emigration offered women significant benefits over remaining in Ireland, what were Irish women seeking from emigration: independence and a career, or marriage? The career/marriage options pop up throughout the literature with the generally unstated assumption that they were mutually exclusive options. Yet given the declining marriage rate in post-famine Ireland, especially rural Ireland, and the importance attached to dowries and arranged matches, it is evident that better marriage prospects, or the freedom to choose a marriage partner, might equally be one of the factors driving male emigration. A secondary question is whether women's motives for emigrating were individualistic or framed within the context of family needs and a family strategy.

Hasia Diner described migration to the USA as 'a "liberating" experience for Irish women. They consciously had chosen to leave a society that offered them little as women to embrace one that proffered to them greater opportunities'. Irish women opted for domestic service 'not only because it blended in with their views of marriage and family but because it offered them a chance to earn money and save as well as providing them with a first-hand peek at how Americans lived'. Diner described Irish women emigrants as civilising Irish emigrant families, transmitting the lifestyle and ambition of upward social mobility to new emigrant families.[33] Janet Nolan agrees with some elements of this thesis, notably the role of domestic service in introducing Irish women emigrants 'to the refinements of the middle-class way of life', thereby enabling Irish mothers 'to speed the assimilation of their American-born children'. But Nolan, unlike Diner suggests that for women in post-famine Ireland emigration to America 'represented a recovery of an opportunity once lost', rather than something new; emigrant women were 'discarding their newly subservient and marginal positions in their home communities, not their traditional expectations'- specifically expectations of early marriage.[34] Perhaps a balance between the two interpretations might be best: we should not overstate the 'liberating' experience offered to a young Irish emigrant on becoming a servant in a Boston middle-class household, yet emigration offered something other than the 'recovery of an opportunity once lost'. Whether a young Irish women in her mid-teens, who emigrated from the west of Ireland in the late nineteenth century chose to leave, or chose her destination is however questionable; this may well have been decided for her by family, both in Ireland and overseas. As for marriage prospects, in 1911, 27 per cent of men and 25 per cent of women aged 45–54 living in Ireland had never married, compared with 22 per cent of Irish-born men and 16 per cent of Irish-born women of similar age in the United States (in 1910). This suggests that emigration increased marriage prospects, though not dramatically, and the proportion remaining single was higher than for native-born Americans and for most immigrant communities, which has led some writers to suggest that Irish emigrants brought their marriage patterns with them when they emigrated. However marriage rates in larger US cities were significantly lower than the US average; in 1910, 17 per cent of native-born

American men and 23 per cent of native-born American women living in the ten largest cities had never married; the comparable figure for Irish emigrants was 18 per cent and 15 per cent.[35] The argument that Irish women emigrated in search of a husband figured prominently in discussions about emigration in mid-twentieth-century Ireland, yet paradoxically, as Spencer shows, based on 1951 Census returns, Irish-born men who emigrated to England saw a much greater increase in their marriage prospects and much earlier marriages than if they remained in Ireland, whereas the benefits for emigrant women were much more marginal.[36]

The juxtaposition of marriage and career is arguably an artificial one, particularly for the many women who took positions as domestic servants. Until the mid-twentieth century domestic service was an occupation that was deemed suitable for women by even the most conservative Catholic commentators and, possibly, for the same reason it met with the approval of Irish farming families: because it was an occupation where women lived and worked in a domestic setting, and where it was believed that they gained skills that would help them to become wives and mothers. The domestic setting was seen as protecting women from the moral dangers associated with factory and urban life, and the risk that they might not develop an interest and expertise in domesticity; the curfews and the other constraints on a servant's private life were also seen as beneficial in protecting the virtue and respectable status of the single women. Domestic service had other practical benefits: it was an occupation that offered board and lodgings, something which was essential to a single woman emigrant; whereas wages for women working in a nineteenth-century textile mill or factory, whether in Belfast, Lancashire or Massachusetts, might not have covered the full cost of board and lodging. Indeed, if food and board are included in the calculation, the wages and living standard of most domestic servants far outstripped that of a female factory worker.[37] By the 1850s, 80 per cent of women working as paid household labour in New York City were Irish born; in 1900 over 60 per cent of Irish-born women in paid employment in the USA were in some form of domestic service.[38] Low outgoings enabled servant girls to save a high proportion of their earnings, either to send home as remittances, or enabling them set up house when they married. Irish servants were much less visible in nineteenth-century British households. In 1881, they accounted for only 2.8 per cent of English servants, rising to 8.8 per cent in the north-west. Walter's study of London-based domestic servants shows that they were significantly older than native-born servants.[39] By the beginning of the twentieth century a growing number of English women were shunning domestic service, because of the lifestyle constraints, so the proportion who were Irish-born rose steadily, because service in Britain offered Irish women much better pay and conditions than they would get in service in Ireland. Indeed by the 1940s the ostensible servant shortage in middle-class Irish households – because large numbers were emigrating to England – was a factor driving criticism of female emigration, to the extent that it was alleged that the servant shortage in Ireland was deterring women (presumably middle-class) from marriage![40] Yet while Diner has represented domestic service as an occupation that exposed Irish women emigrants to the cultural values and aspirations of prosperous US society, Kevin Kenny suggests that there may have been a tendency to overstate the quality of life of Irish servants in the US; he points to the real danger of sexual exploitation, and the fact that American-born women and other immigrants shunned domestic service, as indeed did the daughters of Irish emigrants.[41]

Rising literacy and longer schooling in Ireland opened up prospects of better service jobs (ladies' maids or cooks) and alternatives to service. At the time of the famine, Irish women were less literate than men, by the 1880s however this had changed and young women were tending to spend more years at school than their brothers, partly because they had few opportunities for work, either paid or unpaid. School was also seen as an opportunity to acquire skills that would assist them in emigrating, including knowledge of English, or needlework and home crafts, which was taught in classes offered by the Congested Districts Board, where most attendees planned to emigrate.[42] In the early 1960s girls growing up in rural Ireland were also more likely to remain at school beyond the compulsory school-leaving age of fourteen, and more likely to attend secondary school than their brothers, yet again because there were fewer jobs available locally, but also because further schooling opened the way to clerical jobs or nursing.[43] By the mid-twentieth century women emigrants were more likely to take white-collar jobs than emigrant males. An unpublished 1959 report by the Irish consul-general in New York noted that most of the jobs readily available for Irish male emigrants were 'blue collar jobs. Irish girls coming here as domestic servants have their choice of jobs as so far as qualified secretaries, office workers and salesgirls are concerned, New York City has been a Mecca up to recent months'.[44] For many Irish farmers' daughters, emigration to England offered opportunities for training as a nurse. Admission to nursing in Ireland was highly competitive, generally demanding both a Leaving Certificate (five years of secondary schooling, where fees would have to be paid) and in some instances payment to the training hospital. In England by comparison, where there was a shortage of nurses, one or two years schooling at a traditional secondary school, or even a vocational school, generally sufficed, and the cost of training was covered by the hospital.[45] Nursing was seen as the most desirable occupation for emigrant daughters of respectable Irish farmers and other middle-class families. Like domestic service one hundred years earlier, it offered sheltered employment, with trainee nurses required to live in supervised hostels, subject to curfew and close monitoring of their private lives; and nurses acquired caring and domestic skills appropriate for future wives and mothers. The cover of Enda Delaney's book on *The Irish in Post-War Britain* carries the photograph of three Irish nurses who took the top three places in the British Nurse of the Year Awards in 1964.[46] In 1951 there were 21,672 Irish-born women working as trained nurses and midwives in Britain, 11 per cent of the total.[47] By the 1960s, as Britain came to experience a shortage of trainee teachers, growing numbers of Irish women (and men) were taking these positions. School-teaching was among the favoured occupations among the American Irish, and by the early twentieth century over 2,000 of the 7,000 women teachers in New York City were the daughters of Irish immigrants; in Worcester Massachusetts just under half, 49.6 per cent of women teachers were second-generation Irish.[48]

Although the career choices made by many Irish emigrant women reflected labour shortages and market demand in the country of immigration, the fact that they also conformed to the social and cultural preferences of respectable rural Irish families begs the question as to whether Irish women emigrants were making a dash for freedom and asserting their individual wishes, or were continuing to respect family goals and expectations. The answer is probably elements of both. Evidence collected in England by the Commission on Emigration suggests that women were at least as likely to send money home as men. It was generally acknowledged that the young women who emigrated in their mid-teens did so with parental approval, which made it difficult, if not impossible for the government to impose controls on their departure. So it would be unwise to over-emphasise the extent to which women emigrated in order to assert their independence, or personal goals. One could argue that even the thousands of PFIs – women described by British officials as Pregnant from Ireland – were conforming to family cultural values and wishes – by travelling to Britain, in that by doing so they evaded local censure and a blot on the family's reputation.[49]

Yet once arrived in the USA, Australia or Britain, an emigrant woman, like an emigrant man, had greater personal freedom than if they had stayed at home, including the option to break contact with home, to marry whoever they wished, and to adopt the cultural mores of their destination. Diner suggested that domestic service introduced Irish women to the aspirations and material standards of respectable US society, and that it fostered ambition and consumer standards that Irish women introduced into their homes if they married. Delaney, writing about postwar Britain, noted that women 'were often required to have a greater degree of interaction with the wider society, at work or, as mothers, with the institutions of British officialdom such as schools, hospitals, or doctors, and this required an ability to adapt'.[50] But this integration could take the form of a hybrid identity, retaining links with the country of origin, while integrating into the country of immigration. Diaspora is defined by the maintenance of a link with the place of origin[51] and this can take multiple forms. The more public forms of diaspora culture, such as County Associations or sporting and political organisations were, until recent years, dominated by men, but women accounted for 77 per cent of the 358 US residents to register for Irish citizenship in 1936 – the first time this became possible.[52] And Eamon de Valera went to considerable lengths to ensure that Irish citizenship by descent could pass through the female line at a time when this was at variance with practice in most other countries – action that may reflect the fact that his Irish citizenship derived from his mother.[53]

Less formal connections were also important. Yeo shows how Irish and Jewish women in the family home 'preserve(d) familiar customs in a strange land', and suggests, persuasively, that 'The concept of homeland which is a key construct in diaspora studies … needs to … include other dimensions and especially to accommodate the importance of women in the family home as a constituent of homeland, a link with homeland and even a proxy for homeland'.[54] Andy Bielenberg has alluded to 'the potential significance of the Irish Diaspora as customers for Irish linen in the USA in particular, but also throughout the British Empire'.[55] This would be equally true of demand for Waterford glass in a later generation. Parcels from America were one of the common links with home. Discarded clothing and household goods were shipped to family in Ireland. Given women's superior literacy and schooling they were probably responsible for the bulk of correspondence with family in Ireland from the late-nineteenth century onwards. Women would also have determined whether an immigrant family would provide temporary shelter for a newly arrived relative or invite them to family gatherings. Cultural continuity was also facilitated through children's names and the transmission of an Irish culture, not just in the home, but through parochial schools, which were often staffed by the descendants of Irish immigrants, or even by Irish-born religious sisters, because until the late 1960s, Ireland continued to send large numbers of female and male religious to North America, Britain, Australia, and developing countries in Africa and Asia. Yet in this instance the culture and politics of the country of immigration is important: whereas teachers in parochial schools in the USA and Australia undoubtedly transmitted some form of Irish or hybrid-Irish culture to their pupils, Mary Hickman has shown that this was not so in the UK, where parochial schools encouraged assimilation into British culture – an indication that they were operating in a less welcoming environment and one that was less willing to accommodate hybrid identities.[56]

The almost equal numbers of Irish men and women emigrants – regardless of destination – offered considerable scope for endogamy, and this was probably one reason why Irish emigrants had among the lowest rates of return to the country of their birth. But the extent to Irish immigrants intermarried varied. By 1911 the majority of Irish-born husbands and wives in Australia were married to non-Irish spouses.[57] Byron's study of Albany, New York, a major destination for Irish emigrants in the mid-nineteenth century, shows that 82 per cent of his sample of second-generation Irish married partners of sole or mixed Irish ancestry; for the third generation this had fallen to 72.7 per cent; in the fourth generation to 66 per cent; by 'generation five', the figure was 52.6 per cent. While Byron comments at some length about the level of out-marriage and the factors which drove it, it is the continuing endogamy that is probably more noteworthy.[58] The London-Irish in the mid-nineteenth century married within the Irish community, and a hundred years later marriage records in thirty-seven parishes in Westminster Archdiocese over the years 1948–54 showed that 71 per cent of Irish-born Catholics who married, married other Irish Catholics.[59] By the beginning of the twentieth century the Irish in America were increasingly blending into the wider society: with marriage rates and ages similar to native-born Protestants, combining low rates of residential segregation with high rates of suburbanisation and home-ownership. As for marital fertility, Miller, Doyle and Kelleher cite evidence showing that Irish immigrant birth rates were converging on those of native Americans.[60] Irish migrants in London in the mid-nineteenth century, 'quickly adjusted their demographic behaviour to the urban environment'; with smaller families than in Ireland, and smaller than the average for London.[61] While the Irish in Britain are more elusive, by 1958 the Catholic birth rate in England and Wales was 120 per cent of the national average – most of these infants would have been the offspring of Irish immigrants; before 1914 it was 166 per cent of the national average. Spencer concluded that 'the implication seems to be that the Irish immigrants have to a considerable extent accepted the British ethos of small families'.[62]

Racial and religious prejudice formed part of the emigrant experience, and its expression was at times gendered, though there is no reason to assume that women were especially targeted. The American practice of using Bridget as the generic name for Irish servants,[63] and complaints about 'how unspeakably atrocious the Hibernian maid-of-all work' are indications of the antipathy shown by many Americans towards Irish servants. David Katzman suggests that anti-Catholicism was at the heart of this antipathy,[64] but it also extended to imputations of slovenly standards and lifestyle differences. The fact that New York City's notorious 'Typhoid Mary' – identified as the source of infection of wealthy New Yorkers both on Long Island and New York's Park Avenue, and some years later in a New York maternity hospital – was Tyrone-born Mary Mallon,[65] conjured up evidence of Irish women emigrants as somehow insanitary and carriers of disease. Wartime emigrants from Ireland, male and female, were subjected to mandatory health inspection, including being deloused. In Britain, Irish nurses were represented as carriers of TB, yet the evidence showed that they had been infected in Britain, and were tubercular-free when they left Ireland.[66]

Concepts of contamination and infection operated in both directions. The more emotional rhetoric associated with 'the Flight of the Girls' drew heavily on images of English city life as both physically and morally unhealthy. Yet such criticism drew back from citing statements about Irish women engaging in pre-marital sex, or Irish men who deserted their wives and families in Ireland. When Eamon de Valera made an emotional speech in 1951 about the poor living conditions of Irish emigrants in the English Midlands, based on report sent to him by Maurice Foley, a Catholic social worker, he drew heavily on Foley's descriptions of overcrowded housing, including one instance where men and women shared the same overcrowded bed-room; the women sleeping there at night and the men, working night shifts, using the same accommodation during the day – but he did not mention Foley's concerns over vulnerable young Irish women at risk of pregnancy.[67] There was a similar unwillingness to acknowledge openly that many of the Irish single women giving birth in England were pregnant when they left Ireland; though Irish officials were only prepared to bear the cost of bringing back those babies who were proven to have been conceived in Ireland.[68] Unrestricted entry to Britain for former inmates of industrial schools, absconding husbands or pregnant single women helped Irish society to protect its self-image as morally superior to other societies. Yet the availability of abortion in Britain following the enactment of the 1967 Act was undoubtedly a major factor in the emergence of a more open and tolerant attitude in Ireland towards single women giving birth, though that self-same Abortion Act also meant that Irish society (North and South) avoided having to choose between making abortion available or the horrors of illegal back-street abortions.

Patrick O'Sullivan, in the introduction to the first volume of his series *The Irish World Wide,* draws on Gerda Lerner's broad categorisation of women's history as consisting of oppression, compensation, contribution. In a volume specifically dealing with women's emigration, O'Sullivan suggests that these categories offer appropriate responses to the topic, though not exclusive approaches.[69] The study of Irish women and the diaspora offers a lens on Irish society, and on countries where they settled, and considerable scope for comparative analysis of the impact of different cultures and societies on women's lives. The overall impression is one of complexity; the need to avoid overly schematising female emigrants or their motives, which undoubtedly varied widely, depending on the individual migrant and her personal and family circumstances, the destination and time of departure. With greater prosperity and a more extensive welfare system provided by the state, the financial reliance of Irish families on emigrant daughters and sons has declined significantly, and changing aspirations have tended to favour self-fulfilment over family strategy. The environment for women in Ireland and internationally has changed also – which may mean that contemporary women migrants mark a break with those of earlier generations – but that is a topic for another occasion.

Notes

1 J. F. Maguire, *The Irish in America* (London: Longman's, Green, 1868), p. 319.
2 *Ibid.*, pp. 333–4.
3 *Ibid.*, p. 341.
4 *Ibid.*, p. 343.
5 Report on the welfare of Irish Catholic girls in Britain 1953, by Mrs Elizabeth Fitzgerald, president Archdiocese of Westminster branch of Catholic Women's League, National Archives Ireland, Department of the Taoiseach, S11582 Emigration.
6 Maguire, *The Irish in America*, p. 339.
7 M. E. Daly, *The Slow Failure: Population Decline and Independent Ireland, 1920–1970* (Madison, Wisconsin: University of Wisconsin Press, 2006), pp. 78–82.

8   *Ibid.*, pp. 275–85.
9   L. Earner-Byrne, '"Moral repatriation": the response to Irish unmarried mothers in Britain, 1920s–1960s', in Patrick J. Duffy (ed.), *To and From Ireland: Planned Migration Schemes, c. 1600–2000* (Dublin: Geography Publications, 2004), pp. 155–74.
10 Daly, *Slow Failure*, pp. 43–4.
11 Manuscript Room, Trinity College Dublin, Arnold Marsh Papers, MS8307/3. Transcript of evidence to Commission on Emigration by Irish Housewives Association; Stanley Lyon, 'Survey of living and employment conditions of Irish workers in Great Britain', Marsh Papers, S24B.
12 T. W. Guinnane, *The Vanishing Irish: Households, Migration, and the Rural Economy in Ireland, 1850–1914* (Princeton: Princeton University, 1997), p. 104.
13 D. Fitzpatrick, *Irish Emigration* (Dundalk: Economic and Social History Society of Ireland, 1984).
14 D. H. Akenson, *The Irish Diaspora: A Primer* (Belfast: Queen's University Belfast, Institute of Irish Studies, 1996), pp. 157–87.
15 H. R. Diner, *Erin's Daughters in America: Irish Immigrant Women in the Nineteenth Century* (Baltimore: Johns Hopkins University Press , 1986), p. 31; E. J. Yeo, 'Gender and homeland in the Irish and Jewish diasporas', in M. Schrover and E. J. Yeo (eds), *Gender, Migration and the Public Sphere, 1850–2005* (London: Routledge, 2010), pp. 14–37.
16 Guinnane, *The Vanishing Irish*, p. 182.
17 K. A. Miller, A. Schrier, B. D. Boling, D. N. Doyle, *Irish Immigrants in the Land of Canaan. Letters and Memoirs from Colonial and Revolutionary America, 1675–1815* (New York and Oxford: Oxford University Press, 2003), pp. 257–8; 263. The outcome of Dougherty's petition is not known.
18 R. Kennedy, *The Irish: Gender, Marriage and Fertility* (Berkeley: University of California Press, 1973), p. 82.
19 Akenson, *The Irish Diaspora*, p. 174.
20 D. McLoughlin, 'Superfluous and unwanted deadweight: the emigration of nineteenth-century Irish pauper women', in P. O'Sullivan (ed.), *The Irish World Wide, Vol 4. Irish Women and Irish Migration* (Leicester and Washington: Leicester University Press, 1985), pp. 66–88; D. Fitzpatrick, *Oceans of Consolation: Personal Accounts of Irish Migration to Australia* (Ithaca and London: Cornell University Press), pp. 12–13. Women accounted for more than two-thirds of subsidised passages to Victoria. Given that the majority of those paying their own fares were men, the outcome was parity in numbers of men and women.
21 E. Delaney, *Irish Emigration Since 1921* (Dundalk: Economic and Social History Society of Ireland, 2002), pp. 11–12.
22 L. H. Lees, *Exiles of Erin: Irish Migrants in Victorian London* (Manchester: Manchester University Press, 1979), p. 49; A. E. C. W. Spencer, *Arrangements for the Integration of Irish Immigrants in England and Wales. The First Draft of an Unfinished Unedited Report Prepared by the Newman Demographic Survey for the 1960 Congress of the International Catholic Migration Commission* (Dublin: Irish Manuscripts Commission, 2012), pp. 3–4.
23 M. Fitzgerald, *Habits of Compassion: Irish Catholic Nuns and the Origins of New York's Welfare System, 1830–1920* (Urbana and Chicago: University of Illinois Press, 2006), p. 65.
24 Spencer, *Arrangements for the Integration of Irish Immigrants in England and Wales*, Table 8.
25 B. Morrison, *Things My Mother Never Told Me* (London: Chatto and Windus, 2002); for Malone see K. A. Miller, D. N. Doyle and P. Kelleher, '"For love and liberty": Irish

women, migration and domesticity in Ireland and America, 1815–1920', in O'Sullivan (ed.), *Irish Women and Migration*, p. 60.

26 Miller *et al.*, *Irish Immigrants in the Land of Canaan*, p. 300.

27 M. Kanya-Forstner, 'Defining womanhood: Irish women and the Catholic church in Victorian Liverpool', *Immigrants and Minorities*, 18 (1999), 168–88.

28 S. Morgan, 'Irish women in Port Philip and Victoria, 1840–60', in O. MacDonagh and W. F. Mandle (eds), *Irish-Australian Essays* (Canberra: American National University Press, 1989), pp. 240–5; Diner, *Erin's Daughters in America*, pp. 106–19; C. Cox, H. Marland and S. York, 'Itineraries and experiences of insanity: Irish migration and the management of mental illness in nineteenth-century Lancashire', in C. Cox and H. Marland (eds), *Migration, Health and Ethnicity in the Modern World* (Basingstoke: Palgrave, 2013).

29 D. Fitzpatrick, '"A share of the honeycomb": education, emigration and Irishwomen', in M. E. Daly and D. Dickson (eds), *The Origins of Popular Literacy in Ireland: Language Change and Educational Development 1700–1920* (Dublin: University College Dublin and Trinity College Dublin, 1990), pp. 167–8.

30 K. Miller, *Emigrants and Exiles: Ireland and the Irish Exodus to North America* (New York: Oxford University Press, 1985), pp. 406–8.

31 *Ibid.*, p. 507

32 Miller, *et al.*, '"For love and liberty"', pp. 41–65.

33 Diner, *Erin's Daughters in America*, p. 140.

34 J. Nolan, *Ourselves Alone: Women's Emigration from Ireland, 1885–1920* (Lexington: University of Kentucky Press, 1989), pp. 91–3. For a critique of the arguments set out by Diner and Nolan see Miller *et al.*, '"For love and liberty"', pp. 43–58.

35 Guinnane, *Vanishing Irish*, p. 226.

36 Spencer, *Arrangements for the Integration of Irish Immigrants in England and Wales*, pp. 42–3.

37 K. Kenny, *The American Irish* (Harlow: Longman, 2000), p. 152; M. Hearn, *Below Stairs: Domestic Service Remembered in Dublin and Beyond, 1830–1922* (Dublin: Lilliput, 1993).

38 Kenny, *The American Irish*, p. 152.

39 B. Walter, 'Strangers on the inside: Irish women servants in England, 1881', *Immigrants and Minorities*, 87 (2009), 286–8.

40 Daly, *Slow Failure*, pp. 155–6.

41 Kenny, *The American Irish*, pp. 153–4. There was much greater awareness of the potential dangers of sexual exploitation of Irish servants in Britain in the early and mid-twentieth century.

42 Fitzpatrick, '"A share of the honeycomb"', pp. 170–9.

43 *Investment in Education*, Report of the Survey Team appointed by the Minister for Education in October 1962 (PR 8311), p. 112. In 1963 8,284 boys and 9,984 girls sat the Intermediate Certificate, an examination taken by 15–16 year old pupils.

44 J. M. Conway, 'The Irish in the United States', New York consular area, National Archives of Ireland, Department of Foreign Affairs, Washington Files P115/1.

45 Daly, *Slow Failure*, p. 171.

46 E. Delaney, *The Irish in Post-War Britain* (Oxford: Oxford University Press, 2007), dust jacket.

47 Spencer, *Arrangement for the Integration of Irish Immigrants in England and Wales*, p. 40.

48 Kenny, *The American Irish*, p. 186.

49 S. Lambert, 'Irish women's emigration to England 1922–60: the lengthening of family ties', in A. Hayes and D. Urquhart (eds), *The Irish Women's History Reader* (London: Routledge, 2001), pp. 181–8.

50 Delaney, *The Irish in Post-War Britain*, p. 208.
51 S. Dufoix, *Diasporas* (Berkeley and Los Angeles: University of California Press, 2008), p. 21.
52 M. E. Daly, 'Irish nationality and citizenship since 1922', *Irish Historical Studies*, 32:127 (2001), 398–400.
53 M. E. Daly, 'Wives mothers and citizens: the treatment of women in the 1935 nationality and citizenship act', *Éire-Ireland*, 38 (2003), 244–63.
54 Yeo, 'Gender and homeland', p. 31.
55 A. Bielenberg, *Ireland and the Industrial Revolution: The Impact of the Industrial Revolution on Irish Industry, 1801–1922* (London: Routledge, 2009), p. 178.
56 M. J. Hickman, *Religion, Class and Identity: the State, the Catholic Church and the Education of the Irish in Britain* (Aldershot: Ashgate, 1995).
57 Fitzpatrick, *Oceans of Consolation*, p. 18.
58 R. Byron, *Irish America* (Oxford and New York: Oxford University Press, 1999), pp. 150–4.
59 Lees, *Exiles of Erin*, pp. 153–4; Spencer, *Arrangements for the Integration of Irish Immigrants in England and Wales*, p. 44, footnote 17.
60 Miller *et al.*, '"For love and liberty"', p. 53.
61 Lees, *Exiles of Erin*, pp. 136–7.
62 Spencer, *Arrangement for the Integration of Irish Immigrants in England and Wales*, pp. 51–2.
63 Maguire, *The Irish in America*, pp. 334-6; Kenny, *The American Irish*, pp. 152–3.
64 D. Katzman, *Seven Days a Week: Women and Domestic Service in Industrializing America* (Urbana and Chicago: University of Illinois Press, 1981), pp. 162–3.
65 Kenny, *The American Irish*, p. 187.
66 R. Barrington, *Health, Medicine and Politics in Ireland 1900–1970* (Dublin: Institute of Public Administration, 1987), pp. 1939–40; A. McLellan, 'That "Preventable and Curable Disease": Dr Dorothy Price and the Eradication of Tuberculosis in Ireland, 1930–1960' (PhD dissertation, University College Dublin, 2011).
67 Daly, *Slow Failure*, pp. 275–6.
68 Earner-Byrne, '"Moral repatriation"'.
69 O'Sullivan (ed.), *Irish Women and Irish Migration*, pp. 5–6.

2

Thinking through Transnational Studies, Diaspora Studies and gender

Breda Gray

The 1990s saw a proliferation of studies across disciplines in the humanities and social sciences variously invoking the terms *transnational(ism)* and *diaspora* in accounting for migration and associated phenomena including transgenerational ethnic identities and cross-border practices. These terms are deployed most often as counterpoints to the assimilation model of immigrant incorporation and the container model of the nation-state. As such, they offer resources for rethinking relationships between identity, membership and place and contribute to post-nation(al) and post-ethnic conceptualisations of populations, movement and identity. Paradoxically however, both terms have been criticised for reinforcing national and ethnic boundaries of belonging and for emphasising relationships with the sending state at the expense of those with receiving states and wider multi-local and trans-ethnic connections.[1] Many critics also suggest that these terms are over used, imprecise and indicate nothing new.[2] However, despite the burgeoning of alternative figurations and paradigms, including: 'ethnoscapes',[3] 'cosmopolitanism',[4] 'neo-nomadism',[5] and the 'new mobilities paradigm',[6] the terms diaspora and transnationalism continue to dominate in the domain of Migration Studies.[7]

The overlaps and intersections between the literature in Transnational Studies (TS) and Diaspora Studies (DS) are many. For example, one of the journals in the field is titled *Diaspora. A Journal of Transnational Studies* and the editor, Khachig Tölölyan, noted in the first issue that contemporary diasporas are 'the exemplary communities of the *transnational* moment',[8] Similarly, historian Kevin Kenny calls for a combination of 'the *diasporic or transnational*' and comparative approaches in the historical study of migration.[9] This terminological slippage is variously embraced and challenged depending on the theorist and context. However, in this chapter, I suggest that different (if closely related) work is done by each of these terms and the bodies of literature spawned in each case.

The field of TS focuses on the transnational 'agency' of individuals and groups in shaping cross-border economic, political, social and cultural processes,[10] with some of the literature offering normative models of transnational membership.[11] Although TS and DS are both concerned with the effects of transnational migration, the main focus in DS is on the politics of belonging beyond nation-state boundaries. As such, the politics of boundary formation, maintenance, contestation and dissolution as these interact with questions of membership, de-reterritorialisation, authenticity and belonging are recurring themes in DS. In this chapter, I briefly review key debates in both fields before discussing the particular contribution of DS in framing my 1990s study of migrant and non-migrant Irish women.[12]

As in migration studies more generally, the literature in both TS and DS has only belatedly addressed questions of gender and sexuality. The argument that gender and sexuality need to be thought transnationally and in diaspora, and that transnationalism and diaspora need to be thought through sexuality and gender, has been convincingly made by now.[13] Yet, gender and sexuality continue to be 'naturalised' in mainstream TS and DS via the uncritical adoption and reproduction of normative assumptions with regard to family, kinship and community. Gender and sexuality are ever-present dimensions of transnationalism and diaspora insofar as they underpin related concepts of origins, genealogy, family, continuity, community and identity. It is necessary, therefore, to address the 'patriarchal complicities' that might be at work in transnational and diaspora projects,[14] and how the heteronormative assumptions that tend to underpin notions of national, transnational, diaspora and ethnic communities might be interrogated. By reviewing what is at stake in TS and DS and identifying their different orientations in the early sections of this chapter, I clear the ground for addressing the above concerns in the final section which discusses the gendered heteronormative politics of belonging as these emerged in my own study. As this study was framed by DS, debates in this field are developed in most detail in this chapter.

Transnational Studies

TS scholarship in Migration Studies was pioneered by Basch *et al.* who argued that research on migration should not exclude migrants' relations with their societies of origin. They defined transnationalism as:

> the process by which transmigrants, through their daily activities, forge and sustain multi-stranded social, economic, and political relations that link together their societies of origin and settlement, and through which they create transnational social fields that cross national borders.[15]

Although the early literature implied that transnational practices characterised the lives of most contemporary migrants, evidence suggests that only a minority of migrants and their descendants are transnationally engaged on a regular basis.[16] Nonetheless, the growth of transnational practices and their impact on both migrant adaptation in the receiving country and in the development prospects of sending countries render them an important topic of study.[17] While often assumed to be most prevalent amongst the migrant generation and those who are marginalised and less acculturated, there is much evidence of transnationalism across second and subsequent generations,[18] and Portes found transnationalism to be most prevalent amongst those with secure economic and legal status in the receiving country.[19]

Of course many migrants and their descendants maintained transnational ties in the past and engaged in practices that are not dissimilar to those of the present,[20] but such practices and flows are seen as having multiplied since the end of the twentieth century. This is linked to the internationalisation of markets, globalised media and speeded-up communication and transport facilities, which have created new facilitative infrastructures for long-distance, cross-border activities.[21] Unlike globalisation, which tends to be discussed as a steamroller-like process with the same intensity, frequency and quality everywhere, transnationalism is anchored in specific places, times, processes and relations between specific people and emphasises individual and local agency.[22] Yet, for some, this 'agency-oriented' approach downplays the ways in which such agents must struggle with the tensions and conflicts that arise from the structuring forces of global capitalism and nation-state interests.[23]

As transnationalism emphasises the agency of individuals and groups, it tends to be defined by bottom-up practices and is distinguished from cross-border activities at the level of the state, which are characterised as international.[24] This may account for the tendency in TS to overlook the ways in which states control movement across borders including exit and entry and constrain the 'ability of migrants living "here" to act in ways that yield leverage "there"'.[25] Waldinger and Fitzgerald suggest that TS should attend more to how relations between states politically impact 'the scope for multiple versus exclusive national loyalties'.[26] Yet, the proliferation of dual/multiple citizenships and of transnational social and political movements suggests a more complex picture in relation to the boundaries of the transnational and international. For example, Americans for a New Irish Agenda (ANIA) lobbied Bill Clinton before and after he became President to intervene in the politics of the Peace Process in Northern Ireland leading to the United States state acting transnationally alongside the Irish state in progressing this agenda.[27] In such contexts, questions arise as to where the boundaries are to be drawn between international and transnational. Indeed, the work of Castells on 'the network state' raises further questions about the possibilities of *both* international and transnational state activities.[28]

The focus on 'transnational communities' in early TS scholarship has given way in recent years to a more dynamic emphasis on 'transnational processes'.

These processes are seen as constituting 'transnational social fields' populated by both those who have connections across nations because they are migrants, and those who haven't moved but 'who are linked through social relations to people in distant and perhaps disparate locations'.[29] Thus, the social field is held together by border crossings and the transnational relationships that give rise to and are sustained by these crossings and connections. As such, 'persons in the sending and receiving societies become participants in a single social unit' and the idea of society as bounded by the national territory is challenged.[30] From this perspective then, starting with a focus on the nation-state container would involve a concern with only one level of social experience rather than those locales, populations and spatial practices, including (im)mobilities, that shape the everyday lives of (non)migrant and subsequent generations.[31]

A consensus is emerging that TS offers an optic/lens that never assumes the spatial unit of analysis in advance but sees this as emanating instead from the research questions, context and data.[32] Here, the term transnational, insofar as it references the national, is a misnomer and continues to be used only because of the conceptual and methodological ground already laid down in its name.[33] Thus the term transnational persists as 'a holding term' in the absence of a more adequate conceptualisation.[34] Having acknowledged the limitations of the term, Levitt proceeds to argue that the adoption of a transnational optic or lens generates new 'questions about incorporation and identity and comes up with a different set of answers'.[35] As such, the process and outcome of TS-framed research cannot be anticipated and the results are often 'assemblages' without any obvious logic or coherence, but 'come together within and are made up of elements circulating within these transnational spaces'.[36]

The marginalisation of gender and implicit heteromormativity that characterises much migration studies scholarship is also evident in TS.[37] In one of the few studies relating gender and transnationalism in the Irish context, Louise Ryan found that household strategies and familial networks were most significant in shaping the transnational ties and activities of Irish women who migrated to Britain in the 1930s. She argues that these women's lives involved a 'combination of both active agency and family obligation' lived transnationally.[38] Ryan's analysis moves beyond the container model of nation-state gender regimes, as the concept of the 'transnational family' ensure that attention is given to how both individual and household lives are shaped by transnationally gendered structures and practices of inequality and opportunity.

TS scholarship is at an early stage in addressing those transnational practices that perpetuate or subvert (hetero)normative assumptions around gender, family and kinship.[39] However, such concerns could be rendered mainstream via the interrogation of histories, cultures, and theories of sexuality from a transnational perspective' and of the histories, cultures and theories of TS from queer perspectives.[40] For example, in the context of the 2004 Citizenship Referendum in Ireland, Eithne Luibhéid shows how sexual norms shaped where and how the state drew distinctions between legal and illegal status. Pregnant migrants were constructed as 'paradigmatic figures of illegal immigration, whose arrival and childbearing were to be prevented through changes to citizenship law'.[41] The effects of the subsequent constitutional change, according to Luibhéid, included an expansion of the routes by which migrants could become designated as illegal. It also reworked 'sexual, gender, racial, class, and cultural hierarchies at local, national, transnational, and diasporic scales' in service of the Irish state's racialised politics of belonging and economic neoliberalisation agenda.[42] When the agency and cross-border practices of individual women migrants came into conflict here with state mechanisms to control movement across borders, the state mobilised its power to redefine the boundaries of citizenship. In the following section I review the literature in DS and how questions of gender and sexuality are framed by this field of study.

Diaspora Studies

In reviewing the vast interdisciplinary literature in DS, I take Sudesh Mishra's categorisation of this literature as a starting point and suggest five sub-categories of scholarship: (1) '*diaspora typologists*', who are mainly sociologists and political scientists;[43] (2) those who see diaspora as a displaced ethno-national collectivity that relates to both a territorial homeland and receiving country – what Mishra, following Clifford, describes as the '*dual territoriality*' approach;[44] (3) those who see diaspora as a *hybrid and contingent* notion based on lateral, fluid, multipolar and situational positionings (mainly in Cultural Studies and Anthropology);[45] (4) those who construct diaspora as an autonomous actor and effect of institutionalised *diaspora engagement policies* focused on local and global economic development and (inter)national security (mainly in Development Studies and International Relations);[46] and (5) those who depart from 'general paradigms in favour of an interrogative specificity' by investigating diaspora formation in specific time-spaces, or 'moments' – an '*archival*' approach (historians, social scientists and literature scholars).[47] While there are overlaps between these approaches, I discuss them separately below in order to identify the spectrum of assumptions at play in this domain of scholarship.

Those falling into the category of *typologists* include Safran, Cohen, Vertovec and, to some extent, Dufoix and Brubaker. Here diaspora is deployed primarily as a descriptive term for a specific kind of collectivity/entity formed through dispersal from a real or imagined homeland and which meets further identified ideal-typical criteria. In much of this literature the discussion is limited by a tendency to focus on the characteristics of diaspora and extent to which a specific diaspora meets an identified 'checklist'.[48] Although such criteria are often appealed to in defining the boundaries of identity and belonging, a discussion of typologies and how they are mobilised falls outside the remit of my discussion here.

Sheffer, who falls into the *dual territoriality* category, suggests that ethno-national diasporas attempt to feel at home in their 'host' countries while simul-taneously maintaining close contact with their 'homeland' and promoting its culture and interests.[49] The 'homeland' and receiving/'host' country are imagined as coherent territorialised entities and 'roots' work is mobilised in such a way as to keep the 'homeland' central to diasporic memory and imaginary.[50] Thus diaspora is conceived as an 'ethnically coherent macro subject' occupying a 'zone of tension' between 'homeland' and receiving/'host'-land, but with loyalty to both.[51] This conception of diaspora as suspended between the bipolar territories of homeland and receiving country is seen as producing a sense of 'living without belonging' in the receiving/'host' country while 'belonging without living' in the homeland.[52] Here, diaspora tends to be constructed in terms of 'class-neutral, gender-neutral and generational-neutral ethnic blocks that uncrit-ically project home and host countries as homogeneous territorial entities'.[53]

Those who see diaspora as *hybrid and contingent* emphasise fluidity and deterritoriality and see diaspora as formed in and through the interactions of structural positionings and mobile positionalities that are always contextually specific. For example, the work of Paul Gilroy and Stuart Hall, despite their different emphases, undercuts perceptions of a territorially bound, homogenous nation-state. They argue in different ways that the Black diaspora is unified by experiences of racism, imperialism, oppression and marginalisation and hybrid cultural productions rather than in highly mediated relationship to originary territory, or 'homeland'. For Hall, the Black diaspora in Britain is one in which 'identity and difference are inextricably articulated or knotted together in different identities, the one never wholly obliterating the other'.[54] By adopting the horizontal/lateral conception of diaspora, a logic of assemblage (rather than a logic of roots based on genealogical reproduction of belonging) is suggested that has no necessary unity and can break at any point and connect at any point.[55] As such, an emphasis on routes, boundary erosion and open-ended hybridity emerge from the 'exchanges, crossings and mutual entanglements' that are seen as central to living diaspora.[56]

This approach unsettles binary oppositions between original and copy as, for example, between the 'authentic' Irish-born national and the inauthentic, diasporic 'Plastic Paddy'. Such politics of (in)authenticity across generations and between locations in diaspora arise in the identity claims of second-generation Irish in Britain which are mediated by questions of authenticity insofar as 'one of the major rhetorical arguments used to separate the "authentic" from the "inauthentic" is an allegiance to and knowledge of contemporary Ireland'.[57] So, even at a time when authentic Irishness in Ireland is officially named as diasporic, this rebranding of the Irish nation paradoxically renders Irish identity in the diaspora inauthentic.[58] Such disjunctures and politics of boundary-making within and across groups, as well as between groups, are central to the politics of diaspora. While the emphasis is on fluidity and hybridity, such lateral situational readings of diaspora help unravel the micro/macro power relations that underpin the policing of boundaries and (im)permissible hybridisations in what Avtar Brah calls 'diaspora space'.[59]

Like queer studies, this rendering of diaspora references a mobile category that disrupts fixed identity categories. Indeed, the term 'queer diaspora' emphasises the difference within unity of a dispersed network of queer connections, cultures and 'communities', and challenges the ways in which 'the normal' is underpinned by a naturalisation and culturalisation of gender and heterosexuality in nationalist, racial and ethnic politics of belonging.[60] An analogy is often drawn between queer as that which subverts gender normativity and diaspora as unsettling geographic and national stability.[61] However, Wesling argues that this analogy fails to address the complexities of differently lived experiences and tends to privilege mobility, fluidity and subversion over stasis without critically attending to the actual conditions that enable or constrain mobility and subversion.

In the fourth category of DS literature, diaspora emerges as a discrete actor and effect of *diaspora engagement policy* initiatives. Such policies are evident across the levels of global organisations such as the World Bank, national Aid programmes such as USAID, and in sending state (and local authority) policies. Since the early 2000s, diaspora has circulated in geo-political discourses in three main ways: first, in sending state policies of 'diaspora engagement' promoted by global institutions such as the World Bank and the UN Economic and Social Council; second, in discourses of 'Aid' whereby governments in the Global North channel Aid by mobilising resident diasporic groups from targeted countries; and third, as sites of threat and the focus of securitisation agendas. The Irish state has been to the forefront in actively promoting diaspora engagement as an important strand in its economic development policy since the late 2000s.[62] Although an emergent and increasingly significant aspect of DS with gendered implications,[63] a detailed consideration of this literature falls outside the specific remit of this chapter.

The fifth approach is based on *archival* evidence or original data relating to specific diaspora formations in time and space. It also moves from the general to the particular. As such, those adopting this approach challenge abstract and totalising accounts of diaspora. The focus here is more on the everyday life of diaspora in a particular time-space and the specific practices, institutions and relations that characterise these.[64] Such studies can vary from individual ethnic diaspora histories to similarities and/or differences between specific formations of diaspora and changes in diasporic formation over time. For example, Bronwen Walter's account of how Irish women and men are located differently by their racialisation as white and their class positions in the USA and Britain, and Mary Hickman's comparative study of Irish encounters in the diasporic spaces of nineteenth-century United States and late-twentieth-century Britain, are both testimony to the significance of such intersections and negotiations in the relational politics of diaspora space.[65] (As in my own study discussed below, these studies also draw on other strands of DS in analysis of data and theory development.)

Although attempting to undercut or transcend the nation state, DS, by drawing a boundary around 'a people' as, for example, 'the global Irish', tends to construct internal coherence and unity. Thus, for Ien Ang, diaspora is a double-edged notion that is often 'proto-nationalist in its outlook' because it can be defined by closure,[66] but also holds the potential for hybridisation and radical openness. As such, diaspora potentially entrenches nationalist heterosexual norms of belonging in a new multi-located and multi-generational frame, but also holds out the possibility for new logics of affiliation. In the case of the Irish diaspora, tropes of family reproduce tribe and mother country, and a 'global Irish family' through heteronormative (classed and racialised) promises of belonging. Indeed, as Eithne Luibhéid argues, the political work of boundary-making and logic of diasporic belonging interact closely with heteronormative logics of family, community and nation-state to give 'definition to sexual categories and identities'.[67] As such, the originalities of heterosexuality and nation line up in powerful ways that tend to naturalise gender through national/diasporic belonging and vice versa.

Feminist and queer theory scholarship in Irish DS has begun to address the gender and sexual politics of diaspora by attending to the dynamics of boundary expansion, queering and dissolution.[68] However, the heteronormative logic of Irish diasporic belonging remains hegemonic.[69] In the section that follows I develop these themes with reference to a study I conducted in the mid-1990s. Although an example of archival specificity insofar as it addressed lived diaspora in a specific time-space, the analysis of the data was informed primarily by the *dual territoriality* and *hybrid and contingent* strands of DS scholarship. As such, the study attempted to overcome a 'lack of interconnectedness between the theoretical literature on diaspora and empirical research on "actual" diasporas and their specific geographies'.[70]

Researching gender in diaspora – a case study

My qualitative study of 1980s Irish women migrant and non-migrant experiences of diaspora in the specific transnational space (crossed and connected) or 'diaspora space' (shaped by myriad encounters, claims and counterclaims of belonging, fissures and fusions) of the Republic of Ireland and London/southeast of England was based on focus-group discussions and one-to-one interviews.[71] This study, undertaken in the mid-1990s, was led by three central questions: First, how might we understand Irish migration differently if analysed from the perspectives and experiences of Irish women? Second, in what ways might our understanding of migration as gendered be changed by focusing on the overlooked dynamics between those who emigrate and those who stay put?

And third, how might this particular migrant cohort be understood differently through the lens of Diaspora Studies?

The study aimed to move beyond 'additive' approaches to the study of gender and migration that leave dominant understandings of both in place, by investigating gender as a structuring process. Gender was identified as structuring at a *relational* level, for example, in relations between and amongst men and women migrants, between those who leave and those who stay, between generations of migrants and between migrant groups, as well as between sending and receiving countries and between diasporas. For the purposes of this chapter and to keep the discussion focused, I include three illustrative quotes from the migrant women only below.

Although President Mary Robinson's recognition of the diaspora validated migrant women's claims to Irish identity, the participants in this study articulated split subjectivity in relation to the terms of belonging in Ireland and England. Perceived prospects in relation to belonging in each locale were mediated by expectations of transnational kin work, of 'being there' for family members both in Ireland and in London and the emotional work of maintaining connections. For example, Cath,[72] who worked as a social worker in London at the time of the research, describes her life in London in terms of this split:

> It is very much *a schism of your spirit and everything else when you come over here* because, you definitely do feel pulled … It wreaks havoc with you … you could lead a completely different life over here to the one you were living at home. You could hide so much, and people at home would never know you and people over there would never know the you over here, the one you slip into like me going home and *being a daughter* … I've struggled against that, but I used to feel like it was *two lives*. I worked hard with my mother and father … to get them to see what my life was like over here and to keep saying to them come over … my parents haven't come over, but my sisters have and my brother has … They can feed back to my parents where I live and make a connection because … the tearing is just heart wrenching, you know. It's all about religion and culture … (Interview, London; emphasis added)

This account suggests an over-determination of gender identity by the expectations surrounding Cath's 'daughter' role and the associated work of maintaining and sustaining connection with family in Ireland. Later, Cath notes with regard to the possibility of returning to Ireland, that her London lifestyle (including living with her boyfriend) might not be accepted by her family there. The inhabitance of split subjectivity is described in terms of the work of translating gender and sexual politics across Irish and English locales (dual territoriality) marked by different religions, cultures and gender regimes in an attempt to reconcile her positioning as daughter and adult migrant Irish woman.

The following quote from Fionnuala, a housing manager in London at the time of the study, also points to the complex sense of cut-off and separation produced by the short distance between London and Ireland.

> I came here for a job and if I had found the same opportunities in Ireland that I found here I would … probably have been happier in the long run. Because the practicalities that I have encountered over the last few years with my mothers' failing health, my brothers who have young children and their marriages have split up. I can see where I could have been of assistance and I am not around. And you know, when you have a crisis in your family, as I have had and you are a long way, well, *you're not a long way away, but you're not there.* (Group discussion, London; emphasis added)

To be 'there' at times of 'crisis in your family' in Ireland meant a simultaneous negotiation for Fionnuala of family, work and other commitments in London. In many cases this 'in-between' existence was intensified by new communication technologies, speedier transport and new media. The affordances of these technologies contributed to a heightening of expectations regarding the potential to 'be there' for others in both places at once.[73] The immediacy of expectations on both sides created deep family tensions and constant self-appraisal for migrant women with regard to matching up to the norms of Irish womanhood through notions of the 'good daughter' in particular.

In these accounts, women's identities and belongings are shaped by hetero-normative and ethnicised norms of belonging. As such, kinship and family operate as 'ordering practices' that reproduce gender binaries and the boundaries of intelligible national/diasporic, racial and ethnic subjects. In such dual territorial renditions of diaspora and migration, generations mark the gradual degeneration of an imagined 'original' culture linked to place.[74] For example, many of the accounts articulate anxiety that their actual or potential future children would not be Irish. In this way, the regulatory workings of family and children figured in the women's accounts as dense sites for 'the transfer and reproduction of culture, where "culture" carries with it implicit norms of racial purity …'.[75]

Those women who openly challenged traditional family-oriented versions of Irish femininity were rendered outsiders. For example, Maeve reflected on her experience as a feminist activist in London:

> I've experienced being made to feel that *I'm outside of a recognised Irish identity* even in London by Irish people and groups. And it's … *around feminist issues* where that's been interpreted as an attack on the Irish culture or Irish community … I've felt it as a lack of recognition that here am I, an Irish woman, and this is my experience, and these are my concerns … and then being accused of attacking an Irish identity, of being anti-Irish … Being an Irish feminist is wrong … It's not Irishness it's something else, it's something I've picked up from over here, or it's not recognised as something coming from myself, or from my own experience, and certainly very threatening. (Interview, London; emphasis added)

While some of the women transgressed traditional gender norms and hetero-normative narratives and practices of Irish ethnic belonging, the price was often to have their national/ethnic identity and/or gender identity questioned. Such assumptions of dual territoriality and experiences of split subjectivity emerged as strong themes amongst this cohort of Irish migrant women with gender and diaspora being lived through heteronormative politics of belonging in dispersal.

Although the women's accounts of their lived lives did not, for the most part, suggest a conscious embracing of fluid forms of identity, or anti-essentialist hybridisation, the 'hybrid and contingent' strand of DS literature sensitised my analysis to the regulatory work done by intersecting normative categories of nation, 'race', class, sexuality and gender as these were both sustained and subverted in the lived experience of diaspora. So, for example, returning to Fionnuala's account earlier, her statement that she might have been happier if she had stayed in Ireland is contradicted in many other sections of her account where she asserts her pragmatic adaptation to life in London through conscious performances of 'Anglicisation' and her sense of discomfort and frustration on return visits to Ireland. Thus her account, taken as a whole, suggests oscillations between a subjectivity stretched across dual territories and a more flexible assemblage of subjective (dis)identifications and active avoidance of 'recognisable' gendered Irish identity.

Although Irish diasporic belonging was represented primarily as a pseudo-biological property predicated on genealogy, family and kinship as *lived* did not always map onto such representations.[76] Many of the women anticipated having children with non-Irish partners, which was seen as unsettling the biologically and geographically coded 'origins' of cultural identity. This potential child embodied the uncomfortable 'contact zone' of Anglo-Irish/British-Irish relations and other inter-racial/ethnic relations past and present. The potential of kin or family as a disordering practice in this context often involved unsettling experiences insofar as the necessary hybridity of any future generation cannot produce harmonious merger or fusion, but represents 'complicated entanglement'.[77] This was evident in the accounts of many of the mothers and potential mothers who struggled with both the promise of the normative national/cultural/racial identity (fitting in) and the simultaneous lived discomfort of lack of fit. As such, many of the accounts suggest a lateral moving against teleologies of origin and return as they and their potential children are both separated from and connected to Ireland or London and are differently positioned through locations of gender, class, race and ethnicity. The contested work of boundary expansion and subversion is part and parcel of their everyday lives.

Contemporary contexts of diaspora are seen by Appadurai and Breckenridge as creating the conditions whereby 'women become brokers of new domestic cultures and new kinds of sexual politics'.[78] There is the suggestion here that through the bricolage or assemblage whereby disparate elements are joined in unanticipated forms of reproduction, the gendered heteronormative logics of nationalism and diasporas might be unravelled. However, the gendered imperatives of everyday life make living against the 'intimate normativity' of nation and diaspora an ongoing struggle. These dynamics are reflected in Brah's account of 'diaspora space' as

> where multiple subject positions are juxtaposed, contested, proclaimed or disavowed; where the permitted and the prohibited perpetually interrogate; and where the accepted and the transgressive imperceptibly mingle even while these syncretic forms may be disclaimed in the name of purity and tradition. Here, tradition is itself continually invented even as it may be hailed as originating from the mists of time. What is at stake is the infinite experientiality, the myriad processes of cultural fissure and fusion that underwrite contemporary forms of transcultural identities.[79]

Because diasporas are 'differentiated, heterogeneous, contested spaces, even as they are implicated in the construction of a common "we"', Brah calls on us 'to be attentive to the nature and type of processes in and through which the collective 'we' is constituted'.[80] Women taking part in my study engaged in more and less transgressive ways with the historically shaped politics of location and boundary-making/subversion that marked their diasporic existence. Overall, their accounts suggest women who were both subject to and agents in Irish diasporic politics of belonging.

While TS would have provided a productive framework for my study, the conceptual ground covered in DS, concerned as it is primarily with the dimensions of boundary (un)making and the *politics* of belonging, enabled an analysis of how these dynamics are lived in and through the national, class, ethnic, racial and gender ties that bind identity across borders. Thus diaspora, as a term that signals relations between 'home' and dispersal, global and intimate scales of belonging, as well as tensions between cultural authenticity and hybridity, offered a resonant and capacious analytic frame for my analysis.

Conclusion

Both DS and TS demonstrate the ways in which 'human mobility may reinforce and recreate all kinds of beliefs and –isms, including nationalism, patriarchism, sexism, sectarianism and ethno-nationalism'.[81] Yet they also point to the ways in which such 'isms' are troubled, undermined and transcended through human mobility and encounter. As such, these fields of study interrogate practices and politics of mobility, place and identity, but attend less centrally to how gender, 'race', class, sexuality and generation are mobilised through these practices and politics. Because they have different theoretical starting points, TS and DS are based on distinct ontological and methodological assumptions. While TS might focus on gendered cross-border agency and practices, DS might attend more to the gendered politics of boundary construction and belonging in contexts of complex intergenerational dispersals.

Although collective identity might arise in the cultural aspects of TS which address the 'hybridity or cultural "translations" in which mobile persons are engaged',[82] the boundaries of collective identity and therefore the *politics* of belonging are a central concern in DS. As 'an idiom, stance and claim', diaspora can never be defined *a priori* in terms of specific spatial, ethnic, historical or generational boundaries because it is an emergent and always contingent entity.[83] Indeed, every act of definition involves ongoing work of boundary expansion, disruption, defense or maintenance. Such boundary work always involves gendered assumptions about the nature of collectivity and its reproduction.

The accounts of migrant women taking part in the study discussed above point to the gendered boundary work of diaspora. The ways in which the women negotiate their diasporic belonging profoundly shape their present and projected future lives, as well as that of the collectivity. As such, their self-positionings and negotiations of being positioned can be productively read through the lens of DS. Moreover, their accounts offer a nuanced insight into the dynamics of diaspora which tend to be abstracted in policy discourses and much academic scholarship, often implicitly reproducing naturalised and normative versions of gender and sexuality.

When they saw themselves as falling short of the normative expectations surrounding their gender identities as daughters, mothers or potential mothers, some of the women taking part in this study felt positioned outside, or potentially outside, 'authentic' Irish identity. Their lives, although more connected to Ireland than for previous generations, were marked by an acute sense of dislocation and separation. In many cases, the experience of dislocation was intensified by more frequent contact and connection. In whatever way they engaged in the sexual and gendered politics of diaspora, these women's accounts suggest subjectivities that were variously complicit, split, ambivalent and actively resistant with regard to the hegemonic heteronormative expectations that reproduce nation and belonging in the Irish diaspora.

With the return of net emigration since 2009, gendered *transnational* practices of family, kinship, friendship and community and diasporic politics of belonging are newly inflected by the use of social media and mobile technologies among what is sometimes known as the 'Skype generation'.[84] Moreover, the recent expansion of Irish state diaspora-engagement initiatives, including the funding of welfare and cultural projects in the diaspora, the establishment of the Global Irish Economic Forum and the Global Irish Network and 'The Gathering' tourism initiative for 2013, raise questions about how this new institutionalised infrastructure of *diaspora* reproduces or reorients the boundaries of diasporic belonging in gendered ways. Both TS and DS remain radically open domains of scholarship that are likely to be superseded by more capacious terms and concepts as these emerge in relation to constantly changing social worlds and theoretical debate. However, if the crucial interventions of Feminist, Gender, LGBT and Queer Studies are not engaged more centrally, some of the key forces shaping human mobility and associated sociality and politics will continue to be overlooked.

Notes

1 R. Waldinger and D. Fitzgerald, 'Transnationalism in question', *American Journal of Sociology*, 109 (2004), 1177–95; F. Anthias, 'Evaluating diaspora: beyond ethnicity?', *Sociology*, 32 (1998), 557–80.

2 N. Fonor, 'What's new about transnationalism? New York immigrants today and the turn of the century', *Diaspora*, 6 (1997), 355–75; A. Portes, 'Introduction: the debates and significance of immigrant transnationalism', *Global Networks*, 1 (2001), 181–93; J. E. Braziel and A. Mannur, 'Nation, migration, globalization: points of contention in diaspora studies', in J. E. Braziel and A. Mannur (eds), *Theorizing Diaspora* (Oxford: Blackwell, 2003), pp. 1–22; E. Morawska, '"Diaspora" diasporas' representations of their homelands: exploring the polymorphs', *Ethnic and Racial Studies*, 34 (2011), 1029–48.

3 A. Appadurai, *Modernity at Large: Cultural Dimensions of Globalization* (Minneapolis: University of Minnesota Press, 1996).

4 P. Gilroy, *Between Camps. Nations, Cultures and the Allure of Race* (London: Penguin, 2000); K. A. Appiah, *Cosmopolitanism. Ethics in a World of Strangers* (London: Penguin, 2006).

5 A. D'Andrea, *Global Nomads: Techno and New Age as Transnational Countercultures in Ibiza and Goa* (London: Routledge, 2006).

6 A-M. Fortier and G. Lewis, 'Migrant horizons', *Mobilities*, 1:3 (2006), 307–12; B. Gray, 'Curious hybridities: transnational negotiations of migrancy through generation', *Irish Studies Review*, 14:2 (2006), 207–24; M. Sheller and J. Urry, 'The new mobilities paradigm', *Environment and Planning A*, 38:2 (2006), 207–26.

7 See A. Blunt, 'Cultural geographies of migration: mobility, transnationality and diaspora', *Progress in Human Geography*, 31:5 (2007), 684–94; R. King, 'Geography and migration studies: retrospect and prospect', *Population, Space and Place*, 18:2 (2012), 134–53.

8 K. Tölölyan, 'The nation state and its others: in lieu of a preface', *Diaspora*, 1 (1991), 5 (emphasis added).

9 K. Kenny, 'Diaspora and comparison: the global Irish as a case study', *Journal of American History*, 90:1 (2003), 134 (emphasis added).

10 P. Levitt, 'A transnational gaze', *Migraciones Internacionales*, 6:1 (2011), 9–44.

11 R. C. Smith, 'Migrant membership as an instituted process: migration, the state and the extra-territorial conduct of Mexican politics', *International Migration Review*, 37:2 (2003), 297–343; R. Bauböck, *Transnational Citizenship: Membership and Rights in International Migration* (Aldershot: Edward Elgar, 1994).

12 B. Gray, *Women and the Irish Diaspora* (London: Routledge, 2004).

13 D. L. Eng, 'Out here and over there: queerness and diaspora in Asian American Studies', *Social Text*, 52/53 (1997), 31–52; E. A. Povinelli and G. Chauncey (1999) 'Thinking sexuality transnationally: an introduction', *GLQ. A Journal of Lesbian and Gay Studies*, 5:4 (1999), 439–50; A-M. Fortier, 'Queer diasporas', in D. Richardson and S. Seidman (eds) *Handbook of Lesbian and Gay Studies* (London: Sage, 2002), pp. 183–97; P. R. Pessar and S. J. Mahler, 'Transnational migration: bringing gender in', *International Migration Review*, 37:3 (2003), 812–46.

14 Eng, 'Out here and over there'.

15 L. Basch, N. Glick Schiller and C. Szanton Blanc, *Nations Unbound: Transnational Projects, Post-colonial Predicaments, and Deterritorialized Nation-states* (Langhorne, PA: Gordon and Breach, 1994), p. 6.

16 A. Portes, 'Conclusion: theoretical convergences and empirical evidence in the study of immigrant transnationalism', *International Migration Review*, 37:3 (2003), 874–92; L. Guarnizo, A. Portes, and W. Haller, 'Assimilation and transnationalism: determinants

of transnational political action among contemporary immigrants', *American Journal of Sociology*, 108 (2003), 1211–48.

17 Portes, 'Introduction', 181.

18 Levitt, 'A transnational gaze'; B. Walter, 'Celebrations of Irishness in Britain: second-generation experiences of St. Patrick's Day', in M. C. Considère-Charon, P. Laplace and M. Savaric (eds), *The Irish Celebrating: Festive and Tragic Overtones* (Newcastle: Cambridge Scholars Publishing, 2008), pp. 192–207; M. J. Hickman, 'Census ethnic categories and second-generation identities: a study of the Irish in England and Wales', *Journal of Ethnic and Migration Studies*, 37:1 (2011), 79–97.

19 Portes, 'Introduction', 189.

20 Fonor, 'What's new about transnationalism?'; N. Glick Schiller, 'Transmigrants and nation-states: something old and something new in the U.S. immigrant experience', in C. Hirschman, P. Kasinitz and J. DeWind (eds), *The Handbook of International Migration: The American Experience* (New York: Russell Sage Foundation, 1999), pp. 94–119.

21 S. Vertovec, *Transnationalism* (London: Routledge, 2009); P. Levitt and B.N. Jawarski, 'Transnational migration studies: past developments and future trends', *Annual Review of Sociology*, 33 (2007), 129–56.

22 P. Levitt, 'How sociology is "going transnational": from the study of religious to cultural transformations – in conversation with B. Gray', *Irish Journal of Sociology*, 19:2 (2011), 8–26.

23 T. Faist, 'Diaspora and transnationalism: what kind of dance partners?' in R. Bauböck and T. Faist (eds), *Diaspora and Transnationalism: Concepts, Theories and Methods* (Amsterdam: Amsterdam University Press, 2010), p. 33; Waldinger and Fitzgerald, 'Transnationalism in question'.

24 Portes, 'Introduction', 186.

25 Waldinger and Fitzgerald, 'Transnationalism in question', 1178.

26 *Ibid.*

27 F. Cochrane, *The End of Irish America? Globalisation and the Irish Diaspora* (Dublin: Irish Academic Press, 2010).

28 B. Gray, '"The network state" and diaspora "netizen" members: a case study of Irish state diaspora engagement', *Éire/Ireland*, 47:1&2 (2012), 244–70.

29 N. Glick Schiller, 'Transnationality', in D. Nugent and J. Vincent (eds), *A Companion to the Anthropology of Politics* (Malden, MA: Blackwell, 2004), p. 457.

30 Glick Schiller, 'Transmigrants and nation-states', p. 99.

31 *Ibid.*

32 S. Khagram and P. Levitt, 'Constructing transnational studies', in S. Khagram and P. Levitt (eds) *The Transnational Studies Reader: Intersections and Innovations* (New York: Routledge, 2008), pp. 1–23.

33 Levitt, 'How sociology is "going transnational"'.

34 *Ibid.*

35 Levitt, 'A transnational gaze', 15.

36 *Ibid.*, 11.

37 Pessar and Mahler, 'Transnational migration'; Povinelli and Chauncey, 'Thinking sexuality transnationally'.

38 L. Ryan, 'Family matters: (e)migration, familial networks and Irish women in Britain', *The Sociological Review*, 52 (2004), 351. In a study of postwar Irish migration to Britain, Enda Delaney argues that 'informal personal networks transcended the borders of the nation state' and that 'the Irish in Britain existed in a transnational social space which spanned the Irish Sea and included fellow-migrants, and family and friends living at home'. E. Delaney, 'Transnationalism, networks and emigration

from post-war Ireland', *Immigrants & Minorities*, 23:2–3 (2005), 425.

39 Pessar and Mahler, 'Transnational migration'.

40 Povinelli and Chauncey, 'Thinking sexuality transnationally', 446; R. Diaz, 'Transnational queer theory and unfolding terrorisms', *Criticism*, 50:3 (2008), 533–41; E. Luibhéid, 'Queer/migration: an unruly body of scholarship', *GLQ: A Journal of Lesbian and Gay Studies*, 14 (2008), 169–90; L. Rofel and P. Liu, *Beyond the Strai(gh)ts: Transnationalism and Queer Chinese Politics* (Durham: Duke University Press, 2010). For a broader discussion of transnationalism as shaping Irish feminist politics see N. Reilly, 'The UN "Beijing Platform for Action" 1995–2005: local global political spaces, NGO advocacy, and governmental responses in the Republic of Ireland', *Irish Political Studies*, 20:2 (2005), 187–200, and of the fraught politics of transnational solidaristic feminisms see I. Grewal and C. Kaplan, 'Global identities: theorizing transnational studies of sexuality', *GLQ: A Journal of Lesbian and Gay Studies*, 7:4 (2001), 663–79 and I. Grewal, *Transnational America: Feminisms, Diasporas, Neoliberalisms* (Durham: Duke University Press, 2005).

41 Luibhéid, 'Queer/migration', 179.

42 *Ibid.*

43 A. Weingrod and A. Levy, 'On homelands and diasporas: an introduction', in A. Levy and A. Weingrod (eds), *Homelands and Diasporas. Holy Lands and Other Places* (Stanford: Stanford University Press, 2005), pp. 3–28; G. Sheffer, *Diaspora Politics: At Home Abroad* (Cambridge: Cambridge University Press, 2003) and G. Sheffer (ed.) *Modern Diasporas in International Politics* (London: Croom Helm, 1986); W. Safran, 'Diasporas in modern societies: myths of homeland and return', *Diaspora*, 1:1 (1991), 83–99; R. Cohen, *Global Diasporas. An Introduction* (London: UCL Press, 1997); S. Dufoix, *Diasporas* (Berkeley: University of California Press, 2003).

44 S. Mishra, *Diaspora Criticism* (Edinburgh: Edinburgh University Press, 2006); J. Clifford, *Routes: Travel and Translation in the Late Twentieth Century* (Cambridge, Mass.: Harvard University Press, 1997); Sheffer, *Diaspora Politics*; Sheffer, *Modern Diasporas*. Robin Cohen refers to this perspective as a 'social realist' approach and to the situational laterality perspective as the 'social constructionist' approach. See R. Cohen, 'Interview with Dr Alan Gamlen for the Oxford Diasporas Programme', (2012), available at http://www.youtube.com/watch?v=P8rxYtmJudg, accessed 20 April 2012.

45 Mishra, *Diaspora Criticism*, p. 16; P. Gilroy, *The Black Atlantic: Modernity and Double Consciousness* (London: Verso, 1993); P. Gilroy, *'There Ain't No Black in the Union Jack': The Cultural Politics of Race and Nation* (London: Hutchinson, 1987); Clifford, *Routes*; A. Brah, *Cartographies of Diaspora: Contesting Identities* (London: Routledge, 1986); A. Appadurai, *Modernity at Large. Cultural Dimensions of Globalization* (Minneapolis: University of Minnesota Press, 1996); H. Bhabha, *The Location of Culture* (London: Routledge, 1994); S. Hall, 'Cultural identity and diaspora', in J. Rutherford (ed.) *Identity, Community, Culture, Difference* (London: Lawrence & Wishart, 1990), pp. 222–37; S. Hall, 'The question of cultural identity', in S. Hall, D. Held and T. McGrew (eds), *Modernity and its Futures* (Cambridge: Polity Press, 1992), pp. 274–316.

46 H. De Haas, *Engaging Diasporas: How Governments and Development Agencies can Support Diaspora Involvement in the Development of Origin Countries* (Oxford: International Migration Institute, 2006); D. Ionescu, *Engaging Diasporas as Development Partners for Home and Destination Countries: Challenges for Policymakers* (Geneva: IOM, 2006); Y. Kuznetsov (ed.), *Diaspora Networks and the International Migration of Skills: How Countries Can Draw on Their Talent Abroad, WBI Development Studies* (Washington, D.C.: World Bank, 2006).

47 Mishra, *Diaspora Criticism*, p. 18.

48 K. Butler, 'Defining diaspora, refining a discourse', *Diaspora*, 10:2 (2001), 189–219.

49 Sheffer, *Diaspora Politics*.

50 Clifford, *Routes*.

51 Mishra, *Diaspora Criticism*, p. 28.

52 *Ibid.*, p. 16.

53 *Ibid.*, p. 48.

54 Hall, 'The question of cultural identity', p. 309.

55 Mishra, *Diaspora Criticism*.

56 I. Ang, 'Together-in-difference: beyond diaspora, into hybridity', *Asian Studies Review*, 27:2 (2003), 141–54.

57 M. Scully, 'The tyranny of transnational discourse: "authenticity" and Irish diasporic identity in Ireland and England', *Nations and Nationalism*, 18:2 (2012), 206.

58 *Ibid.*; Gray, '"The network state"'.

59 Brah, *Cartographies of Diaspora*.

60 Fortier, 'Queer diasporas'; Eng, 'Out here and over there'; G. Gopinath, *Impossible Desires: Queer Diasporas and South Asian Public Cultures* (Durham, NC: Duke University Press, 2005).

61 M. Wesling, 'Why Queer Diaspora?', *Feminist Review*, 90 (2008), 30–47.

62 Gray, '"The network state"'.

63 B. Mullings, 'Governmentality, diaspora assemblages and the ongoing challenge of "development"', *Antipode*, 44:2 (2011), 406–27.

64 Mishra, *Diaspora Criticism*.

65 B. Walter, 'Whiteness and diasporic Irishness: nation, gender and class', *Journal of Ethnic and Migration Studies*, 37:9 (2011), 1295–312; M. J. Hickman, 'Diaspora space and national (re)formations', *Éire-Ireland*, 47:1&2 (2012), 19–44.

66 Ang, 'Together-in-difference', 144. See also Anthias, 'Evaluating diaspora' and R. Brubaker, 'The "diaspora" diaspora', *Ethnic and Racial Studies*, 28:1 (2005), 1–19.

67 E. Luibhéid, *Entry Denied. Controlling Sexuality at the Border* (Minneapolis: University of Minnesota Press, 2002), p. x.

68 B. Walter, *Outsiders Inside. Whiteness, Place and Irish Women* (London: Routledge, 2001); B. Walter, *Irish Women in London* (London: London Strategic Policy Unit, 1988); I. O'Carroll, *Models for Movers: Irish Women's Emigration to America* (Dublin: Attic Press, 1990); A. Rossiter, *Ireland's Hidden Diaspora: The Abortion Trail and the Making of a London-Irish Underground, 1980–2000* (London: IASC Publishing, 2009); A. Rossiter, 'Bringing the margins into the centre: a review of aspects of Irish women's emigration from a British perspective', in A. Smyth (ed.), *Irish Women's Studies Reader* (Dublin: Attic Press, 1993), pp.177–202; P. O'Sullivan, (ed.) *Irish Women and Irish Migration* (London: Leicester University Press, 1995); Gray, *Women and the Irish Diaspora*; Ryan, 'Family matters'; Luibhéid, 'Queer/migration'; E. Luibhéid, 'Nationalist heterosexuality, migrant (il)legality, and Irish citizenship law: queering the connections', *South Atlantic Quarterly*, 110:1 (2011), 179–204.

69 Luibhéid, 'Queer/migration'; Luibhéid, 'Nationalist heterosexuality'.

70 S. Carter, 'The geopolitics of diaspora', *Area*, 37:1 (2005), 55.

71 Gray, *Women and the Irish Diaspora*. A total of 111 women took part in the study, thirty-six in London and the south-east of England and seventy-five in the Republic of Ireland. The latter group included seventeen women who had migrated and returned and sixteen Traveller women, eight of whom had lived in Britain at some stage in their lives. Women from urban and rural backgrounds were fairly equally represented in both national locations. Nine per cent of the women in Ireland and 3 per cent of those in London came from non-Catholic, mainly Protestant backgrounds. Forty-nine per cent of the England-based cohort and 64 per cent of

those based in Ireland identified themselves as Catholic. Based on their current occupation I estimate that 60 per cent of the sample was middle class. No black or Jewish women were included in the study.

72 All names are pseudonyms.
73 B. Gray, '"Generation emigration" and social reproduction in twenty-first century Ireland', *Irish Studies Review*, 21:1 (2013), 20–36.
74 A-M. Fortier, *Migrant Belongings. Memory, Space, Identity* (London: Berg, 2000).
75 J. Butler, *Undoing Gender* (New York: Routledge, 2004), p. 10.
76 Gray, 'Curious hybridities'.
77 Ang, 'Together-in-difference'.
78 A. Appadurai and C. Breckenridge, 'On moving targets', *Public Culture*, 2:1 (1989), ii.
79 Brah, *Cartographies of Diaspora*, p. 208.
80 *Ibid.*, p. 184.
81 Faist, 'Diaspora and transnationalism', p. 15.
82 *Ibid.*, p. 21.
83 Brubaker, 'The "diaspora" diaspora', 1.
84 Gray, '"Generation emigration"'.

PART II

Irish women and the diaspora in Britain

3

Exploring religion as a bright and blurry boundary: Irish migrants negotiating religious identity in Britain

Louise Ryan

We were very holy in those days. (Dympna, nurse, migrated 1950s)

I used to go to church every morning, I was holy in those days, to the Brompton Oratory. (Fiona, nurse, migrated 1950s)

This chapter uses the sociological concept of boundaries to explore the processes through which migrants may be included in or excluded from national, ethnic and religious collectivities. In so doing, the discussion examines how, on the one hand, religion can work as a means of building bridges across communities of insiders and outsiders, overcoming the potential divisions of ethnicity and nationality. However, on the other hand, religion may also be used to build walls, dividing people, emphasising differences and reinforcing processes of exclusion. Thus, using the work of Alba, I will argue that religion can be both a 'bright' and a 'blurry' boundary.[1] As the case study of the Irish in Britain shows, these processes are not mutually exclusive but can occur simultaneously. This chapter suggests that religion, ethnicity and nationality intersect in ways that are complex and dynamic and which may also be gendered in particular ways.

The chapter draws on oral histories interviews undertaken with Irish women migrants in Britain. All the research participants mentioned religion as a site on which they confronted and negotiated their identity as Irish women in Britain. Irish migrant belonging and integration had to be negotiated across various ethnic and religious boundaries.[2] The research indicates the ways in which boundaries are not stable but can be experienced as bright or blurry, stable or shifting in different sites. As Catholics the women could be both insiders (within a universal Catholicism) and outsiders (in a Protestant and/or secularised Britain). As Irish people they occupied a complex and indeed contradictory position both as white, European insiders but also as former colonial outsiders.[3]

This chapter suggests the complex and dynamic relationship between national, religious, ethnic and gender boundaries. In so doing, it aims to contribute to wider theoretical debates about the multilayered and shifting processes of belonging and unbelonging.

Theorising boundaries

Boundaries are a way of marking processes of inclusion and exclusion. The boundary separates insiders and outsiders and in so doing defines collectivities of 'us' versus 'them'. For migrants in particular, moving to a new country may redefine their relationship to ethnic and national collectivities as they move from being part of 'us' (their relevant national collectivity) to 'them', the outsiders, newcomers, aliens (within a new national environment). In developing an understanding of how ethnicity is perceived and experienced, the work of the anthropologist Fredrik Barth has been influential.[4] Barth highlights the interplay of self-description and ascription by others in the formation of ethnic identity. In particular, he has highlighted the role of boundaries in forming ethnic insiders and outsiders. Anthias and Yuval-Davis have similarly argued that ethnicity 'can be internally constituted by the group or externally imposed, or both'.[5]

However, membership of an ethnic group does not imply that ethnicity is homogeneous, rather it may be experienced and defined very differently within a specific ethnic group.[6] Ethnic identity interacts with other facets of identity such as class, gender and religion. Articulations of identity emerge 'out of multiple social positionings and the interplay between these positionings in the formations of selves'.[7] Ethnic identity cannot be seen as given or fixed; despite evocations of tradition rooted in the distance past, ethnicities are dynamic and change both temporally and spatially. As Alba indicates, expressions of ethnicity will vary in different social contexts.[8] For example, the way ethnic identity is expressed in an ethnic social club may differ markedly from how ethnic identity is expressed in a more diverse environment such as the work place.

Boundaries are constructed around many different facets of identity – religion, language, nationality – to name a few. These boundaries do not necessarily overlap, so that one may be marked as an outsider on different levels but may be able to negotiate insider status around some key aspects of identity. For example, white migrants may claim insider status in a white majority society, while other aspects of their identity, such as language and nationality, may mark them as outsiders.[9]

The work of Zolberg and Long provides a conceptual starting point for discussing how boundaries are constructed and change over time. They ask the question, 'who can become a member of society and what are the conditions for membership?'[10] In answering this question, they point to the dialectic processes of self-identification and ascription by others – 'involving elaborations of the boundary that defines who we are and who we are not'.[11] Of course boundaries are not necessarily fixed entities, they may be permeated and changed in various ways.

Richard Alba has further developed the conceptualisation of boundaries by arguing that processes of change depend upon how the ethnic boundary is configured and institutionalised in different domains of society.[12] He distinguishes between two main types of boundaries. First, 'bright boundaries': 'the distinction involved is unambiguous, so that individuals know at all times which side of the boundary they are on'.[13] He gives the example of citizenship status which is institutionalised in particular ways that make it more or less accessible in different societies. Secondly, 'blurry boundaries' involve 'zones of self-presentation and social representation that allow for ambiguous locations with respect to the boundary'.[14] These could involve various aspects of culture, food, dress, and music. Religion in different contexts could be either a bright or a blurry boundary or oscillate back and forth between the two.

This conceptualisation of boundaries is useful and indeed has the potential to be taken much further in exploring multifaceted identities. In fact, the theories put forward by Barth, Alba and Zolberg and Long are quite gender neutral and do not explore how men and women may be positioned differently in relation to particular boundaries, such as religious or ethnic boundaries. The work of Anthias and Yuval-Davis is important in conceptualising the gendering of ethnic boundaries.[15] They argue that women are expected to play a key role in the boundary maintenance of their ethnic groups. 'The boundary of the ethnic is often dependent on gender ... much of ethnic culture is organised around rules relating to sexuality, marriage and the family.'[16] However, these rules do not apply equally to men and women. 'Women's membership in their national and ethnic collectivities is of a double nature. On the one hand, women, like men, are members of the collectivity. On the other hand, there are always specific rules and regulations which relate to women as women'.[17]

A plethora of boundaries exist not only between 'immigrant' and 'native' but also within immigrant communities. It is important to see immigrant or ethnic communities as dynamic and diverse rather than static and cohesive.[18] Drawing on the work of Zolberg and Long and Alba, I examine the role of religion in defining boundaries of identity and belonging and also explore how religious identities intersect with ethnicity and gender. Is religion a marker of difference, demarcating those who do not fit in, outsiders, aliens, or can be religion be used as a means of facilitating belonging and inclusion?

I use data from research with Irish women in Britain to explore the dynamic relationship between ethnic and religious boundaries. Focusing on nurses, I examine how religion was negotiated in a work environment and how assumptions about religious practices impacted on constructions of professional identity. Walter has provided a thorough analysis of racialisation of the Irish and, while much of this was embedded in colonialism, in the decades following Irish independence there was a notable increase in tendencies to racialise Irishness within British public discourses.[19] Images of the Irish as not merely inferior but also as violent, drunken and dirty 'savages' proliferated throughout the British popular press in the early twentieth century.[20] For the Irish in Britain, religion has been a key marker of identity and difference.[21] While the Catholic Church may have used religion to try to integrate Irish migrants into British society, it is apparent that being Catholic continued to define Irish people as outsiders in opposition to a historically constituted Protestant Englishness.[22] As discussed at length in the following section, religious labels are used to denote social boundaries as religious identity constructs a symbolic divide between in-group and out-group.[23]

Religion and migration

Peggy Levitt has called for more 'empirical, grounded' research on migration and religion.[24] For too long, she argues, social sciences and migration studies have paid insufficient attention to the importance of religion in the everyday lives of many migrants. Perhaps academic scholars have ignored the importance of religion in people's lives because these scholars usually come from a secular tradition.[25] As Bilge argues, most feminist and liberal scholars seem unable to engage seriously with the religious beliefs of their research participants.[26]

In addition, religious belief is also quite difficult to research. As Levitt notes, religion is not a fixed entity 'but a dynamic web of shared meanings used in different ways in different contexts'.[27] Levitt goes on to argue that it is more about 'individualised, interior, informal practices and beliefs' than about formal, institutional structures and organisations.[28] Hence, it involves something personal and intimate and may be difficult to talk about and verbalise: 'the unobservable dimensions of religious life have often been given short shrift because the analytical tools we have to study them are undeveloped or undervalued.'[29] Levitt argues that in order to understand the role of religion for migrants we must 'build from the ground up' by examining how 'ordinary individuals live their everyday religious lives across borders'.[30]

Religion may perform many different roles in the migratory experience and, indeed, migration may in turn shape religious expression. For example, religion may play a significant role in enabling migrants to imagine themselves within collectivities that span beyond the nation-state.[31] Church-going may fulfil many functions for migrants, not only spiritual, but also practical and social.[32] As Stanczak argues, religious organisations can provide an 'exploratory space for maintaining, reclaiming, and altering aspects of racial and ethnic identity'.[33] Religion can provide a means for maintaining and expressing continuity of faith and practice post migration. In addition, religious beliefs may offer 'protection' from the 'corrupting, inferior values' of that new society.[34] This is not to suggest that religion necessarily leads to separatism but instead, Stanczak suggests, 'religious authority legitimizes the attempts to integrate the community'.[35]

My research suggests that Catholic parishes in Britain have sought to embed migrants within the local context through emphasising the universalism of the Church.[36] No matter where one comes from one is a member of the Catholic family and so will fit into the familiarity of the Church community at local level. In addition, there is recognition of specific liturgical traditions and rituals. These may be maintained and reinforced by ethnic and linguistic chaplains from the sending country.[37] During the post-World War Two period, due to the increasingly diverse migration to Britain,[38] Irish migrants in Britain may have found themselves both grounded in a particular local context – such as an Irish parish in North London – while simultaneously worshipping alongside Catholics from far flung parts of the world, thus locating them within a global religious community that superceded national boundaries.

The aim of the Irish Chaplaincy in Britain has been to care for the Irish abroad and in practice this usually meant 'helping the newly arrived emigrant to adapt and integrate into new surroundings' – there was a strong emphasis on providing practical assistance such as information on 'suitable' employment and accommodation.[39] Fr O'Shea concludes his history of the Irish Chaplaincy by suggesting that since the 1950s many Irish migrants have settled down into their local parishes and to this extent the scheme has achieved its main goal, 'integration into the community'.[40] Thus, the ethos of the Chaplaincy has been, and remains today, one of integration across ethnic and national divisions.[41] This approach fits closely with the policy of the British Catholic hierarchy and the Vatican in strongly advocating that ethnic chaplains should be builders of bridges not walls.[42]

However, I suggest that while Catholicism represents a form of continuity with the homeland, it can also be experienced as a site of difference within the context of migration. Thus despite the apparent universalism of the Catholic Church, religious practices and identities are not always experienced in the same way in every context. I argue that the meaning of a particular religious identity may be experienced differently and negotiated in specific, perhaps unanticipated, ways at the local level in the new society. For example, Catholics arriving in Britain may experience, for the first time, being part of a religious minority. Rather than focusing on religious practices and rituals per se, I am interested in how identity is placed, expressed and experienced through religion in the context of migration. Just as identity is an ongoing dynamic process of formation, so too the relationship between religious and ethnic identity may take on new meanings and manifestations in different social and geographical contexts. Therefore, as Levitt notes, 'Religion plays a critical role in identity construction, meaning making and value formation. Migrants may use religion to create alternative allegiances and places of belonging.'[43] Levitt argues that more work is needed on untangling the relationship between ethnic and religious identities. However, this may not be easy, as my discussion below illustrates that identities are not composed of discrete elements which can be prised apart and analysed separately.

The study

This chapter draws on data from an oral history project with twenty-six Irish nurses in Britain. With the exception of one woman in Birmingham and one in Coventry, all the others were based in the south-east of England, fifteen in London. Four of the women had arrived in Britain in the 1940s, fourteen in the 1950s, three in the 1960s, four in the 1970s and one in the 1980s. The participants ranged in age from 84 to 35 years and the average age was 64 years. The interviews were largely unstructured with a brief topic guide and so tended to be fairly free-flowing narratives. Most of the women were interviewed in their own homes and this setting, plus the flexibility of the interview schedule, usually resulted in a relaxed, informal atmosphere. Looking back on past events involves some of the advantages of hindsight and mature reflection but also some of the complications of how the past is remembered. In a previous paper I have discussed the issues involved in migrants recalling and retelling their early experiences of migration.[44] My interest in this chapter is not the veracity or reliability of their memories but rather how these women made sense of their encounters with and negotiations of Irishness in Britain.

Although I did not specifically ask the women about religion, it is striking that almost all of them introduced the subject in one way or another. For many of the women religion was a taken for granted part of their lives. It shaped their belief systems and framed their weekly rituals and observances. As migrants in Britain, Catholicism provided continuity with their past lives in Ireland. The familiarity of mass, prayers and hymns, as well as the opportunity to meet with other Irish people, helped to provide an important framework for making sense of their new environment. However, the women's narratives also reveal that religion could be a site of contestation and tension as Catholicism defined Irish migrants as foreign, alien and 'other' in Britain.

In the following sections, I explore the women's accounts of how religion was negotiated and expressed in different social spaces and how this both shaped and was shaped by their migratory experiences.

Hospitals and boundaries of inclusion and exclusion

For these nurses, religion had been experienced in complex ways in particular hospitals. It could simultaneously act as a boundary marking difference from non-Catholic colleagues but also a marker of shared belief systems with other Catholics. The extent to which these boundaries were experienced as sites of power or powerlessness depended upon the rank of the individual actors. This is clearly illustrated in an incident described by Dympna who worked in a hospital with large numbers of Irish nurses:

> Then I went on a ward, and they were all Irish you know, it was the capital of Ireland … we used to put our prayer books on the side and we'd go to mass, she [the sister] threw our prayer books down the ground. So we went to Matron. Matron was a Catholic so she said 'I'll see to that' so she did and after that the sister didn't touch our prayer books again. (Dympna)

In this context, the Catholic matron outranked the non-Catholic ward sister and could challenge anti-Catholic behaviour. In hospitals with a strong tradition of recruiting Irish and/or Catholic nurses, religious identity could be constructed and experienced very differently. Orla trained in a hospital that actually encouraged students to attend mass. 'The matron was very strict, she always tried to get us to go to Mass early in the morning before we started work.' Thus some hospitals could be described as sites in which Catholic identity was not only encouraged but also positively reinforced.[45]

Bernadette was recruited directly from Ireland to work at a hospital in Coventry in the 1950s: 'the matron used to go to convents up and down Ireland to recruit people and say it was an Irish Catholic hospital they were being brought to.' As a result of these recruitment strategies there were large numbers of Catholic staff employed at the hospital and this meant that mass attendance was strongly encouraged:

> When I was on an early shift I would go to half 6 mass, Sister Morgan was a Catholic, the Matron was a Catholic, Sister Broderick was a Catholic, so I suppose they wouldn't be too happy if they thought you stayed in bed. (Bernadette)

It is important to remember that most of these student nurses were recruited at a young age and many went to Britain directly from school. Clearly some parents regarded Catholic hospitals as a safe and suitable environment for their young daughters. Aisling recalled that her mother had encouraged her to go to a partic-ular hospital in London:

> because it is a Catholic run place, it was run by nuns, so it was very strict. We came from a very strict up bringing, very Catholic up bringing, to a Catholic environment and the reason we went into that environment was to keep us off the street, we had to be in at a certain time. (Aisling, migrated 1970s)

Thus, it was assumed that hospitals run by Catholics would envelop the young nurses within a safe environment, erecting a protective boundary from the dangers which lurked outside the hospital walls. The Catholic Church did not simply provide religious services to the young student nurses. There was also an important social aspect to the church. Many of the women recalled attending dances and other social activities in the local church hall: 'We were allowed to go to the church youth club, a grand crowd' (Eithne). Several women met their future husbands at the local Catholic dance. For example, Clodagh recalled: 'I met Gerry weeks after I started nursing, we used to go, like good Catholic girls, to St Augustine's club in Hammersmith.' These social spaces were usually regarded by the women as a safe place where they could relax, have fun and socialise with other young people. These were also spaces where they could express their Irishness in a familiar and friendly environment.[46]

However, while Catholicism was positively reinforced in some hospitals, in others it became a source of tensions, discrimination and resistance. Many women described encounters with colleagues which highlighted boundaries of difference and similarity, exclusion and inclusion based on religion. In most cases, their ethnicity and religion were conflated.

> The matron didn't have a lot of time for Irish people, you knew the feeling, you were like something that came off the sole of her shoe. So I showed her my papers and she said 'oh I suppose you want to go to church'. I said yes and she said 'well you can go to church on your day off'. And I said 'I will go to church every Sunday'.
> (Kathleen, migrated 1949)

Although she was young, newly arrived and 'didn't know a soul' in the hospital, Kathleen challenged the authority of the matron. Her identity, as an Irish Catholic, was more important to her than the rules of the hospital. Kathleen went to nursing headquarters in Portman Square and arranged to transfer to a different hospital where she completed her training.

In their study of Irish Catholics in Scotland, Walls and Williams interviewed a Protestant nurse, now retired, who complained that Catholic nurses always wanted extra time off to attend church.[47] Indeed, many of the older nurses in my study said that their requests to attend mass every Sunday were often regarded as unreasonable and inconvenient. Sheila recalled that although there was a Catholic church 'across the road' from the hospital, it was very difficult for the Catholic students to get time off to attend mass as the matron said 'we were wasting time' (Sheila, migrated 1952). She also suggested that Catholic nurses may have encountered discrimination in particular hospitals: 'a Catholic never got promoted there, at least that was the view, how true that is I'm not sure, but it looked like that and I heard that, and you know, rumours don't go around that easy.'

The apparent conflation of ethnic and religious boundaries meant that Irish nurses were often implicated in stereotypes which were assumed to undermine their professionalism and commitment to their job.

> There was a big thing made about the Irish Catholic nurses and you don't have to have anything to do with anybody having a termination, and I said I'm not there judging and I don't know why they ended up in that bed having to have an abortion,

it is not my place to judge them. I said you don't have to worry about me ... but they assumed that the Irish Catholics would have a big problem with it. But one of my friends tried to get out of the gyny ward but she was allocated to it anyway. (Cliona, migrated 1970s)

Cliona's story suggests not only that Irish Catholics were expected to have a 'big problem' with abortion, but that they were allowed to excuse themselves from this area of work. Nonetheless, her friend had tried and failed to avoid work on the gynaecology ward. Siobhan described how her assumed belief system was discussed when she went for a job interview:

the person who interviewed me she said 'you have one child and you're going to have more, obviously you are a Catholic so you won't be using contraceptives'. Yeah, this was said to me ... That wouldn't happen today but that was said to me. I didn't know what to say...Anyway, I got the job, but those were the sort of things that we said to you. (Siobhan, migrated 1960s)

The interview panel simply took for granted that an Irish woman would strictly adhere to Catholic dogma on family planning. Siobhan's ethnicity was thus used to place her within a particular religious boundary – she was 'obviously a Catholic' – and to draw a firm conclusion about her behaviour – hence she would not be 'using contraceptives'. This put Siobhan in the difficult position of needing to explain her family planning strategy in relation to Church teaching, either by affirming her religious observance or by explaining her decision to break with Catholic teaching on this sensitive issue. She was left not 'knowing what to say'.

Bright and blurry boundaries

As noted earlier, religious beliefs and worship can be fluid and change in different contexts and at different points through the life course. Religious identity and expression may change in the context of migration. This is clearly demonstrated by Sinead, the youngest woman in my study and also the one who spoke most openly about her religious beliefs:

my sense of identity is quite bound up in going to mass, so I had done the rebellious thing and hadn't gone to mass for years, so I decided I would go to church and I went after a year of being in England, so I went to mass and that was how I maintained my sense of identity. (Sinead, migrated 1980s)

Sinead sees a strong link between her ethnic and religious identity: 'I am very much an Irish person, I would never play my Irishness down or adapt or change my accent to accommodate people I am Irish and that's it and I am a Catholic and I am very proud.'

However, it is apparent that she also sees religion as a bridge that can foster links across ethnic groups.

> I became very friendly with a girl from the West Indies so I very much got into understanding the West Indian community and I didn't really hang around with so many of the Irish girls. The girl from Trinidad was my friend and we were great friends actually she was all the way from Trinidad and ... she was a Catholic as well so we had that commonality through our faith. (Sinead)

Their shared Catholicism united these two young nurses across their different ethnicities. Religion created a bridge across their different ethnic and national histories fostering commonality and understanding which lead to a meaningful friendship. It is also clear that religion can divide people who share the same ethnic identity.

> There were two girls, one from Wexford, she was Church of Ireland so we had commonalities but there was still a sense that we were the same but a bit different because the rites of passage were different, communities that we mixed in and things I felt important we wouldn't necessarily have shared. (Sinead)

For Sinead it is apparent that religion is a bright boundary of difference. While she can relate to someone from a different ethnicity through a shared religion, it is clear that she finds religious difference a barrier to meaningful friendships within ethnic groups. Thus, one could argue that, for Sinead, religion is a more powerful marker of identity than ethnicity in this context.

Hence, it is necessary to question the conflation of ethnic and religious boundaries. Not all the women in my study were simply placed or positioned themselves within a collective Catholic identity. Dympna had a particularly unusual surname which meant people 'didn't know whether I was Catholic or Protestant'. She went on to explain: 'My great grandfather was a Presbyterian and he married an Irishwoman and she converted him to Catholicism.' Although this Protestant relative had been a distant ancestor, his surname continued to mark out her identity with a somewhat ambiguous, blurry boundary. Dympna was not the only participant to have had a Protestant ancestor.

Noreen's 'grandparents were Protestant, Church of Ireland, and my mother had become a Catholic to marry my father'. Noreen's parents lived on the farm with her grandparents: 'I think my father found it difficult living in a Protestant household.' Noreen attended the local Catholic school but found some tensions between the doctrine taught by the nuns in school and her life on the farm with her Protestant grandparents:

> There was this very strict nun and ... she said nobody can go to heaven unless they are baptised into the Catholic church, well I thought of my lovely grandmother and grandfather and I thought well I'm not going to heaven because I wouldn't want to

go where they weren't, you know, as a child my mind worked like that, so I began to question things. (Noreen, migrated 1946)

Thus, Noreen had an ambiguous relationship with Catholicism and could be said to experience religion as a blurry, rather than a bright, boundary. Noreen's story also demonstrated that boundaries do not simply divide people; they can also be crossed so that people move from an out-group to part of the in-group. In the case of religious boundaries this can be achieved through conversion. While Noreen's mother converted to marry her father, several of the nurses in my study had sought to convert their husbands.

Although most of the women married Irish-Catholic men, several had 'married out', i.e. married Protestants. These 'mixed marriages' had to be carefully negotiated with in-laws on both sides of the family. Bernadette's marriage to an English Protestant encountered some opposition from her future in-laws in Coventry but more especially from her parents back home in Ireland: 'I was marrying the first non-Catholic within the family and my mother went up to see the nuns, you know, and they all said "well, knowing Bernadette she will probably have him a Catholic within 6 months".' Thus the local nuns in Ireland reassured Bernadette's mother about the wedding by saying that the husband could be persuaded to cross the religious boundary. Bernadette's husband did convert but only many years later. What is interesting about this story is that Bernadette's marriage in Coventry had to be discussed in such detail with religious leaders in the local village in Ireland. Through religion, the local and the transnational become interconnected in ways that strengthen bonds across national boundaries.[48] By converting her husband, Bernadette enabled him to cross the bright boundary of religion from being a religious outsider within an Irish-Catholic family to a Catholic insider.

Interestingly, Eithne also 'married out' and her husband converted quite quickly to Catholicism but with unexpected consequences: 'My husband converted to Catholicism, which was a mistake in my eyes, contraception wise, because I was a bit more liberal than that. He seemed so surprised.' Given the comments earlier about Siobhan and her use of contraception, it is interesting that Eithne defines herself as 'liberal' on the issue of birth control. Her husband's conservative views on family planning were a source of tension in the marriage. Eithne had wanted to continue working but her career was cut short by pregnancy and child rearing. In subsequent sections the issue of combining work and motherhood will be discussed in more detail.

Encountering religion in new contexts

Many of the women moved to new locations upon marriage. For several women this was the first time they had lived outside the nurses' home and, as I have discussed elsewhere, it required considerable readjustment.[49] Getting to know a new place, making new friends, navigating unfamiliar terrain was often discussed in terms of Catholic institutions: the Church, school and social clubs. Eileen was typical of many participants:

> There was a new school up here, Our Lady of Grace, opened. So it was the first Catholic school up the road and my first child went there. And there were a lot of the mothers, you know, mainly Irish because the majority (at the school) were Irish. We formed a group then. I was on the first PTA in the school and we used to do church cleaning and all that and then we started ladies night. (Eileen, migrated 1950s)

As the mother of young children in a new area, Eileen made friends and established herself in a community through the local Catholic school and church. Because of the ethnic make-up of the area in north London, Eileen inhabited a mainly Irish world where ethnicity and religious identity were reinforced.

Most of the women spoke about sending their children to Catholic schools, attending mass and feeling part of a local Catholic community. For those women like Eileen who had young children in the 1950s-60s, many of these Catholic parishes, especially in London, were largely Irish. Hence their Irishness and Catholicism were conflated.

Nonetheless, not all women felt included within the local Irish-Catholic community. Tricia, whose children attended the local Catholic school, described how there was a network of Irish mothers at the school. But she felt excluded from this 'clique'. None of these women offered her friendship or any sort of practical support. Tricia worked an early shift at a prestigious London hospital. She recalls: 'not one of the Catholic mothers offered to help me although I had helped them quite a lot and I had delivered one of the women's babies, but not one of them offered to take my children to school.' Tricia believed that these women disapproved of her because she worked full time:

> The Irish were great for it, if they weren't working themselves ... There was a very catty atmosphere, they were the type of individuals who went to church and would never miss church but then they thought that gave them the right to stand and criticise everybody else who wasn't conforming to their rigid rules. (Tricia, migrated 1953)

Tricia started work at 7am and some of the local mothers were suspicious that she was leaving her children at home alone to get themselves ready for school. Someone contacted the local health visitor to make a complaint. 'The Irish women went and told that I was leaving my children on their own in the flat, they forgot that my husband was working nights and he was there with them.' Tricia's husband was at home when the health visitor called and he explained that he was always arrived back home before Tricia left for work. Tricia's domestic arrangements contravened societal expectations of the period. It seemed impossible for '*the mothers at the school gate*' to imagine that Tricia's husband could be looking after the children and getting them ready for school each morning.

Clearly these mothers had a particular view about how Catholic mother-hood should be expressed. As Anthias and Yuval-Davis have argued, ethnic and religious boundaries are gendered in ways that place a heavy weight of expecta-tion on women's social obligations.[50] Tricia contravened those expectations and was shunned by the group. She crossed a boundary which marked her as an outsider, not 'one of us'.

Tricia also felt that the nuns at the school, several of whom were also Irish, disapproved of her working full time. Tricia's experiences suggest that shared ethnicity is no guarantee of friendship and support. As Sarah Holloway has noted, there are local childcare cultures that create 'a moral geography of mothering'.[51] Of course these discourses around motherhood were not unique to Catholic communities of the period. The social and historical context of postwar British society forms the backdrop to many of the nurses' stories. As described by Wendy Webster, the 1950s discourses of the ideal housewife and mother were encouraged by the state, churches, the media and an array of experts including, most notably, the psychologist John Bowlby whose 1953 book *Childcare and the Growth of Love* became a best-seller.[52] Many of the women I interviewed wanted to pursue their nursing careers after they had children. However, their decisions and opportunities were influenced by public discourses and social policies idealising the 'stay-at-home' mother.

While the Catholic Church regarded itself as a source of spiritual and in many cases practical support for its parishioners, it is apparent that not all the women could comfortably claim their position within the Catholic community. In addition, some women felt disappointed that the Church had not responded to them in a time of particular need. Sheila's husband died at a young age, leaving her alone with five young children to support.

> I didn't get any help at all from the Catholic Church, the only people who gave me anything, I remember, they used to bring a hamper every Christmas were the Presbyterians, the church the other side of Camden Tube station. The Catholic Church never brought anything to this door and that is what I hold against them more than anything ... Oh they'd ask you why you didn't go to church and why the kids weren't at church and all that, but as far as any practical help, nothing like that. (Sheila)

It is noteworthy that Sheila lived in Camden, not far from the Irish Chaplaincy, yet she felt no connection and received no practical support from this service. Like Tricia, Sheila is suggesting that membership within the boundary of the Catholic community was conditional on conformity to particular social norms. She was busy and did not attend mass regularly, for which she was criticised by the local clergy. Instead of receiving help from the Catholic community around her, Sheila instead was offered and accepted support from a local Protestant group. Tricia and Sheila both lived within the geographical locale of a Catholic community. However, for different reasons both felt excluded, unsupported and criticised by their Catholic brethren. Thus they did not belong within the boundaries of the community.

Conclusion

This chapter has used the concept of boundaries to explore the processes through which Irish migrants in Britain have both positioned themselves and been placed by others in relation to religion and ethnicity. I suggest that boundaries are a useful way of capturing the dynamic processes that shift both temporally and spatially as religious and ethnic identities take on distinct meanings at different times and places. For migrants, in particular, moving to a new place may mean that aspects of identity are experienced and expressed in different ways; taking on new significance and meanings. Religious practices may forge a link with the sending country. Regular mass attendance, the familiarity of rituals, hymns and prayers, provide a sense of continuity with 'home' in a new and strange environment. As Richard Alba has noted, participation in such collective rituals enables the expression of a shared identity.

However, as well as continuity and shared identity, religion may also be experienced as a marker of difference. Upon arrival in Britain many of the nurses in this study were confronted by 'bright' ethnic and religion boundaries which were defined by stereotypes and discriminatory practices. Mass attendance was frequently mentioned as a practice through which boundaries of identity were constructed and, in several cases, hotly contested. Hospitals became defined as either pro- or anti-Catholic depending on how mass attendance was facilitated, encouraged or impeded. However, boundaries of religious identity extended beyond Sunday mass. Their professionalism as nurses and their individualism as women could be undermined by assumptions about how their beliefs and practices were defined by strict adherence to Catholicism. Family planning, contraception and abortion in particular were topics which were used to define boundaries of insiders and outsiders.

While religion may be experienced as a marker of difference; defining outsider status, it can also become a channel for integration. As Peggy Levitt has argued, within the universal Catholic family migrants may negotiate their belonging in their new environment while simultaneously maintaining links with their traditional beliefs and practices.[53] Thus, as Stanczak suggests, religion becomes a mechanism through which migrants may be both integrated and 'protected' from the 'corrupting' influences of the host society.[54] The Irish Chaplaincy, particularly, in the 1950s and 60s, regarded its role as one of supporting migrants to remain faithful to their religion, while at the same time becoming active members of British society.

Certainly, many of the participants in my study created a sense of community and belonging in local neighbours through their active involvement in Catholic schools and parishes. Depending on the areas in which they lived, these parishes may have been spaces where both religious and ethnic identities were reinforced. In more ethnically diverse areas, Catholic parishes could provide a space in which religion fostered a sense of 'commonality' across ethnic boundaries.

For many of the women religion was a bright boundary that could only be crossed by the long and complex process of conversion to Catholicism. However, for others religion was a more blurry boundary. Some women, especially those who had Protestant relatives, did not have a fixed Catholic identity. Others, in particular those who were critical of the Church or felt unsupported by the clergy, had a relatively weak sense of affiliation to religious institutions. It is also apparent that perceived deviation from gendered Catholic norms and practices could result in a process of boundary shifting, as one woman in particular felt excluded from the local Catholic clique.

Thus, to conclude, I suggest that a boundaries perspective helps us to capture the complexity of multifaceted identities. Although Irishness and Catholicism are often conflated, it is important to understand the dynamism of the temporal and spatial interplay between these two boundaries. In different places and at different times these identity markers may take on distinct meaning and significance. They may be experienced as bright, fixed, impermeable boundaries demarcating clear lines of inclusion or exclusion or, alternatively, as blurry and ambiguous. In addition, it is necessary to remember that religion and ethnicity intersect in complex ways with other markers of identity such as age, marital status, parenthood, profession.[55] My analysis illustrates the significance of gender in negotiations of religious and ethnic boundaries. The role of gender has been underplayed in the theorisation of Alba and Zolberg and Long. Thus, drawing on the work of Anthias and Yuval-Davis, this chapter suggests that positioning and belonging within specific religious and ethnic collectivities is informed by gendered norms and roles. The extent to which women conform to these gendered discourses both shape and are shaped by religious identifications. My work further reveals the dynamism of these processes as affiliation to religious institutions and conformity to religious norms may change with particular life circumstances associated with marriage and motherhood. Hence, this chapter highlights the weakness in gender-neutral conceptualisations of ethno-religious boundaries. The narratives of these Irish nurses suggest the different ways in which they not only confronted but also constructed their multiple identities. Their position within and beyond ethnic and religious boundaries cannot be taken for granted but involved active and ongoing processes of negotiation through the life course.

Notes

1 R. Alba, 'Bright versus blurry boundaries: second-generation assimilation and exclusion in France, Germany and the United States', *Ethnic and Racial Studies*, 28:1 (2005), 20–49.

2 M. J. Hickman, *Religion, Class and Identity: the State, the Catholic Church and the Education of the Irish in Britain* (Ashgate: Aldershot, 1995).

3 B. Walter, *Outsiders Inside: Whiteness, Place and Irish Women* (London: Routledge, 2001).

4 F. Barth, 'Ethnic groups and boundaries', in J. Hutchinson and A. D. Smith (eds) *Ethnicity* (Oxford: Oxford University Press, 1996), pp. 75–82.

5 F. Anthias and N. Yuval-Davis, *Racialised Boundaries: Race, Nation, Gender, Colour and Class and the Anti-Racist Struggle* (London: Routledge, 1993), p. 4.

6 K. R. Lacy, 'Black spaces, black places: strategic assimilation and identity construction in middle-class suburbia', *Ethnic and Racial Studies*, 27:6 (2004), 908–30; A. Wimmer, 'Does ethnicity matter? Everyday group formation in three Swiss immigrant neighbourhoods', *Ethnic and Racial Studies*, 27:1 (2004), 1–36; S. Castles and M. Miller, *The Age of Migration: International Population Movements in the Modern World* (Basingstoke: Palgrave, 2003).

7 B. Gray, *Women and the Irish Diaspora* (London: Routledge, 2004), p.19

8 R. Alba, *Ethnic Identity: The Transformation of White America* (Yale University Press: London, 1990).

9 L. Ryan, 'Becoming Polish in London: negotiating ethnicity through migration', *Social Identities*, 16:3 (2010), 359–76.

10 A. Zolberg and L. Witt Long, 'Why Islam is like Spanish: cultural incorporation in Europe and the United States', *Politics and Society*, 27:1 (1999), 8.

11 *Ibid.*, 28.

12 Alba, 'Bright versus blurry boundaries', 21.

13 *Ibid.*

14 *Ibid.*, 22.

15 Anthias and Yuval-Davis, *Racialised Boundaries*; N. Yuval-Davis, *Gender and Nation* (London: Sage, 1997).

16 Anthias and Yuval-Davis, *Racialised Boundaries*, p. 113.

17 Yuval-Davis, *Gender and Nation*, p. 37.

18 C. Alexander, R. Edwards and B. Temple, 'Contesting cultural communities: language, ethnicity and citizenship in Britain', *Journal of Ethnic and Migration Studies*, 33:5 (2007), 783–800.

19 Walter, *Outsiders Inside*; R. Douglas, 'Anglo-Saxons and Attacotti: the racialisation of Irishness in Britain between the World Wars', *Ethnic and Racial Studies*, 25:1 (2002), 43.

20 L. Ryan, 'Aliens, migrants and maids: public discourses on Irish immigration to Britain in 1937', *Immigrants and Minorities*, 20:3 (2001), 25–42.

21 P. Walls and R. Williams, 'Sectarianism at work: accounts of employment discrimination against Irish Catholics in Scotland', *Ethnic and Racial Studies*, 26:4 (2003), 632–62.

22 M. J. Hickman, 'Reconstructing deconstructing "race": British political discourses about the Irish in Britain', *Ethnic and Racial Studies*, 21:2 (1998), 289–307

23 Lacy, 'Black spaces'.

24 P. Levitt, 'Religion as a path to civic engagement', *Ethnic and Racial Studies*, 31:4 (2008), 766–91.

25 S. Bilge, 'Beyond subordination versus resistance: an intersectional approach to the agency of veiled Muslim women', *Journal of Intercultural Studies*, 31:1 (2010), 9–28.

26 *Ibid.*

27 P. Levitt, 'You know Abraham was really the first immigrant: religion and transnational migration', *International Migration Review*, 37:3 (2003), 869.
28 *Ibid.*
29 *Ibid.*, 851.
30 P. Levitt, 'Redefining the boundaries of belonging', *Sociology of Religion*, 65:1 (2004), 5.
31 *Ibid.*
32 Zolberg and Long, 'Why Islam is like Spanish'; Levitt, 'Religion as a path to civic engagement'.
33 G. Stanczak, 'Strategic ethnicity: the construction of multi-racial/multi-ethnic religious community', *Ethnic and Racial Studies*, 29:5 (2006), 857.
34 Levitt, 'Redefining the boundaries', 13.
35 Stanczak, 'Strategic ethnicity'.
36 L. Ryan and P. Hatziprokopiou (with A. Castro-Ayala), *Ethnic and Linguistic Chaplains: A Research Study*, Commissioned by the Catholic Bishops Conference of England and Wales (2010).
37 *Ibid.*
38 For an overview see L. Ryan and W. Webster (eds), *Gendering Migration: Masculinity, Femininity and Ethnicity in Post-War Britain* (Ashgate: Aldershot, 2008).
39 K. O'Shea, *The Irish Emigrant Chaplaincy Scheme in Britain, 1957–82* (Naas: Printed by the Leinster Leader, 1985), p. 61.
40 *Ibid.*
41 For a discussion of the ongoing work of the Irish Chaplaincy, mainly supporting older Irish people, see Ryan and Hatziprokopiou, *Ethnic and Linguistic Chaplains*.
42 Erga Migrantes Caritas Christi, *Pontifical Council for the Pastoral Care of Migrants and Itinerant People* (Vatican City, 2004).
43 Levitt, 'Religion and transnational migration', 851.
44 L. Ryan, 'Navigating the emotional terrain of families "here and there": women, migration and the management of emotions', *Journal of Inter-cultural Studies*, 29:3 (2008), 299–314.
45 L. Ryan, 'Who do you think you are?: Irish nurses encountering ethnicity and constructing identity in Britain', *Ethnic and Racial Studies*, 30:3 (2007), 416–38.
46 *Ibid.*
47 Walls and Williams, 'Sectarianism at work'. As noted by Walls and Williams the sectarian context in Scotland is quite distinctive and different in many ways from the situation in England.
48 Levitt, 'Religion as a path to civic engagement'.
49 L. Ryan, 'Migrant women, social networks and motherhood: the experiences of Irish nurses in Britain', *Sociology*, 41:2 (2007), 295–312.
50 Anthias and Yuval-Davis, *Racialised Boundaries*.
51 S. Holloway, 'Local childcare cultures: moral geographies of mothering and the social organisation of pre-school education', *Gender, Place and Culture*, 5 (1998), 31.
52 W. Webster, *Imagining Home: Gender, Race and National Identity, 1945–64* (London: University College London Press, 1998).
53 Levitt, 'Redefining the boundaries of belonging'.
54 Stanczak, 'Strategic ethnicity'.
55 Ryan, 'Who do you think you are?'.

4

Irish-Catholic women and modernity in 1930s Liverpool

Charlotte Wildman

World War One 'marked the beginning of a Catholic revival' in Britain and America suggests Patrick Allitt, reflected by 'a period of bolder social policy, accelerated institutional growth, and a new concern with intellectual life'.[1] The confidence of the Catholic Church was particularly striking because of the notable number of high-profile religious conversions made by public intellectuals in the two decades after 1918: Evelyn Waugh, Graham Greene, Ronald Knox and Edith Sitwell all became Roman Catholics and T. S. Eliot and C. S. Lewis became Anglo-Catholics. Although the spiritual experience and religious identity of these Catholic converts has attracted scholarly attention,[2] historians of twentieth-century Britain, including those writing about the Irish diaspora,[3] have largely neglected the role of popular or working-class Catholicism except in relation to sectarianism.[4] However, recent debates regarding secularisation, led by Callum Brown's work that argues Britain did not become a secular country until the 1960s,[5] suggest it is time to reconsider the nature, strength and influence of Catholicism more generally between the two world wars, as well as the Church's relationship with broader social and cultural changes.[6]

The scholarly neglect of popular Catholicism reflects broader cultural stereo-typical understandings of the religion during the early twentieth century. Adam Schwartz highlights the criticisms Catholic converts received from their peers and quotes Virginia Woolf's horrified response to the 'shameful and distressing' news of Eliot's conversion in 1928, declaring 'he may be called dead to us from this day forward … there's something obscene in a living person sitting by the fire and believing in God'.[7] Criticisms of the non-elite Roman Catholic population were even more damning and, for example, became the focus of Marie Stopes's birth control campaign after 1918: she constantly vilified their 'soiled, diseased, desperate, and misbegotten reproductions'.[8] Such attitudes have since shaped historical scholarship, which has typified interwar Catholicism as 'parochial, legalistic and utterly third rate'.[9]

These stereotypes have contributed to the perceived close association between secularisation and modernity since, as Adrian Hastings claims, 'modernity had simply no place for religion in general or Christianity in particular'.[10] British modernity tends to be associated with the decline of the role of the Church from the late nineteenth century, alongside the rise in mass consumerism, changes in women's roles and rights, a new imperialism, new innovations in technologies and accompanied by a sense of crisis as contemporaries attempted to make sense of these changes.[11] Schwartz suggests Roman Catholicism was inherently anti-modernity and therefore explains the very attraction for intellectual converts such as Greene; 'it was precisely Roman Catholicism's perceived willingness to swim against what these converts considered their day's prevailing cultural currents that made this "rejected minority" so compelling to them.'[12] Key texts on British modernity are notable in that they do not address Catholicism, the Irish diaspora or even religion.[13]

Yet Joshua Landy and Michael Saler's recent edited volume, *The Re-Enchantment of the World*, argues that modernity is 'defined less by binaries arranged in an implicit hierarchy, or by the dialectical transformation of one term into its opposite, than by contradictions, oppositions, and antinomies: modernity is messy'.[14] Their collection develops a growing acceptance amongst scholars 'that there are forms of enchantment entirely compatible with, and indeed at times dependent upon, those features of modernity usually seen as disenchanting the world'.[15] Their work suggests that not only does the relationship between modernity and religion in England need to be re-addressed, but, by implication, the very definition of modernity, and its perceived close association with secularisation, needs to be reconsidered also.

Catholic women, in particular, have been characterised by historians as being alienated from the processes of modernity and isolated from the emerging new opportunities presented to them in mass culture, employment and education, which are considered to be inherently secular and non-spiritual.[16] Maryann Valiulis, for example, argues the Catholic Church in Ireland constructed a form of womanhood during the 1920s, which 'represented a bulwark against modernisation'.[17] Yet Louise Ryan's study of newspaper debates over the 'modern girl' during the mid-1920s, suggests there were tensions 'between the need to assert traditional Irish values while, at the same time, negotiating modern cultural influences'.[18] The work of anthropologist Roberto Orsi on Italian-Catholic women migrants in early twentieth-century New York City, also shows how they were able to balance their Catholic identity with the changing world around them.[19]

Influenced by Orsi's and Ryan's approaches and alongside the scholarship of Landy and Saler, this chapter uses Irish-Catholic women in 1930s Liverpool to challenge the perceived binary between religion and modernity and to undermine stereotypes about popular Catholicism amongst the Irish diaspora in

Britain. I argue that Catholic leaders in Liverpool became increasingly relaxed about modernity and its impact on women and, furthermore, were keen to carve out roles and responsibilities for women that merged their Catholicism with emerging opportunities in paid work, civic duties and leisure and consumer culture. My approach not only encourages a renegotiation of the relationship between modernity and religion but also offers a new way of thinking about the experience of the Irish diaspora in Britain and, in particular, offers Irish–Catholic women more agency and authority than historical scholarship tends to allow. Rather than perceiving Irish women's diasporic identification as the product of late-twentieth-century modernity, as scholars have a tendency to do, my research suggests that Irish women's diasporic identity helped to produce and shape the form and nature of late modernity.[20] Using the programme of Catholic Action, implemented by Liverpool Archdiocese during the 1930s, the chapter illustrates the positive contribution Irish-Catholic women made to public life in Liverpool as an implication of the Church's strategy towards modernity.

The Irish-Catholic diaspora in Liverpool

The Catholic population in England rose from 2.5 million in 1920 to 3 million in 1940, largely due to Irish migration.[21] Catholic communities were found throughout the country, but especially in London and Lancashire. Liverpool Archdiocese was created in 1924 with an official population of 183,811, but this figure excluded Birkenhead, North Liverpool, and most of the area beyond the immediate city centre.[22] One estimate counted 249,000 Catholics living in the three- to four-mile radius surrounding the Town Hall in 1925,[23] whereas a separate survey suggested Liverpool was home to 400,000 Catholics in 1934.[24] Within a general population of around 750,000 therefore, Liverpool's Catholic community encompassed at least a third and possibly over a half of the population interwar. Liverpool's other majority religion was Protestantism, and there were notable numbers of Presbyterians and Methodists, and a significant Jewish community.

Liverpool's Catholics were mainly concentrated in the Scotland Road area between the city centre and the docks. Scotland Road was home to 75,000 of Liverpool's Catholics, which made it larger than the Dioceses of Cardiff, Shrewsbury, Portsmouth and Middlesbrough combined.[25] Everton was one of the few districts of Liverpool that was home to significant numbers of skilled and 'respectable' Catholics.[26] Broadly speaking, middle-class Catholics did tend to leave Scotland Road, wishing to distance themselves from the area's working-class social network and culture.[27] Yet although considered the 'black spot on the Mersey',[28] Scotland Road should not be presented within the context of the typical myths relating to slums and ghettoes that dominate historical accounts of the Irish experience in Britain.[29] Many people chose to live there because of the support network offered[30] and the area should be seen as a micro-society, with an independent form of hierarchy and social stratification.[31] Inhabitants were, however, united by Catholicism and close links with Ireland. As John Belchem writes, 'there would be no place for Protestants in the Irishness of the diaspora: ethnic and religious identity were increasingly interwoven, a symbiotic relation- ship which "made Irish, Catholic and Catholic, Irish"'.[32]

P. J. Waller's classic *Democracy and Sectarianism* illustrated the strong influence of the Irish-Catholic diaspora on local politics in Liverpool. One commentator in the 1920s 'likened the monthly Labour meetings to "a lesson in apartheid", where members segregated themselves according to religion and politics'.[33] There was an Irish nationalist MP for Liverpool, 1885–1929, and concerns about the Labour Party's secularism prevented the Party from taking over the city's administration until 1955.[34] Although there was less explicit violence than before 1918,[35] sectarian tensions prevailed throughout the 1920s and 1930s.[36] In partic- ular, Protestants in Liverpool campaigned against the provision of Catholic schools and the perceived burden on the rates caused by Irish immigrants.[37] Catholic leaders in Liverpool were enthusiastic to improve the image of the Church and sought to move away from the sectarian violence that had dominated the city in the pre-World War One years. This strategy was typical during the energetic and ambitious leadership of Archbishop Doctor Richard Downey (1881–1953) from 1928, who was keen that Catholics should be less involved with local politics and banned priests from involvement in municipal elections.[38] Nevertheless Irish-Catholics in Liverpool suffered from greater sectarian prejudices during the interwar period as the city was badly hit by economic depression in the two decades that followed 1918:[39] unemployment rates remained higher than average throughout the 1930s, hitting 33 per cent in 1932 compared with 22.7 per cent nationally.[40] Liverpool's Irish-Catholic community was not only worse affected because of their reliance on low-paid, low-skilled jobs such as dock work, but they were also often blamed for the city's problems.[41] The Irish-Catholic diaspora has also led historians to characterise Liverpool as being 'exceptional' or separate from broader British political and social culture and goes some way to explain the scholarly neglect of the diaspora (and of Liverpool) in discussions of British modernity.[42] Looking at Irish- Catholic women in Liverpool however, draws similarities with broader social and cultural changes in Britain that shaped ideas about women's roles after World War One.

The problem of modernity: Catholic women in the postwar world

As peace finally fell throughout Europe in 1919, the Catholic Church was one of many institutions that looked to reassert traditional gender relations in response to the chaos and destruction of World War One.[43] In 1919, Pope Benedict XV outlined his perceived evils of the modern world in an address titled 'Women's Mission in Modern Society'. Pope Benedict specifically warned women against 'those exaggerations of fashions', declaring, 'we are filled with amazement at seeing those who communicate the poison seem not to realise its malignant action, and those that set the house on fire seem to ignore the destructive force of the fire'.[44] According to Rome, women's interest in fashion made them agents of immorality and invested them with the 'poison' of corruption. In response to this apparent problem, Pope Benedict called on all Catholic women to form leagues promoting decent fashions and to 'fulfil the strict duty of not giving scandal, and of not becoming a stumbling block to others in the path of virtue'.[45] The Pope's association between fashion, the emerging consumer culture, and women's ability to manifest moral corruption, was to have important consequences for the way Catholic leaders considered women's place in the postwar world.

Pope Benedict's assertion led a group of women in Ireland to form an official league against 'Immodest dress'. Their oath pledged to avoid 'all impropriety in the matter of dress and to maintain and hand down the traditional purity, and modesty of Irish womanhood'.[46] There was also a meeting in Ireland in opposition to 'the introduction of new forms of dancing into the city of Dublin', and an association was formed 'to place on record its apprehension that nightclubs such as exist in other places may be introduced into the city, and respectfully urges the citizens to take strenuous measures to prevent such an evil'.[47] In Ireland, the association between the emerging consumer cultures, fashion and leisure with immorality was clear and the large number of Irish immigrants and their descendants in north-west England were also affected.[48] Opposition to women's interest in leisure and consumerism was not limited to the Catholic Church and Penny Tinkler argues that secular concerns and discourse over women's leisure peaked during World War Two.[49] Within specifically Catholic discourse, however, these fears were very prominent during the immediate postwar years.

In Manchester for example, Salford Diocese was clearly influenced by events in Ireland and Rome. In a Christmas pastoral letter to his diocese in 1919 the Bishop of Salford, then Louis Charles, called on women of the diocese to form a league 'against the evils of fashion'.[50] During the immediate postwar years, the perceived link between fashion and corruption was strong within Salford Diocese. In 1921, his command was repeated through the Lenten pastoral letter: 'it has been reported to us on credible authority that at some of the dances among Catholics certain of these young people have appeared in costumes utterly repugnant to Christian modesty.'[51] Bishop Charles went further and claimed that the modern world was in opposition to the Catholic idea of womanhood.

> there is the matter of amusement, frivolity, worldliness … there is an excess, resulting in a craving for constant, daily amusement, which grows like a taste for alcohol and drugs, and leads to a frivolous and dissipated state of mind, to extravagance and religious carelessness.[52]

The Bishop advised women to abstain from attending the theatre, cinema and dances during Lent. As I have shown elsewhere, women in Manchester forged an episodic religious identity, which meant they could move between secular and religious spheres of culture at particular moments. Unlike Liverpool, Manchester's Catholic population was more cosmopolitan and was made up of not only Irish-Catholics but also Italians and Eastern Europeans, which created a less fixed and more flexible form of religious shared identity.[53] As Louise Ryan's chapter in this book also shows, the broader nature of migration in cities and communities shaped the nature of Irish diasporic identities. In contrast to other cities, the cohesive and tightly knit nature of the Irish-Catholic diaspora in Liverpool led Catholic leaders to develop a far more comprehensive and assertive approach to the changing world.

Catholic Action in 1930s Liverpool

Liverpool was the focus of a wider sense of confidence within the Catholic Church in Britain around the centenary anniversary of Catholic emancipation in 1929. The celebrations saw 400,000 Catholics gather in a Liverpool park,[54] where 'rich and poor, young and old, the educated and ill, stood shoulder to shoulder'.[55] The celebrations were described in detail within a souvenir publication of the event and the jubilant scenes in Liverpool were considered to epitomise the sense of triumph of the Church's survival within a Protestant country:

> And now in a blaze of glory, with heads held high, 400,000 Catholics had gathered to celebrate the Sacrifice of the Mass, the cynosure of all eyes in England and abroad. Surely this was the most eloquent vindication of the tireless efforts of Wiseman, Newman, Manning, and those other pioneers who saw in England a field while for the harvest. Assertion, without aggression had been their policy then; an exhibition of a living faith with aggression to no man was the picture gathering.[56]

Although celebrations were held elsewhere in the country, especially in Westminster, Liverpool witnessed the grandest events and drew the greatest crowds, suggesting they held particular value to Liverpool Archdiocese.

Mass attendance records suggest there was a broader growth in popular Catholicism in interwar Liverpool, which was reflected in the enthusiasm expressed through the 1929 celebrations. In 1908, the average Catholic in Liverpool attended mass ten times a year, but by the period 1915–24 it had risen to twenty-five times a year.[57] In the early 1920s, there were sixty-four convents in Liverpool Archdiocese and eighty-two by 1940.[58] 'Dominic's Day', which was a time of pilgrimage for a popular saint, saw 2,500 people take to the city's streets in 1925, which rose to 10,000 in 1939.[59] Such vibrant popular religiosity was fundamental to local Irish-Catholic shared identity and did much to boost the confidence of the Archdiocese.

This confidence was epitomised by the Catholic Church's attempts, led by Rome, to formalise the strength of Catholicism in England. Pope Pius XI announced a programme of 'Catholic Action' in 1931, which aimed 'to marshal the organised Catholic forces for the spread of religious and moral principles in all spheres of life: individual, family, professional, civic'.[60] In response, Liverpool Archdiocese embarked on a comprehensive programme of provisions for Catholic social groups, welfare services, education and leisure activities to foster their form of Catholic Action. As the Liverpool Board of Catholic Action explained, '[it] means that we are to be apostles always, not merely for a week or a day, or for an hour or so each day, but for every day of the week and every hour of the day'.[61] Catholic Action was not, Downey stressed, a method for attacking others, it was not political in any way and was not merely a system of good deeds, rather 'it is essentially a constructive movement with the definite aim of re-Christianising society; it is a scheme of co-ordinated effort for a common spiritual end'.[62]

Fundamental to Catholic Action was the cultivation of a stronger Catholic presence in public and civic life in Liverpool. As the President of Liverpool's Catholic Service Committee explained, Catholics in the city were encouraged 'to take up representative positions on public bodies, including local councils, trade unions, professional societies, charity and social organisations' and also 'to encourage the cultivation of the spirit of public responsibility among Catholics'.[63] One of the most striking aspects of the programme, which encompassed the desire to involve Catholics in all forms of public and civic life, was the establishment of a Social Service Bureau in Liverpool city centre in 1937, which offered advice on non-religious issues such as pensions and unemployment relief.[64] The Bureau was an immediate success and struggled to deal with demand in the weeks after it first opened.[65] Downey claimed it was 'doing excellent work in assisting the perplexed or distressed'.[66] Liverpool Archdiocese also opened a Catholic college that aimed to produce 'a well-informed Catholic laity' and sought to recruit both men and women 'from every walk and station of life and from every calling'.[67]

Crucially, the architects of Catholic Action claimed that there was a need to define distinct roles for men and women.[68] In particular, the programme assigned a great responsibility to women not just in the private sphere of the home, where their roles as wives and mothers were crucial to safeguarding the morality of their family, 'But publicly also, and as a body, the Catholic women of this nation, and particularly the married woman, ought to be much stronger and more active than they are'.[69] Women's public role was fundamental to the success of Catholic Action, argued Catholic leaders, because 'if the women are sound on these points the men will fall into line; it is when women fall away that a nation falls'.[70] These beliefs paved the way for Irish-Catholic women in Liverpool to take an active and assertive role in developing the work and activities of Catholic Action, which in turn, extended their presence and influence in public and civic life.

Irish-Catholic women: mothers in the home and in the city

Women's roles as wives and mothers were perceived by the architects of Catholic Action to be the moral and spiritual foundations for the Irish-Catholic community more generally. In 1937, a report by the Catholic Action Committee revealed,

> All the efforts, public and private, of Catholic women today ought to be devoted to upholding or restoring family life. (If a mother) wisely and prudently looks after their reading and amusements, and invites their companions into the home so that she may judge whether they are good companions, she may save her son or daughter from many a sin.[71]

Women's spiritual role as mothers and guardians of public life was both formalised and extended under Catholic Action and the Union of Catholic Mothers was especially present and influential within the programme.

The Union of Catholic Mothers (UCM) was founded by the Catholic Women's League in 1913 (in response to a request by Cardinal Bourne) but was reorganised in 1923 and a constitution formalised in 1929. The objects of the UCM, described by Catholic leaders as 'a spiritual dynamo',[72] were:

1 Band together Catholic mothers to raise children who would be 'good Catholics and public-spirited citizens'.
2 Uphold the 'sacramental character and permanence of marriage and the observance of God's natural laws in the married state.'
3 'To secure a Catholic education for their children, and to guard them from immoral companions, amusements, and literature.'[73]

Liverpool Archdiocese looked to the UCM to lead women's involvement in Catholic Action and was seen to be crucial to its success: 'All Catholic *married* women, whatever class they may belong to socially, should belong to this Union.'[74] The language of classlessness and inclusivity was reiterated by Liverpool Archdiocese: 'There are no class distinctions in the UCM, it is for rich and poor alike' and the Liverpool UCM groups included a broad range of activities such as dressmaking, saving clubs and clothing clubs, which could appeal to the many rather than the few.[75] By 1935 the UCM in Liverpool had a membership of 2,421. A report by the UCM in the magazine *Catholic Mother* reported the scale of the group's activities: 'exceedingly generous contributions have been made by Foundations towards the needs to their Parish churches; these are usually the result of Social evenings … Quarterly meetings for Parish Offices continue to be very successful. Highly successful summer outings have been organised.'[76]

Catholic Women's organisations in Liverpool, such as the UCM, became increasingly autonomous from the national associations by implication of Catholic Action. In 1936, Liverpool Archdiocese formed its own Catholic

Women's League (CWL), which focused on providing a practical support network for Irish-Catholic women, particularly those new to the city. The CWL was pleased with its work with young women and girls arriving in Liverpool from Ireland and was keen to intervene in certain cases such as returning runaways to their families, and described a case where 'one girl travelling to America to join her intended husband against the wishes of her parents was, after much correspondence, dissuaded from her waywardness'.[77] The range of activities by Catholic women and girls' organisations in Liverpool was impressive by the late 1930s and included fifty-eight companies of Catholic Girl Guides by 1938, along with the Ladies of Charity, Legion of Mary, Federation of Children of Mary and the Catholic Needlework Guild.[78] Yet Catholic Action also sought to extend women's influence beyond that of the home, with a particular interest in women's paid work.

Work, leisure and pleasure

As historians such as Selina Todd and Sally Alexander have shown, the interwar period was also marked by the emergence of greater opportunities in paid employment for women, particularly in nursing, teaching, clerical work and the 'light' industries.[79] Some of these new areas of employment were subjects of concern within Liverpool Archdiocese. Downey estimated there were 150,000 to 200,000 working girls and 'even a few enquiries are sufficient to verify the fact of the lamentable consequences of all this: the moral abandonment, promiscuity, depraved conditions in which these girls are compelled to work in to earn their living'. Downey suggested there were 87,000 girls in factories, performing 'work that is so mechanical and brutalising amidst the noise and nerve-wracking rush of the machine in an environment that is indecent, promiscuous and disorientating, that it rapidly defeminises the young girls completely, at the precise age when their nature as women should be awakened and developed'.[80] Similarly, the office environment was criticised because it was seen to encourage 'flirtation … as the normal relationship between young people and even between married men and girls, a recherché toilette made up simply to attract attention, conversation enlightened only by obscenity'.[81]

Liverpool Archdiocese was by no means opposed to women's paid work however; Catholic leaders were very sensitive to the harsh economic conditions Scotland Road inhabitants were often in and understood that most Irish-Catholic families needed women to work. The Archdiocese therefore sought to encourage women to choose particular careers that permitted them to incorporate their religious duties: for example, in March 1937, the CWL opened an Occupational Centre for Women and Girls on Brownlow Hill (just above the city centre). The Liverpool-based Young Catholic Workers even set up their own magazine, *The Young Working Girl*, to encourage Catholic girls into appropriate forms of employment.[82] The Archdiocese especially encouraged young women to become teachers or nurses as both occupations were seen as ways to ensure that Catholic doctrine would suffuse society more generally.[83] Nursing was defined by the Archdiocese as being a specifically woman's role and identified that 'the well-educated Catholic girl [is] whom we must entice into the profession'.[84] Guilds for Catholic nurses and teachers were established in the Archdiocese and in 1938 the Liverpool and District Catholic Teachers Association was celebrated for his success in an annual report: 'There is no more flourishing Catholic organisation in the Archdiocese, and in true zeal for Catholic Action and in constant devoted loyalty for H. C. the Archbishop, the Liverpool Association claims to be second to none.'[85] These guilds were fundamental to women's involvement in the Catholic Action Public Service committee which aimed 'to encourage the cultivation of the spirit of public responsibility among Catholics'.[86]

Historians have linked women's greater employment opportunities and financial autonomy with a rise in mass consumer culture and a democratisation of glamour, which offered young, working-class women, in particular, greater access to fashionable clothes and cosmetics.[87] Catriona Clear's work shows how Irish women's dress became more strongly influenced by international shifts in fashion culture from the 1940s with a greater emphasis on cosmetics and grooming, which was linked to broader shifts in women's increased presence in economic and public life.[88] During the 1930s however, women's interest in fashion and consumer culture was, to some extent, perceived as a matter of concern to Liverpool Archdiocese because Catholic leaders feared it hindered religious faith: one article published in the *Liverpool Cathedral Record* in 1935 warned 'for one woman who ever thinks beyond her world of superficialness – you will find ninety whose whole concern is their hair, nails, eyebrows, toes, lips... the fashion, the cult of the hour'.[89] Again, a couple of months later, the *Liverpool Cathedral Record* complained, 'if the idle mind is the devil's workshop then the modern woman is free from its snares. By the time she has visited the hairdresser, the manicurist and the beauty specialist and done her work she must be glad to sleep'.[90]

In response to these anxieties, there was a clear attempt to foster a model of Catholic womanhood that transcended modernity. As one journalist in the *Liverpool Cathedral Record* complained, 'I am convinced that "modern" woman is what she is because she lacks an ideal of womanhood which is independent of fashion, change, time or tide'.[91] Liverpool Archdiocese looked to nurture a more stable Catholic form of womanhood for women to aspire to imitate. The Virgin Mary was chosen to do this, yet Liverpool Archdiocese emphasised that she was not necessarily anti-modern but transcended cultural and social changes over time. The *Liverpool Cathedral Record* explained,

> In the 'Maiden' of Nazareth she has the model of every virtue, of every line of
> physical loveliness, grace and beauty. During all the centuries of change, this model

has endured … The model woman does not exist in this sense outside the Catholic Church.[92]

The clergy of Liverpool were reminded by the Archbishop of Liverpool to read the Pope's instructions against immoral dress on the feast of the Immaculate Conception, which was a celebration of the Virgin Mary and her modesty.[93] However, the image of womanhood promoted by the Catholic Church in Liverpool was by no means backward looking, particularly in comparison with the Catholic Church in Ireland.[94] The Archdiocese was notable in producing Catholic forms of leisure organisations, especially for young girls, and there were fifty-eight Catholic Girl Guides clubs in Liverpool by 1938.[95] A Junior League of CWL was founded nationally in 1932: the Liverpool branch was one of the strongest and its leaders emphasised the importance of Catholic girls' involvement in local clubs, advising that 'every member can find something suited to her time, purse and tastes … such as becoming the secretary or coach of the dramatic or sports sections of a girls' club'.[96]

Concerns about fashion, leisure and shopping did not stop Liverpool Archdiocese from encouraging women to embrace the new mass consumer culture, albeit in acutely Catholic terms. Most notably, Catholic leaders in Liverpool became increasingly enthusiastic towards to idea of a specifically Catholic shopping culture (aimed at women) in order to fund their most ambitious part of the 1930s programme of Catholic Action: the campaign to build the second largest cathedral in the world. Designed by Edwin Lutyens and expected to cost £3 million, most of which would come from the local Catholic population, the cathedral fundraising campaign exposes a distinct shift in Catholic leader's attitudes towards consumer culture. The Archdiocese had first raised plans to build a cathedral in the late nineteenth century, but was hindered by a much more pressing need for Catholic schools and churches. The cathedral remained a desirable project amongst Downey's predecessors and as a way to mark Irish-Catholic presence in the city, although little real progress was made. Archbishop Whiteside, whom Downey succeeded, described his hopes for a cathedral in 1922:

> If a new Catholic Cathedral means that amongst Catholics there has been deliberately brought about less drinking and betting, less luxury and more self-denial, a football match foregone one week, a packet of cigarettes the next, a new jumper sacrificed without a feminine sigh … then will the projected cathedral be well and nobly built.[97]

The cathedral was therefore conceived by Whiteside as a way to focus the attention of Liverpool Catholics away from the appeal of cheap amusements.

In contrast, Downey actively sought to harness working-class consumer culture for the cathedral campaign: One of the most ostentatious forms of mass consumer culture incorporated into the cathedral project by the Archdiocese was the production of 'Cathedral Cigarettes'. At a cost of 6d for ten or a shilling for twenty, they allowed Catholics the opportunity to fund the building of the Cathedral as they smoked. Similarly, the Archdiocese approved the sale of 'Cathedral Tea', which cost 4d a quarter and was promoted as 'The tea with double the appeal … Every quarter sold adds to the Metropolitan Cathedral Appeal … Good Cause for an Extra Cup'.[98] In July 1933, 5,000 pounds of cathedral tea was sold every week and Downey was told to expect sales to double in volume over the following months.[99] Research by Moya Kneafsey and Rosie Cox has shown that food was used by women of the Irish diaspora 'knowingly, as well as unconsciously, to create a sense of Irishness'.[100] The practice of homemaking through foodstuffs may have helped to consolidate the importance of items such as cathedral tea and cigarettes for Irish women in Liverpool. Crucially, these items could be incorporated into everyday spending habits and as tea and cigarettes were fundamental to working-class patterns of consumption, did not add extra burdens to most Catholics' pockets.

There was the opportunity to subscribe to the 'Golden Book': 'As builders of the Sanctuary and Blessed Sacrament Chapel your name and the names of your relatives or friends, living or dead, would be inscribed therein FOR EVER'.[101] The Archdiocese also established a scheme that gave people a replica model of the cathedral in return for collection boxes. 'Be a leader … Say with pride in years to come: "I helped to raise this, the second *largest* of all Cathedrals"', proclaimed the advert for collection boxes.[102] Between 1 March and 30 June 1933, over £600 was raised through these collection boxes alone.[103] The range of products and spending opportunities allowed Catholics to demonstrate their Catholic identity through their purchases, no matter how modest their income was.

The selling power of the cathedral project did not go un-noticed by other businesses in Liverpool and was used as a publicity tool during the 1930s. Throughout 1931, Coopers, one of Liverpool's more working-class, inexpensive department stores, made a direct appeal to its Catholic customers when it printed special vouchers on boxes of tea. The voucher could be exchanged for an etching of the new cathedral. 'Coopers offer them to their thousands of Catholic customers **entirely free of charge**', described the advert.[104] Many opportunities appeared in Liverpool for Catholics, especially women, to become involved with the Cathedral through shopping. In September 1933, there was a two-day sale arranged by the Catholic Police Guild to raise money.[105] A Christmas Club appealed for agents using the Cathedral fund as an incentive:

> If you want to help the Cathedral fund why not organise a Club and give the profits? Out of all the cash received from agents who mention 'Cathedral Record' on the order, an extra 2 ½ per cent will be sent directly to the Cathedral fund.[106]

A Catholic form of consumer culture, and even spectacle, developed in Liverpool by the 1930s in a way that is seemingly at odds with existing stereotypes about the Irish-Catholic diaspora in Britain.

Catholic women were especially encouraged to use the new consumer and leisure opportunities to aid the cathedral campaign. An article in the *Liverpool Catholic Parishioner* in 1931 was one of many that specifically asked women to raise money, writing that it 'would like to bring to the notice of ladies the possibilities of considerable additions being made to the building fund', giving the example of a group of ladies who made children's clothes and raised £58 for the cathedral fund.[107] Similarly, the publicity campaign asked ladies to organise 'Snowball Teas', where six ladies from a parish organise tea for six ladies each who pay one shilling and each of those ladies does the same for another six ladies.[108] Whereas there were never any direct appeals to lay men, Catholic women appeared to embrace their role as consumers to aid the cathedral project. From the mid 1930s it was popular for women to bequest donations to the Cathedral fund on their death and in 1934, for example, a Miss A. G. M. Standish left her entire jewellery to the fund.[109] Nor was she a rare case and the donation of jewellery was a very popular form of supporting the cathedral; as early as 1930 the *Liverpool Post and Mercury* reported that 600 to 700 items had been submitted to the fund in lieu of money.[110] The opportunity to become Cathedral builders was not limited to wealthy women. In 1935, the *Daily Mail* reported that a woman from Scotland Road had raised £200 by collecting and selling jam jars.[111] No such references made about the money made raised by (lay) men for the Cathedral fund seem to exist. Furthermore, archived accounts also show that of the different chapels in the cathedral, most of the subscriptions were by women to Chapels that reflected their identity. For example, by 1939 the Union of Catholic Mothers had donated £144 10s to the Lady's Chapel.[112] The energetic fundraising efforts of Catholic women, from a range of class backgrounds, illustrates the way popular support for the cathedral was mobilised to great effect and shows how women's roles as shoppers and consumers was fundamental to the fundraising campaign.

Conclusion

Although the Catholic cathedral project was halted by the coming of World War Two and eventually abandoned because postwar inflation made Lutyens' ambitious plans unworkable, it was largely down to Liverpool's Irish-Catholic women that £1,000,000 (a third of the way towards the Archdiocese's target) had been raised by 1939.[113] The war did not halt the work of Irish-Catholic women in Liverpool's civic and public culture and, in contrast, did much to enhance it. Downey was very quick to mobilise the many Catholic women's organisations (which were at the peak of their strength by 1939) for the war effort. In 1939 the Archdiocese reported 'Liverpool CWL were making a special effort to co-operate in every worthy civic activity' and had organised knitting parties to make blankets for soldiers and had campaigned for Catholic canteen huts for Catholic soldiers in army camps.[114]

By the time World War Two broke out, Irish-Catholic women held a strong and assertive role in local civic culture, employment and welfare services, which would eventually permit them to shape and implement the types of auxiliary services associated both with the Home Front and the subsequent foundation of the welfare state. In 1940 Downey established a Temporary Diocesan Board of the Union of Catholic Women (UCW) for the 'promotion and co-ordination of Catholic Action among the Catholic women of the Archdiocese'.[115] The Board brought together all the women's societies with the aim to ensure their presence in the Home Front. The CWL advocated that women should 'try to get appointed to Evacuation and Reception Committees and do your upmost to see that Catholic children are sent to areas where facilities for the practice of their religion are at hand' and help working girls new to town and Catholic girls in forces. They cautioned women to 'never neglect an opportunity for taking an active part in civic affairs; Catholics should be represented on town councils and on local committees'.[116] Nor did the importance of keeping local religious and ethnic bonds wane after the outbreak of war: the UCW was praised by the Archdiocese for refusing to permit Catholic children to be 'merged' with non-Catholics during evacuation.[117] Greater research is needed to understand fully the contribution made by the Irish-Catholic diaspora in Liverpool's war effort and to examine how the welfare provisions associated with Catholic Action evolved in conjunction with the development of the welfare state. What is clear, however, is the positive contribution Irish-Catholic women made in Liverpool's religious, public and civic life during the 1930s, which ensured they were well placed to respond to the demands of 'Total War' and the subsequent postwar 'New Jerusalem'.

The chapter has also shown that Catholic leaders in Liverpool became more relaxed about modernity and sought to encourage a specifically religious form of consumer culture, which allowed women to merge their roles as shoppers and Catholics. Writing in 2004, Frank Trentmann highlighted the need for a greater understanding of the historical relationship between religious groups and consumption.[118] My research on Catholic Action in Liverpool has started to consider how Catholic women could merge their religious identities with new roles as shoppers, paid workers and within civic and public life. If we take the centrality of the emergence of modern forms of consumer culture to British modernity (and the great weight placed by historians on looking at women's experiences of modernity by focussing on the department store, for instance) alongside women's greater presence in the public sphere, then the work of Irish-Catholic women in Liverpool suggests the link between secularisation and modernity is not so clear.[119]

Together, the chapter suggests that a more nuanced approach to the study of the Irish diaspora is needed to understand further Irish-Catholic women's experiences of and relationship with modernity. As Martin Daunton and Bernhard Rieger have suggested, British modernity should be studied 'through close readings within specific locales and venues'.[120] Liverpool's tightly knit Irish community, with its strong links to both Ireland and Catholicism, do suggest that a comprehensive programme of Catholic Action and a more relaxed attitude towards modernity were unique to the city, although my study of Manchester suggests a similarly increasingly relaxed attitude was displayed in slightly different ways.[121] Nevertheless, a comparative approach, particularly between British north-west and American east coast cities, would be especially useful to explore how typical the experience of Liverpool's Irish diaspora and women's experience of leisure, consumer, employment and civic culture was. What is clear however, is that the scholarly neglect of women in the Irish diaspora has not only marginalised their place in understandings of British modernity but that greater intellectual engagement with their experiences can revise the very definitions of modernity itself. As this chapter has shown, Irish-Catholic women possessed significant agency and were able to shape and contribute to public and civic life in Liverpool. Their influence on local urban culture uncovers a larger story about the relationship that migrant communities had with the populations they joined. As a case study, Irish-Catholic women in Liverpool suggest that conceptual and theoretical understandings of diasporic histories need to incorporate greater attention towards gender in order to acknowledge the agency and influence of women migrants, who too often remain 'hidden' from histories.

Notes

1 P. Allitt, *Catholic Converts: British and American Intellectuals Turn to Rome* (London: Cornell University Press, 1997), p. 3.

2 See A. Schwartz, *The Third Spring: G.K. Chesterton, Graham Greene, Christopher Dawson, and David Jones* (Washington D.C.: Catholic University of America Press, 2005); I. T. Ker, *The Catholic Revival in English Literature, 1845–1961: Newman, Hopkins, Belloc, Chesterton, Greene, Waugh* (Notre Dame: University of Notre Dame Press, 2003); J. R. Lothian, *The Making and Unmaking of the English Catholic Intellectual Community, 1910–1950* (Notre Dame: University of Notre Dame Press, 2009).

3 Writing in 2000, Don MacRaild criticised the history of the Irish diaspora in Britain for neglecting the spiritual aspect of Catholicism. D. M. MacRaild, 'Introduction', in D. M. MacRaild (ed.), *The Great Famine and Beyond: Irish Migrants in Britain in the Nineteenth and Twentieth Centuries* (Dublin: Irish Academic Press, 2000), p. 8.

4 F. Neal, *Sectarian Violence: The Liverpool Experience, 1819–1914: An Aspect of Anglo-Irish History* (Manchester: Manchester University Press, 1988).

5 C. G. Brown, *The Death of Christian Britain: Understanding Secularisation, 1800–2000* (London: Routledge, 2000), p. 164.

6 For a helpful overview of the secularisation debate see J. Morris, 'The strange death of Christian Britain: another look at the secularisation debate', *Historical Journal*, 46 (2003), 963–76.

7 Virginia Woolf to Vanessa Bell, 11 February 1928. As quoted in Schwartz, *Third Spring*, p. 1.

8 M. Stopes, *Roman Catholic Methods of Birth Control* (London: Davies, 1933), p. 220.

9   A. Hastings, *A History of English Christianity 1920–2000* (London: SCM Press, 2001), p. 287.

10 *Ibid.*, p. 224.

11 See M. J. Daunton and B. Rieger, 'Introduction', in M. J. Daunton and B. Rieger (eds), *Meanings of Modernity: Britain from the Late Victorian Era to World War II* (Oxford: Berg, 2001), pp. 1–21.

12 Schwartz, *Third Spring*, p. 7.

13 The neglect of religion is clear in the following: Daunton and Rieger (eds), *Meanings of Modernity*; M. Nava and A. O'Shea (eds), *Modern Times: Reflections on a Century of English Modernity* (London: Routledge, 1996); B. Conekin, C. Waters and F. Mort (eds), *Moments of Modernity: Reconstructing Britain, 1945–1964* (London: Rivers Oram Press, 1999).

14 J. Landy and M. Saler, 'Introduction: The varieties of modern enchantment', in J. Landy and M. Saler (eds), *The Re-Enchantment of the World: Secular Magic in an Rational Age* (Stanford: Stanford University Press, 2009), pp. 6–7.

15 *Ibid.*, p. 7.

16 There is some outstanding research on women and modernity, which influences my approach. See, in particular, B. Soland, *Becoming Modern: Young Women and the Reconstruction of Womanhood in the 1920s* (Princeton: Princeton University Press, 2000) and L. Conor, *The Spectacular Modern Woman: Feminine Visibility in the 1920s* (Bloomington: Indiana University Press, 2004).

17 M. Valiulis, 'Neither feminist nor flapper: the ecclesiastical construction of the ideal Irish woman', in M. O'Dowd and S. Wichert (eds), *Chattel, Servant or Citizen: Women's Status in Church, State and Society* (Belfast: Queen's University of Belfast, Institute of Irish Studies, 1995), p. 175. Similarly, Victoria de Grazia has described the attempts of Mussolini's Italian-Catholic regime to restore patriarchal authority and reinforce women's maternal role, drawing attention to their strategy of creating a national dress that was distinct from connotations with the perceived excess of consumer culture. V. de Grazia, *How Fascism Ruled Women: Italy, 1922–1945* (Berkeley: University of California Press, 1992), p. 233.

18 L. Ryan, 'Negotiating modernity and tradition: newspaper debates on the "modern girl" in the Irish Free State', *Journal of Gender Studies*, 7 (1998), 182.

19 R. Orsi, *The Madonna of the 115th Street: Faith and Community in Italian Harlem, 1880–1950* (London: Yale University Press, 1985); R. Orsi, *Thank You, Saint Jude: Women's Devotion to the Patron Saint of Hopeless Causes* (New Haven: Yale University Press, 1996).

20 See B. Gray, *Women and the Irish Diaspora* (London: Routledge, 2004), pp. 22–6.

21 This migration accelerated after 1940 and the Catholic population rose by 2 million by 1970. R. McKibbin, *Classes and Cultures: England, 1918–1951* (Oxford: Oxford University Press, 1998), p. 273 and pp. 285–6.

22 Very Reverend Canon Hughes, *A Concise Catholic History of Liverpool* (Liverpool, 1926), p. 41.

23 *Ibid.*, p. 43.

24 As quoted in *Daily Dispatch Cathedral Supplement*, p. 1, c.1934 in Liverpool Central Library Local Studies Collection (LCL LLC) Cuttings: *Cathedral Collection*, 1929–1957.

25 Hughes, *A Concise Catholic History of Liverpool*, p. 43.

26 T. Lane, *City of the Sea* (Liverpool: Liverpool University Press, 1997), p. 108.

27 J. Belchem, *Merseypride: Essays in Liverpool Exceptionalism* (Liverpool: Liverpool University Press, 2000), p. xv.

28 For an overview of these stereotypes, see J. Belchem, *Irish, Catholic and Scouse: The*

    History of the Liverpool Irish, 1800–1939 (Liverpool: Liverpool University Press, 2007), pp. 1–8.

29 G. Davies, 'The Irish in Britain, 1815–1939', in A. Bielenberg (ed.), *The Irish Diaspora* (Harlow: Longman, 2000), p. 19.

30 John Belchem emphasises the parish-based support network established by the Catholic Church in Liverpool where a report published in 1883, *Squalid Liverpool*, described the Catholic priest as 'the parson, the policeman, the doctor, the nurse, the relieving officer, the nuisance inspector, and the school board inspector all rolled into one.' Quoted in Belchem, *Merseypride*, p. 120.

31 See T. Cooke, *Scotland Road 'The Old Neighbourhood': The Yesteryears of Liverpool's Famous Scotland Road* (Birkenhead: Countyvise, 1987).

32 J. Belchem, 'Irish and Polish migration: some preliminary comparative analysis', in J. Belchem and K. Tenfelde (eds), *Irish and Polish Migration in Comparative Perspective* (Essen: Klartext-Verlag, 2003), p. 14.

33 P. J. Waller, *Democracy and Sectarianism: A Political and Social History of Liverpool, 1868–1939* (Liverpool: Liverpool University Press, 1981), p. 325.

34 Lane, *City of the Sea*, p. 99.

35 The decade before 1914 was particularly violent. See J. Bohstedt, 'More than one working class: Protestant-Catholic riots in Edwardian Liverpool', in J. Belchem (ed.), *Popular Politics, Riot and Labour: Essays in Liverpool History, 1790–1940* (Liverpool: Liverpool University Press, 1992), p. 216.

36 Sectarian tensions inhibited the building of Liverpool's war memorial until 1930. See J. O'Keefe, 'First World War Memorials and the Liverpool Cenotaph, 1917–1934' (MA dissertation, University of Manchester, 2004).

37 '10 Reasons why Roman Catholic Schools Should Not be Built Out of the Rates', *Protestant Times*, 9 October 1937, p. 8 and 'The Man with a Load of Mischief', *Protestant Times*, 20 April 1935, front cover.

38 Waller, *Democracy and Sectarianism*, p. 304.

39 The port lost an average of 1 per cent of trade per annum to other British ports in each year from 1919 to 1939. D. E. Baines, 'Merseyside in the British economy: the 1930s and the Second World War', in R. Lawton and C. M. Cunningham (eds), *Merseyside: Social and Economic Studies* (London: Longman, 1970), p. 60.

40 S. Davies, P. Gill, L. Grant, M. Nightingale, R. Noon, and A. Shallice, *Genuinely Seeking Work: Mass Unemployment on Merseyside in the 1930s* (Birkenhead: Liver Press, 1992), p. 13; D. Aldcroft, *The Inter-War Economy: Britain, 1919–1939* (London: Batsford, 1970), p. 41.

41 Belchem, *Irish, Catholic and Scouse*, pp. 297–8.

42 Belchem, *Merseypride*, p. xi.

43 Susan Kingsley Kent argues there was an attempt to remedy the havoc caused by World War through a desire to restore 'gender peace' in Britain. S. K. Kent, *Making Peace: The Reconstruction of Gender in Interwar Britain* (Princeton: Princeton University Press, 1993).

44 Pope Benedict XV, 'Women's Mission in Modern Society', *The Tablet*, 4 January 1919, cxxxiii, p. 559.

45 *Ibid.*

46 *Catholic Herald*, 10 January 1920, p. 1.

47 *Ibid.*, p. 6.

48 Relations and links between Irish immigrants, their descendants and their home country remained strong and are stressed in personal testaments of Irish people living in England throughout the twentieth century. See S. Lambert, *Irish Women in Lancashire 1922–1960: Their Story* (Lancaster: Centre for North-West Regional

Studies, 2001); M. Lennon, M. McAdam and J. O'Brien, *Across the Water: Irish Women's Lives in Britain* (London: Virago, 1988); J. Devane, 'Irish roots? Evaluation of the Preston-Irish community identity', *Sociology Working Papers*, University of Manchester, 5 (1998).

49 P. Tinkler, 'Cause for concern: young women and leisure, 1930–50', *Women's History Review*, 12 (2003), 233–62.

50 L. Charles, Bishop of Salford, '*Regina Pacis*: An Advent Pastoral Letter', *The Acta*, 1919, Salford Diocesan Archive (SDA).

51 L. Charles, Bishop of Salford, 'Lenten Pastoral Letter', *The Acta*, 1921, SDA.

52 *Ibid.*

53 C. Wildman, 'Religious selfhoods and the city in interwar Manchester', *Urban History*, 38 (2011), 103–23.

54 Archbishop Robert Downey, 'Foreword', *Catholic Times Souvenir of Thingwall Park Centenary Celebrations*, 1929, p. 3, Liverpool Archdiocesan Archive (LAA) S2 V D12.

55 L. J. Sullivan, 'The Scene at Thingwall park: An Impression', in *Catholic Times Souvenir of Thingwall Park Centenary Celebrations*, p. 23, LAA S2 V D12.

56 *Ibid.*

57 This statistic was derived from the total number of recorded communions taken each year divided by the number of attendants at mass on Easter Sunday. For example, in 1924 there were a total of 6,535,000 communions given out; this number was divided by 258,000, the number of attendants at mass on Easter Sunday. Taken from Hughes, *A Concise Catholic History of Liverpool*, p. 43.

58 P. Doyle, *Mitres and Missions in Lancashire: The Roman Catholic Diocese, 1850–2000* (Liverpool: Bluecoat Press, 2005), p. 135.

59 *Ibid.*, p. 150.

60 Monsignor Fontenelle, *Little Catechism of Catholic Action* (Dublin, 1933), p. 12, in Downey Papers 1928–1953, LAA S1 VI A2.

61 Liverpool Archdiocesan Board of Catholic Action, *Catholic Action: A Simple Explanation* (Liverpool, 1937), p. 4, LAA S1 VI A7.

62 Archbishop Richard Downey, 'Address on Catholic Action', 5 December 1937, p. 4, LAA S1 VI B4.

63 P. Taggart, 'Catholic Action Public Service Committee', January 1937, LAA S1 IX A1.

64 'Catholic Action in the Liverpool Archdiocese', Sir John Reynolds, Demonstration in St George's Hall 6 December 1937, Liverpool CA Congress Report, December 1937, p. 21, LAA S1 VI B7

65 Catholic Services Bureau Report, April 1937, LAA S1 XI A5.

66 Downey, 'Address on Catholic Action', 5 December 1937, p. 5, LAA S1 VI B4.

67 Downey, 'Address to Catholic Action College, Liverpool', 13 March 1938, LAA S1 VIII C1.

68 Rev. Father R. Kothen, 'Principles of Catholic Action' address delivered at the Adelphi Hotel, 5 December 1937, Liverpool CA Congress Report December 1937, LAA S1 VI B7.

69 'Women in Catholic Action', Archbishop of Birmingham to Women's Demonstration in St George's Hall Tuesday 7 December 1937, Liverpool CA Congress Report, December 1937, LAA S1 VI B7.

70 *Ibid.*

71 Liverpool Catholic Action, *Congress Report* 1937, LAA S1 V1 B7.

72 Circular letter to UCM Feast of Immaculate Conception, 1929. UCM National Archive, LAA R AS5 471 B2.

73 LAA R AS 547/1/ AS.

74 *Ibid.*
75 Catholic Women's League (CWL), UCM, Easter 1935, LAA R AS 547/1 AS.
76 UCM Liverpool Report, *The Catholic Mother*, Christmas 1935, p. 9.
77 CWL Liverpool Archdiocesan Branch, 26th Annual Report 1936, LAA S1 XI A18.
78 LAA S1 IX A1.
79 S. Todd, *Young Women, Work, and Family in England, 1918–1950* (Oxford: Oxford University Press, 2005); S. Alexander, 'Men's fears and women's work: responses to unemployment in London between the wars', *Gender & History*, 12 (2000), 401–25.
80 Archbishop Richard Downey, 'The Papal Teaching on CA and the Experience of the Jocist Movement', LAA S1 VI A13.
81 'Papal Teaching on Catholic Action and the Experience of the Jocist Movement', *c.*1930 Downey Papers 1928–1953, LAA S1 VI A15.
82 Catholic Action Notes, October 1940, LAA SI VII B3.
83 CWL UCM pamphlet, May 1927, LAA R AS 547/1 AS.
84 'The Position of the Catholic Nurse', Delivered to Catholic Medical Guild, 28 November 1926, LAA S1 IX A17.
85 Liverpool and District Catholic Teachers Association, 3 October 1938, LAA S1 IX A1.
86 Catholic Action Public Service Committee, January 1939, LAA S1 IX A1.
87 S. Alexander, 'Becoming a woman in London in the 1920s and 1930s', in D. Feldman and G. Steadman Jones (eds), *Metropolis: London, Histories and Representations* (London: Routledge, 1989), pp. 245–71; S. Todd, 'Young women, work, and leisure in interwar England', *Historical Journal*, 48 (2005), 789–809.
88 C. Clear, '"The minimum rights of every woman"? Women's changing appearance in Ireland, 1940–1966', *Irish Economic and Social History*, 35 (2008), 68–80.
89 *Liverpool Cathedral Record (LCR)*, October 1935, 1771.
90 *LCR*, December 1935, 1831.
91 *LCR*, October 1935, Vol. V, 1771.
92 *LCR*, October 1935, Vol. V, 1772–3.
93 LAA, *Pastoral Letters 1932–1938.*
94 Maryann Valiulis argues that the Catholic Church in Ireland promoted a specifically anti-modern image of womanhood in the 1930s, alongside a campaign against modern forms of leisure and consumer culture. Valiulis, 'Neither feminist nor flapper', pp. 168–78.
95 First Report of the Archdiocese Girl Guides, Conference of Catholic Action, 1938, LAA S1 IX A1.
96 Report from Liverpool Branch of Junior League of CWL, *Awake, Catholic Youth*, Summer 1932, p. 46, LAA S1 XI A21.
97 *Catholic Times*, 27 May 1922, 11.
98 *LCR*, February 1933, inside page.
99 Report to Downey, 3 July 1933, LAA S2 B13.
100 M. Kneafsey and R. Cox, 'Food, gender and Irishness: how Irish women in Coventry make home', *Irish Geography*, 35 (2002), 11.
101 *LCR*, July 1933, back inside page.
102 *LCR*, April 1931, front inside page.
103 Report to Downey, 3 July 1933, LAA S2 B13.
104 *LCR*, February 1931, 1558.
105 *LCR*, September 1933, 75.
106 T. C. Morris, *LCR*, September 1933, 79.
107 'Ways and Means', *Liverpool Catholic Parishoner*, April 1931, 1558.
108 'Snowball Teas', LAA S2 V A4.

109 LAA S2 V B11.
110 *Liverpool Post and Mercury*, December 1930, LCL LSC Cuttings: Cathedral Collection 1929–1957.
111 *Daily Mail*, 21 March 1935, LCL LSC Cuttings: Cathedral Collection 1929–1957.
112 'Ways and Means', LAA S2 V B11.
113 The cost was estimated at £27,370,438 in 1954, Architect's Report, 13 September 1954, LAA S2 VI C2.
114 CWL, 29th Annual Report 1939, LAA S1 XI A18.
115 Temporary Constitution of the Diocesan Board of Union Catholic Women Appointed by His Grace, the Archbishop of Liverpool, May 1940. LAA S1 VIII D1.
116 *Ibid.*
117 Catholic Action Notes, October 1940, LAA S1 VIII.
118 F. Trentmann, 'Beyond consumerism', *Journal of Contemporary History*, 39 (2004), 379.
119 As Mica Nava has argued, it was through consumer culture and spectacle that 'large numbers of ordinary women were most deeply affected by the process of modernity'. M. Nava, 'Modernity's disavowal: women, the city and the department store', in Nava and O'Shea (eds), *Modern Times*, p. 46.
120 Daunton and Reiger (eds), 'Introduction', p. 3.
121 Wildman, 'Religious selfhoods and the city in interwar Manchester'.

5

The thermometer and the travel permit: Irish women in the medical profession in Britain during World War Two

Jennifer Redmond

The study of women in the Irish diaspora has developed a significant historiography yet there are still gaps in our knowledge and stories to be told about women. As Louise Ryan has cogently argued, theories developed to explain migration flows in the twentieth century often take men as their model for analysis, thereby excluding the specific experiences of women:

> Despite the apparent 'gender-neutrality' of many of these mainstream theories of migration, this individual economic migrant has usually been constructed as male, thus tending to exacerbate the exclusion of women from analyses of migration. Notwithstanding the impact of recent feminist research, there remains a tendency to consider women migrants within narrow domestic and familial contexts: playing supporting roles as wives and home-makers.[1]

Yet as Breda Gray has written, women have left Ireland involuntarily and voluntarily under a variety of circumstances and in large numbers over the last two centuries, many as single women in search of opportunities outside their reach at home.[2] Women have thus been an integral part of the 'complex migratory activities that link societies of origin and settlement'[3] and which have resulted in a global community of people claiming Irish identity, the Irish diaspora. Indeed, women have often constituted the key linkage between diasporic communities and homelands through the regular sending of remittances, trips home to provide or receive care or to socialise their children within the kith and kin networks of their birthplaces, all sites of cultural preservation and continuity of tradition identified by Gray as contributing hugely to formations of the diaspora.[4] Ryan's argument that women emigrants were also economic migrants and that they played roles beyond the domestic sphere is attested to in my research on women in World War Two Britain. Indeed, the single status of many of these migrant women placed them outside the realm of the traditional as they forged new paths for Irish women in the British medical field.

Drawing on the recent scholarship of historians such as Greta Jones and Louise Ryan, this chapter examines new source material related to Irish women working as doctors and nurses in Britain during World War Two.[5] Women played an active and vital role in the British medical service at this time and this chapter seeks to highlight the diversity of this group, their agency and the ways in which their profile disrupts stereotypical narratives of immigrant women occupying marginal sectors of major economies. These women also defy characterisation as either 'sexual or maternal creatures, juxtapositions which tap into the historical trope of the Madonna versus the Magdalene, or the mother versus the whore'.[6] These women, for the most part single, were professional women working in a high-pressure environment at a time of 'total war' affecting civilian populations. They are thus an entirely different group to examine in comparison with domestic servants, or the other group that has received attention, unmarried mothers.[7]

The tendency to focus on domestic immigrant workers is not unique to Irish historiography and has been noted by Schrover and Yeo as understandable due to their historical and contemporary predominance in the sector. However, as Schrover and Yeo note, 'the huge research concentration gives a greater importance to domestic service than is true in reality and diverts attention away from migrant women who work in other sectors'.[8] This need not be the case for Irish women emigrants as the evidence of their propensity to work in British hospitals avows. As Greta Jones' work has highlighted, medical migration from Ireland has a long history, although patterns of migration can be seen as distinct from general trends in post-Famine migration from Ireland for such persons. Laura Kelly's work on Irish students travelling to Scotland for medical education has revealed that between '1859 and 1900, 182 students of Irish birth attended the University of Glasgow to study medicine', and highlights the strong networks of education and employment which existed for Irish people in the medical system of Great Britain since the seventeenth century.[9] In the case of women in the nursing profession, migration may have occurred to embark on the chance to become a qualified professional rather than after training in Ireland, and in this sense they can be viewed as becoming part of what I have termed 'Ireland's medical diaspora'. By this term, I am referring to the dispersal of Irish-trained or Irish-born migrants working as doctors, nurses and other kinds of medical professionals throughout the world in the nineteenth and twentieth centuries. As in Ryan's oral histories with female emigrants of the 1930s, 'these stories begin to suggest the ways in which women's active agency continued to be framed by gendered relations with both their home and their new life abroad'.[10] The return of these women to Ireland in this period, whether temporarily or permanently, demonstrates the ways in which nurses operated within the nexus of home, Britain, diaspora and family, maintaining 'lengthened family ties', to paraphrase Sharon Lambert.[11]

The context of World War Two also deserves some attention: the nature of nursing changed to meet the exigencies of the war and many women were engaged in front-line medical activities in Britain wholly different from their training, and perhaps their expectations. This chapter examines the profile and history of Irish women working as nurses and doctors in Britain during World War Two by analysing information taken from the travel permit applications of those who wished to return to Ireland. Travel permit applications were administrative forms used by Irish people living in Britain who wished to return to Ireland either permanently or temporarily. All citizens, apart from men in the armed forces, needed a travel permit with an exit permit in order to undertake travel between Britain and Ireland during the war. Such permits were instituted in order to ensure security between the two countries and required the submission of a fee of five shillings, a photograph and proof of birth details. Travel permits and exit permits were issued by the Irish High Commissioners Office and the British Passport Office respectively and were used in lieu of a passport, the only time at which this happened and the only time at which travel was so strictly regulated between the two countries during the common travel area period. As the forms required applicants to state their occupation, data on women working in the medical field in Britain can be captured and indeed women working as nurses were the largest cohort of working women in the collection of over 23,000 individual files held by the National Archives of Ireland. While the files do not explicitly reveal where medical training was obtained, they do reveal patterns of origin, age, marital status and current place of residence and are thus an invaluable resource for contributing to our knowledge of the Irish in World War Two Britain.[12]

This chapter will apply a prosopographical approach in order to build a profile of Irish women in the medical profession in Britain. Out of the 23,040 travel permit applications that were analysed, over two-thirds (15,252) were from women, a reflection of their greater propensity to be involved in the evacuation of children and the greater numbers of women who were not working outside the home and thus could travel more easily.[13] Greater detail can be obtained about women due to the fact that the forms detail their name/maiden name and their husband's nationality.[14] The forms also asked applicants to state their county and date of birth, occupation, their reason for travelling home and whether or not they were travelling with children. In many instances, the files also contain personal letters which reveal more information about a particular case and add to the richness of the source material.[15]

The data the records contain is extremely important, offering an insight into Irish emigrants in the 1940s unavailable from any other source. Contextualising the material in the scholarship of emigrants in the medical field, this article draws on the new demographic data revealed in the source material, in addition to using a case history approach to illustrate individual stories and experiences. Such an approach aims to provide a nuanced and detailed account of the lives of Irish women in Britain during the tumultuous period of World War Two.

Figure 5.1   Travel permit belonging to Mary Nugent, issued 1941

Source: Author's collection. Permission to photograph and use given by Mary Nugent's grandson, Joseph Glennon.

In terms of their general profile, the average age of all female applicants was thirty-one years; the most common county of origin was Cork; July 1941 saw the peak in applications for travel permits; the greatest number of female applicants were based in London at the time of application. Female applicants were more likely to be single than married and the most commonly cited reason for requesting a travel permit was to return for a holiday or temporary visit. This is reflective of the fact that nurses (the largest cohort of working women in the files) were given holiday leave and often travel subsidies by their employers.

Profile of Irish women in the medical field

Before discussing the larger categories of persons reporting occupations in the medical field in Britain, a broad profile of the applicants is provided in Table 5.1 below. A total of 4,456 women were categorised as in the medical field. In common with the overall profile of women, most were in London (24 per cent) and hailed from Cork (11 per cent), with Mayo (7.8 per cent) and Galway (6.9 per cent) as the next most popular counties, although as these figures indicate, the cohort was quite geographically dispersed in terms of origins. Almost all (97.4 per cent) were single, with just 104 cases of married women and ten widows. This is unsurprising given their age profile: 54 per cent were under the age of twenty-five at the time of their application.

Table 5.1   Travel permit applications from Irish women in the medical field (N=4,456)

Employment category	Number of female applicants for travel permits
Air Raid Protection Nurse/ Civil Nursing Reserve/ First Aid Nurse/ Red Cross Nurse	38
Ambulance attendant	9
Ambulance driver	9
Dentist	2
Doctor	12
First Aid Post Worker	3
Maternity ward nurse/midwife/pupil midwife	47
Matron	22
Nurse (State Registered/Staff Nurse)	3105
Nurse assistant	119
Nurse companion	9
Nurse probationer (trainee)	742
Orderly	10
Private Nurse	68
Radiographer	5
Religious in Nursing	14
Specialist nurse (e.g. TB)	152
Ward Sister	90
Total	4456

Source: Department of Foreign Affairs Travel Permit Files, National Archives of Ireland. Central Statistics Office, *Statistical Abstract of Ireland 1949*, Table 32 (Dublin: Government Stationery Office, 1950).

In presenting this data a number of caveats must be provided in order to properly contextualise what is represented and to highlight its limitations. First, the records only reflect those persons who wished to obtain a travel permit; they do not, therefore, represent the total numbers of Irish women involved in any given occupation. Second, the analysis of the applications are limited to the time period for which they are still extant (1940 to 1942) and thus different statistical patterns may have emerged by studying alternate temporalities or by analysing the entire cache of applications if either existed. Third, the applications are just that – a request for permission to travel, not confirmation that travel actually took place.

One other point arises in relation to the categorisation of the occupations which occurred for methodological reasons. In some cases the number of individual cases was too small for practical purposes to constitute its own category and thus figures are presented in grouped form, such as the figures for nurses in the maternity field. The descriptions of occupation are given by the applicants themselves and have been presented here as faithfully as possible to the wording used by them, including the term 'probationer' to indicate a trainee nurse.

As can be seen from Table 5.1, qualified nurses were by far the largest category within this group with just a handful of other occupations such as dentists, doctors and radiographers. These smaller groups of professional women are harder to research given their low numbers and the absence of records available to study their lives and experiences. However, the female doctors in the files constitute a unique and interesting group and will be discussed in more detail later in the chapter. As the largest category within the source material, however, nurses will be discussed first and in greater depth.

Nurses

Throughout the war years the number of women going to England to domestic service jobs greatly outnumbered those going to agricultural, nursing and factory work, yet nursing remained an attractive option for many female emigrants. There were 61,580 female domestic servants who emigrated between 1941 and 1948, representing 56 per cent of the total (109,507) recorded number of women issued travel documentation from Ireland.[16] In contrast, nursing accounted for 17,840 women obtaining travel permits representing only 16 per cent of the female cohort,[17] although many of these applicants may have had no prior experience of nursing and merely put down the occupation they were intending to take up.[18]

The wartime context of nursing in Britain is particularly important to consider. Although the regulations on Irish persons working in Britain may have seemed prohibitive and demanding due to the previous freedom with which Irish people lived and worked in Britain, Irish nurses experienced far less restrictions than those placed on the over 1,000 refugee nurses from Europe during the same period.[19] They also enjoyed favourable conditions such as paid travel and generous holidays. The most important consideration, however, may have been the reciprocal registration arrangements whereby nurses trained in Britain could register with the Irish General Nursing Council, allowing for the possibility of return should economic conditions improve. Furthermore, the war appeared to allow the transition from lower status occupations into nursing as revealed by some travel applications, accompanied by original permits used to gain entry to Britain, listing other employment, including domestic service as their original occupation.

Within the nursing profession Irish women occupied an incredible range of roles in the British medical system and their labour undoubtedly contributed to the British Home Front war effort. As Yeates has argued, the space left by the shortage of British women interested in nursing was ably and enthusiastically filled by Irish nurses and Irish women who wanted to train as nurses:

Britain consistently drew on Ireland (and other current and former colonies) for its supplies of trained and intending nurses and midwives during World War II and throughout the post-war period. Its need to recruit overseas care labour to fill professional nursing posts in the NHS resulted from the failure to remedy what was perceived by British women as a poorly paid and less attractive occupation.[20]

In this sense nursing was comparable with the domestic service industry, also abandoned by British women and supplemented by Irish immigrants, themselves fleeing relatively and substantively poorer pay and conditions in Ireland.

The report of the 1937 Congress of the International Council of Nurses suggests that nurses working in British hospitals enjoyed a higher social status than those in other countries as the writer observed in the following remark: 'The prestige enjoyed by English nurses has long been a source of envy to their sisters in other countries'.[21] This again suggests that a 'pull factor' for many Irish nurses may have been their perception of nursing as occupying a higher social position in Britain than in Ireland, or allowing access for unskilled women into a well-respected occupation. Coupled with this were two important factors: first, Irish women's greater access to nursing education in Britain and second, the increasing importance of nursing during World War Two.

Thus despite any negative connotations associated with nursing by British women, it provided a valuable opportunity to Irish women to train for a professional career. This was unavailable to many in Ireland due to some institutions' stricter entry requirements, the training fees and the loss of income whilst training in comparison with the free fees and the payment received whilst undergoing training in Britain. The necessity of having a Leaving Certificate qualification in Ireland was a barrier for many, and while many of the teaching hospitals in England also required high levels of education, many of the regional hospitals were prepared to take women without these.[22] The tragic circumstances of the war thus inadvertently created opportunities for the professional development of Irish women unattainable at home or in other time periods. Such was the impact of nursing on the profile of Irish female immigrants in Britain that in 1951, 22 per cent of Irish-born women in paid employment in Britain were engaged in professional occupations, mainly in nursing and midwifery.[23]

The travel permit records confirm Louise Ryan's findings on the familial networks that Irish nurses created, where 'a broad range of actors such as siblings, cousins and aunts in transnational kinship networks … encourage and enable women to become economically active migrants'.[24] Many of the records are of sisters or women from the same locality in Ireland working in British hospitals as well as in other professions, particularly domestic service. For example, two sisters from Roscommon, applicants 10238 and 10239, were living and working in Sussex as nurses. Aged twenty-seven and thirty-five at the time of application in August 1940, both were returning home, the older sister stating that she was returning permanently (the other sister's form did not state a reason for return). The desire for permanent return may strike one as odd given the attractive pay and conditions nurses received, but it is a reminder again of the wartime context. Sussex was a key site in the Battle of Britain, the major air battle between Britain and Germany in the summer of 1940, due to the presence of the Tangmere airbase near Chichester. Although no space is available on the forms for detailed reasons for applications, the war was mentioned by many as the main reason they wish to return, either through direct bombings on their homes or because of the nervous tension (often termed 'war strain') they experienced as a result of constant air raids. The Roscommon sisters may simply have had enough of their nursing careers in such a dangerous area and wished for the peace of their parents' home.

Wages were an important motivation for most migrants, and in nursing the disparity between Ireland and Britain in financial compensation was even starker than for domestic service, not to mention the gender disparity in wages in Ireland. Female rates of pay in Ireland throughout the 1940s up to the 1960s were between 53–57 per cent of those of men.[25] The propensity for Irish people to migrate from rural to urban locations also impacted on wage rates; as Hatton and Williamson have posited, this generally results in a doubling of wages.[26] Women entering nursing in Britain were thereby responding to 'relative wage signals', and the 'large relative wage gap between Ireland and the countries which received Irish immigrants' that led to mass emigration from Ireland.[27] Not only was training provided for free in Britain, but nurses received much higher wages, even when they were not fully trained.[28] Jane Bruder, for example, left the Richmond Asylum in Dublin where she was paid thirty shillings a week to go to the Horton War Hospital in Epsom where she received £5 per month plus board, food and uniform.[29] In 1944, a concerned reader of *The Irish Catholic* saw fit to write a letter about the wages and working conditions of nurses in Ireland, highlighting the relatively poor conditions nurses in Irish hospitals endured:

> Surely it is time to improve the working conditions and salaries of nurses in Ireland. They are amongst the worst paid of all professions when one considers the long time of training, the large entrance fee and the long working hours. Some of the nicest girls from our secondary schools enter that profession. And one can never pay a good nurse sufficiently in coin. Moreover, is it not a work of mercy that is always needed, for the sick like the poor are always with us? Yet, no pensions are allowed, and £65 p.a. [per annum] is still considered princely remuneration for a qualified nurse.[30]

Britain was the predominant location for both Irish trained nurses and those undertaking training. As Yeates found, over the period from 1929 to 1951 between 8 and 14 per cent of Irish-registered nurses were working abroad, the vast majority (89 per cent in 1951) in parts of Great Britain.[31]

Yeates' data clearly shows the increasing predominance of Britain throughout the war years as a site of training for women on the General Nursing Council register, indicating both the demand for nurses in Britain and the demand for training by Irish women eager to take up the opportunity. The war proved a

Table 5.2   Place of training of Irish nurses registered with the General Nursing Council,
selected years, 1929–1951

Year	Total registered	Total trained abroad	Trained abroad as % of total registered	Trained in Northern Ireland	Trained in England, Scotland or Wales
1929	2,244	344	15.3%	113	190
1934	2,320	395	17.0%	116	241
1939	2,788	493	17.7%	122	341
1944	3,164	713	22.5%	82	610
1949	3,676	876	23.8%	90	766
1951	4,060	1,058	26.0%	88	952

Source: Table adapted from N. Yeates, 'Migration and nursing in Ireland: an internationalist history',
Translocations: Migration and Social Change, 5 (2009), Table 2, 8. Yeates' table includes data from North
America, France, Africa, Australia/New Zealand and India which are not represented here, but the
figures were substantially lower for any of these locations.

pivotal point in this history: as Scanlan has found, in 1945 3000 Irish women
took up nurse training in Britain[32] and in 1949, 236 nurses (36 per cent) of a
total of 654 registered in Ireland that year had trained abroad.[33] The
overwhelming majority of the nurses who were registered in Ireland listed their
place of training in the UK, as detailed in Yeates' data represented in Table 5.2.

It is clear that nursing continued to attract proportionately high numbers of
women to work in Britain in the postwar period, even those who had qualified
in Ireland. In evidence to the Commission on Emigration and Other Population
Problems, the Irish Nurses Organisation (INO) stated that Irish training hospitals
did not have enough jobs to subsume their graduates, much like the medical
schools for doctors, as discussed below.[34] This ruled out personal choice as to
where to work as Mrs Grogan, representing the INO, plainly stated in addressing
the Commission:

> I don't think it is the experienced people who emigrate; it is, invariably, the younger
> nurses who have just finished their training. They have no choice – a sufficient
> number of vacancies do not exist here. They take up an English nursing paper where
> they find 8 or 9 pages of advertisements for nursing posts. Of necessity they emigrate.
> In the case of most Irish nurses, they would prefer to work in their own country but,
> as I say, they have no choice in the matter.[35]

Mrs Grogan further estimated that only 10 per cent of a group of graduate nurses
were likely to be employed within their training institution, making migration a
reality for the vast majority of nurses. Thus there was a dynamic relationship
between the British and Irish medical systems in the exchange of nurses.

The evidence of the INO to the Commission is interesting from another perspective: the position of women who worked as 'nurse assistants' in British hospitals, a category of worker that did not exist in Ireland. The spectrum of nursing in Britain included the nurse assistant category, women engaged primarily in the more domestic chores associated with nursing which required fewer qualifications. It did, however, offer the chance to work in a medical setting and to perform work of a higher social status than ordinary domestic service. Fr Counihan, a Commissioner, questioned the INO on female emigrants who fell into this category, and his class bias is evident in the language he chose to discuss 'these girls':

> To come back to the problem of this Commission, i.e. the question of emigration, it seems to me that you have several different types of girls leaving the country. You have the good type who is unable to afford a premium in order to train as a nurse; you have, also, the good type who leaves training because she cannot secure a well paid position as a trained nurse in this country […] While there is a certain drain, particularly of the better type of girl, the main concern of this Commission is the drain of the poorer type. The premium which is required to keep up the standard with regard to education, class etc., weighs against her. Consequently she is ruled out and she has no option but to go to England. Simultaneously with the heavy outflow of these young girls I understand there is a great shortage of attendants, wardsmaids, domestic servants, etc. Do you not think something should be done in this country to establish a professional grade? […] If you are going to keep these girls here you must give them a status and if you call them nurses of a certain type you are distinguishing them.[36]

The INO and Commissioners went on to discuss this problem, highlighting that having a grade below a fully trained nurse and above the status of a domestic (but who did much of the domestic work) may, particularly in the view of Fr Counihan, retain more girls at home. The INO did not seem keen on the introduction of such a grade, perhaps because of its proximity in status to an untrained domestic worker and the fact that fees were paid by nurses in Irish hospitals to attain their training. A certain 'dilution' in the status of Irish nursing may have been perceived if such a grade were implemented. The fact that Irish women could transition from unskilled, domestic work to a career as a nurse by going to Britain heightens this proximity in perception and was exemplified in a comment by Dr Doolin, also a Commissioner, who stated: 'Recently my wife had some trouble with a recalcitrant maid who threatened to go to England to take up nursing.'[37] The existence of a lower category of qualification for women interested in nursing appears to have been significant, however, as an outlet for those who either did not wish to complete full training or who were unsuccessful in their final examinations. In 1959 it was reported that approximately one student out of every three joining the training schools of general hospitals in Britain failed to complete the prescribed course for varied or unspecified reasons.[38] The ability to continue working in a hospital (if desired) must have

Table 5.3   Analysis by Department of Social Welfare of *Irish Independent* advertisements by type of job advertised, 1947

Sex	Nurses, probationers and and student nurses	Industrial workers	Domestics for institutions
Male	Nil	Nil	3
Female	286	30	23
Total			342

Source: Arnold Marsh Papers, 8304/46, Trinity College Dublin Manuscripts Department.

been an important factor for working–class women who needed to work, and, within the records analysed here, was a source of steady employment for over one hundred Irish women.

The discussion of Britain as a 'lure' for Irish women was a constant feature of government reports in the post-independence period and nursing always featured as a particularly prime 'pull' factor. Even before the Commission on Emigration and Other Population Problems was established, the Irish government was interested in monitoring the degree to which women were being influenced to leave Ireland for Britain for employment. In 1947, for example, the Department of Social Welfare conducted an analysis of seventy-six issues (three months) of the *Irish Independent* in 1947 in order to assess whether advertisements were acting as an inducement to Irish people emigrate. Table 5.3 details the range of employments they found to be publicised in larger advertisements, which were in addition to the small personal advertisements.

The Department's memo noted that the increased demand for female labour was due to the ending of the restrictions on women's travel to and from Britain which occurred in the summer of 1946. The memorandum simply laid out the facts contained in the advertisements, who placed them and gave examples of the advertising copy. The memorandum did not state what action was taken as a result of this analysis. It is likely, however, that it related to the proposed ban on female emigration indicated in a memorandum from 1948, by the office of the Minister for External Affairs and circulated by D. J. O'Donovan from the Employment Branch of the Department of Social Welfare to the Commission on Emigration and Other Population Problems.[39] Such a ban did not come to pass, but the feeling that nursing was an area of employment drawing Irish women away was articulated throughout the Commission's report. No such commentary existed about female doctors, and although this can be explained partially by their rarity, professional emigrants such as doctors were not lamented in national discourses about emigration in the same way as working-class migrants. Although there may be many reasons for this, the fact that they had more resources due to their education and training, and that they rarely created the kind of social problems that navvies and domestics did while in Britain meant that they were a silently assimilated cohort who rarely surfaced in discussions about emigration.

Doctors

Although few in number in the records under analysis here, Irish women working as medical practitioners in various parts of Britain are revealed in the travel permit applications and are also of interest in considering the Irish medical diaspora. They are interesting not only because professionals in general have been somewhat invisible in studies of Irish migration, but also because women professionals were rarely discussed in either contemporary or historical accounts of Irish migration. As Louise Miskell has noted, the 'role of the Irish middle class in the cultural, political and social life of migrant communities is still largely obscure' despite the widening of research on Irish migrants over the last few decades.[40] This is despite the fact that like nursing, Irish hospitals produced more doctors than they could provide jobs for and doctors were forced to migrate to find work, a problem that affected women as well as men as Laura Kelly's work on Irish female doctors has revealed.[41]

In Greta Jones' study of medical graduates from Irish hospitals between 1860 and 1960 about 41 per cent of the cohorts examined were practising outside Ireland, a decade later with a further 15 per cent unaccounted for.[42] England was the primary migration destination for doctors trained in Irish institutions, military service accounting for the majority of others residing outside of Ireland. As the records examined in this chapter show, Britain continued to constitute a draw for men and women in the medical field throughout the twentieth century; it predominated as the destination of choice until the 1950s and 1960s when North America emerged as an alternate destination for doctors, although not for nurses.[43] The reciprocal registration arrangements between Britain and Ireland negotiated in the 1920s assisted the migration of Irish doctors throughout Britain and the cohort within the travel permit files benefited from this flexibility.[44]

The emigration of doctors was not an unexpected phenomenon; it was widely recognised that Irish medical schools produced a greater number of doctors than the Irish medical system could subsume.[45] As Oscar Gish pondered in the 1960s, 'it is not clear whether Ireland must overproduce because so many emigrate, or so many emigrate because of the overproduction', but whatever the motivating principle it resulted in Irish doctors making a 'substantial contribution to medical care in Britain as well as in other countries'.[46] Much like Irish nurses, Irish doctors constituted a significant minority working in the British health system in the postwar period. More striking, however, is the fact that there were more Southern Irish physicians practicing in Britain (2,700) than in the Republic (2,600) by 1966.[47]

For some this migration reflected a personal choice in pursuit of greater professional opportunities; for others, it was adopted after failed attempts at establishing a thriving surgery in Ireland. Both options faced Irish medical graduates in the time period under study here as Jones has observed: 'Though the decision to emigrate arose, in some cases, after protracted attempts at setting up practice in Ireland, in other instances, it was expected and planned for.'[48] Furthermore, the monetary gains to be made in setting up practices in the burgeoning British towns would have acted as a specific draw and it is likely that the larger annual incomes were well known among medical students and recent graduates, as Jones has commented: 'even those who worked in poorer parts of urban England could tell tales of medical prosperity'.[49]

The women doctors in the permit files are revealed to have a diverse demographic profile. Of the eleven Irish women applicants, seven were single and four were married.[50] Of those that were married all four had Irish-born husbands, showing a propensity for endogamous marriage, although this small number does not allow for any claims to a wider applicability of this finding. They ranged in age between twenty-five and forty-one years, and as with the overall cohort and the profile of nurses, the greatest proportion of the group (four women) were from Cork, the others being from Galway, Cavan, Dublin, Clare and Kilkenny. At the time of application, five were in the Greater London area, and there was one applicant in Staffordshire, Devon, Yorkshire and Glamorgan, with two applicants in Warwickshire. Their reasons for return also showed some variety; although five of the group reported going for holidays, one was returning to visit relatives and to rest for health reasons, and another was visiting a chronically ill relative. Of most interest, however, are the two cases where the women doctors reported evacuating their children; one bringing a child to Ireland, and one bringing a child and visiting another child previously evacuated.

There were two ways in which Irish children were evacuated from Britain during World War Two: either through personal arrangements by their parents or through the official British evacuation scheme. The official evacuation scheme began on 1 September 1939, and moved 1,473,000 children and adults from the crowded cities of Britain. Undoubtedly parents were urged on by propaganda depicting Hitler's glee at targeting children in British cities who had not yet been evacuated. The majority of these mothers and children were transferred to Reception Areas before war was declared two days later, on 3 September 1939.[51] A second wave of evacuations took place the following year in September from London, which saw 1,250,000 adults and children moved, and a further evacuation from this city occurred in July 1944.[52] The extant travel permit evacuation files cover the second wave of evacuations only, although throughout 1941 Irish parents were evacuating their children in regular numbers to go to relatives in Ireland, according to the records.

In the first case referred to above, applicant 20021 was a twenty-seven-year-old doctor from Cavan. Married to an Irish-born doctor, she was evacuating her child to her parents' home, away from war conditions in Staffordshire where they were based at the time of her application in December 1940. Her file mentions that her husband was also applying for a travel permit, suggesting that they were planning to travel together home to Ireland. In the second case, applicant 25466 was a thirty-six-year-old doctor from Dublin bringing one child, a three-year-old boy, with her on a trip to visit her two other children who had been evacuated from Warwickshire. Although it is not stated, it is likely they were with family members. In the case of this applicant, she had some trouble renewing her permit as she originally intended because there were so many stamps on it, suggesting that she was regularly returning to Ireland to see her children.

Evacuees going privately arranged their own accommodation and the British government provided free travel vouchers and a lodging allowance to be paid to the homeowner they and/or their children were going to. Interestingly, this could be a family member, thus in applying this policy the British government were funding family reunification in the case of Irish immigrants who had been working in Britain. There is no official commentary on this arrangement – either from the Irish or British perspective – that could be found as part of this research. It is yet another strange anomaly in the post-independence relationship between Britain and Ireland which saw Irish citizens in Britain benefit fully from British social policies without themselves being British citizens.

The lodging allowances were five shillings per mother and the same for children fourteen years and over, with three shillings per week being allowed for children under fourteen years. This was half the rate that would have been paid in allowances if they had stayed in Britain, which may explain the motivating factor for the British government to provide such assistance. In this way the two Irish women doctors in these files were facilitated to return to Britain and continue their work while ensuring the safety of their children. In this context they were assisted to be working mothers, evidence again of the exigencies of the war that needed all available 'manpower', particularly in hospital settings hit by air raid casualties.

Conclusion

While women in the nursing profession may have held a more visible position in ethnic archetypes and the cultural memory of Irish people in Britain, little has been researched or written on women in the wider medical field. While this is partly due to their low numbers, it is noteworthy that Irish women working as doctors or dentists, for example, are rarely mentioned within accounts of either medical migration or Irish migration in general. Moreover, we lack a comprehensive understanding of how Irish women came to inhabit such a significant place in nursing in Britain. As Miskell has pointed out, the Irish in Britain were often posited as the receivers of medical care rather than the providers, reflecting ethnic biases on the 'problem Irish'.[53] Thus, it is necessary to emphasise that although the poor health status of Irish migrants in Britain has in recent years been a focus of study, their historical importance as providers of medical care in Britain must not be forgotten.[54] Their subsequent invisibility in the historical record may therefore be the result of 'ethnic fade' in middle-class Irish immigrant communities, a strategy employed to avoid discriminatory attitudes. As Janes Yeo has reminded us, the periods of peak Irish migrations 'were not periods of multicultural toleration of ethnic difference'.[55]

Although more is known about Irish women working as domestics or nurses, they have become somewhat of a cultural stereotype that has yet to be fully interrogated to explore the totality and nuance of their experiences. The research presented in this chapter provides a 'chink of light' on to the many histories of women in the Irish global medical diaspora, yet many questions emerge as to their migration trajectories and lives after the 'snapshot' provided by the travel permit forms. To what extent did their sense of nationality, ethnicity or 'Irishness' become emphasised or de-emphasised in hospital settings? Given the preponderance of British hospitals that specifically recruited from Ireland, it is likely that many hospitals had a strong Irish influence or cultural ethos, yet little is known about this beyond some of the oral history studies that have been completed. The Christopher Maggs collection at the British Library includes an interview with a British nurse who found herself working at what was commonly referred to as the 'Irish Hospital' due to the prevalence of Irish nurses and the fact that the Matron went on recruiting missions to Ireland, locating 'Irish farm girls and girls from convents you know, all mad keen to get to London' through local priests.[56] Mrs Maden's interview reveals that in her particular case, the 'Irishness' of the hospital was imbricated with a religiosity that saw patients having different coloured medals to indicate their faith, and the meting out of religious-based punishments to nurses who made mistakes:

> As many of them [nurses] were Roman Catholic they were given many penances to do and many hours of prayer to do … when they did anything wrong. I remember one nurse who flirted with a doctor and she had to take a cold bath every morning at six in the morning and they made sure she did it … I would fall over nurses who were kneeling because they would be told to pray at certain times! … I was in the wrong hospital, I really was![57]

To what extent this kind of culture was familiar to Irish women working as nurses or doctors, or whether it was idiosyncratic to that particular hospital, is difficult to establish given the paucity of evidence. Further studies investigating the 'Irishness' of British hospitals are necessary to fully contextualise this anecdote, but it raises interesting possibilities of how the working lives of Irish nurses and doctors were affected by the migration of Irish people into the British medical system, or the Irish medical diaspora as I have termed it. Questions also arise as to how the Irish influence or atmosphere of a hospital was impacted by the political context of Ireland's neutrality during the war and whether this proved problematic or not for Irish staff members dealing directly with wounded soldiers and civilians.

The travel permit application files, unfortunately, do not provide us with any detail of what happened next: did the women in these files return to Ireland permanently after the war? Or did the opportunities for jobs and career advancement available in Britain in the postwar period constitute not just a pull factor but a 'root' factor, promoting the desire to stay in Britain? As was stated in the British *Economic Survey for 1947* the industries most seriously in need of labour were those likely to 'have a paralyzing effect on the whole of the rest of the economy' if shortages were to occur and for women, this included textiles, nursing, and domestic service.[58]

Medical migration was a phenomenon that persisted throughout the twentieth century. As Jones' work has shown, significant numbers of doctors migrated in the nineteenth century and a London School of Economic survey found that over 6,100 doctors trained in medical schools in Great Britain and Ireland left the British Isles in the ten years 1952–61 and were still abroad in July 1962.[59] The interconnected nature of the Irish and British medical professions continued after Irish independence and the impact of migration in this process cannot be underestimated: a staggering '71 per cent (2,025) of the Irish graduates of the Republic's medical schools between 1950 and 1966 – an average of 127 per year – had left Ireland and gone abroad'.[60] Although often undertaken individually and through personal choice, migration to the nursing profession, for example, 'was organised, extensive and sustained, and was formative of the Irish nursing profession and nursing institutions, at home and abroad'.[61]

Yeates has asserted that 'migration has been important in the history of nursing in Ireland since the early nineteenth century'.[62] This chapter seeks to contribute to the literature on Irish women in the medical profession by outlining the demographic profile of women found across the British medical field. It is clear that further work is needed to draw out the more liminal areas of Irish female migration in Britain, which may be accomplished through specific hospital studies, further oral histories or through uncovering as-yet undiscovered official records. Irish women's particular contribution to the British medical field during World War Two (and throughout the twentieth century), and their impact on the National Health System was recognised in contemporary accounts but has been sadly obscured in the historical record. Travel permits are just one way to illuminate the histories of such an obvious immigrant minority; the challenge to scholars interested in migration and women's history is to find other ways to elucidate the lives of these women in ways that fully recognise the important role they have played as part of Ireland's medical diaspora.

Notes

1 L. Ryan, '"I had a sister": family-led migration, social networks and nurses', *Journal of Ethnic and Migration Studies*, 34 (2008), 454.
2 B. Gray, *Women and the Irish Diaspora* (London: Routledge, 2004), p. 1.
3 *Ibid.*, p. 2.
4 B. Gray, '"Too close for comfort": re-membering the forgotten diaspora of Irish women in England', in W. Kokot, K. Tölölyan and C. Alfonso (eds), *Diaspora, Identity and Religion: New Directions in Theory and Research* (Routlege: London 2004), p. 34.
5 The research on which this chapter is based is taken from a wider postdoctoral project, 'Regulating Citizenship: Irish Travel and Emigration Arrangements in the Second World War' funded by the Irish Research Council for Humanities and Social Sciences and held by the author at the Department of History, NUI Maynooth (2009–2011). My thanks are due to Catriona Crowe, Head of Special Projects at the National Archives for access to the records. At present, the records are closed and thus all cases in this chapter are discussed in aggregate form or anonymously. For the purposes of this article, Greta Jones' most relevant works are, '"Strike out boldly for the prizes that are available to you": medical emigration from Ireland 1860–1905', *Medical History*, 54 (2010), 55–74 and '"A mysterious discrimination": Irish medical emigration to the United States in the 1950s', *Social History of Medicine*, 25 (2012), 139–56. Louise Ryan's work on Irish nurses in Britain has examined the issue from both a historical and sociological perspective, for example, L. Ryan, 'Migrant women, social networks and motherhood: the experiences of Irish nurses in Britain', *Sociology*, 41 (2007), 295–312.
6 M. Schrover and E. J. Yeo, 'Introduction: moving the focus to the public sphere', in M. Schrover and E. J. Yeo (eds), *Gender, Migration and the Public Sphere, 1850–2005* (New York: Routledge, 2010), p. 4.
7 A range of research exists on Irish unmarried mothers either fleeing to Britain or participating in the repatriation scheme operated between the Catholic hierarchy in Britain and Ireland. For more on this topic see J. Redmond, 'In the family way and away from the family: examining the evidence in Irish unmarried mothers in Britain, 1920s–40s', in E. Farrell (ed.), *'She Said She was in the Family Way': Pregnancy and Infancy in the Irish Past* (London: Institute of Historical Research, 2012); L. Earner-Byrne, '"Moral repatriation": the response to Irish unmarried mothers in Britain, 1920s–1960s', in P. J. Duffy (ed.), *To and From Ireland: Planned Migration Schemes c.1600–2000* (Dublin: Geography Publications, 2004), pp.155–74.; and L. Ryan, '"A decent girl well worth helping": women, migration and unwanted pregnancy', in L. Harte and Y. Whelan (eds), *Ireland Beyond Boundaries: Mapping Irish Studies in the Twenty-first Century* (London: Pluto Press, 2007), pp. 135–53.
8 Schrover and Yeo, 'Introduction', p. 5.
9 L. Kelly, 'Migration and medical education: Irish medical students at the University of Glasgow, 1859–1900', *Irish Economic and Social History*, 39 (2012), 40. Note that women were not allowed to attend the school until 1892.
10 L. Ryan, '"I'm going to England": women's narratives of leaving Ireland in the 1930s', *Oral History*, 30 (2002), 52.
11 S. Lambert, 'Irish women's emigration to England, 1922–1960: the lengthening of family ties', in A. Hayes and D. Urquhart (eds), *Irish Women's History* (Dublin: Irish Academic Press, 2004), pp.152–67.
12 It may be possible to examine the forms in greater detail to detect where training took place but the information on past residences was not uniformly filled out by applicants and was thus not recorded by the author. The applications are held by the National Archives of Ireland in the Department of Foreign Affairs collection and

relate to the period between 1940 and 1942, thus they do not constitute the entire cache of records as travel permits for women were issued up to 1946, and for later still for men whose labour was more strictly regulated at this time.

13 There were 745 cases where this information was missing from the application form, thereby creating a valid sample of 22,295 individual cases.

14 For the most part marital status for women can be known either through a direct statement on the form or through the signature of the applicant, although some versions of the form did not ask this.

15 The records have not been previously used by historians as the National Archives has never had a complete catalogue and has decided thus far to keep the records private; I was given special permission to use the records and created a catalogue of the records as part of my research.

16 These women are different than those applicants who specifically stated that they were a First Aid Nurse.

17 Central Statistics Office, *Statistical Abstract of Ireland 1949*, Table 32 (Dublin: Government Stationary Office, 1950).

18 J. Meenan, *The Irish Economy Since 1922* (Liverpool University Press: Liverpool, 1970), p. 211. James Meenan was one of the serving Commissioners on the Commission on Emigration and Other Population Problems. This tendency is also discussed by Enda Delaney, see E. Delaney, *Demography, State and Society: Irish Migration to Britain, 1921–1971* (Liverpool University Press: Liverpool, 2000).

19 J. Stewart, 'Angels or aliens? Refugee nurses in Britain, 1938 to 1942', *Medical History*, 47 (2003), 150.

20 N. Yeates, 'A dialogue with "global care chain" analysis: nurse migration in the Irish context', *Feminist Review*, 77 (2004), 86.

21 '"Dear sisters of the world": notes on the Congress of the International Council of Nurses, London, July 19–24, 1937', *The American Journal of Nursing*, 37(1937), 999.

22 M. Daniels, *Exile or Opportunity? Irish Nurses and Midwives in Britain*. Occasional Papers in Irish Studies Number 5 (Liverpool: University of Liverpool, 1993), p.10.

23 Yeates, 'A dialogue with "global care chain" analysis', 87.

24 Ryan, '"I had a sister in England"', 455.

25 R. King and H. O'Connor, 'Migration and gender: Irish women in Leicester', *Geography*, 81(1996), 313.

26 T. J. Hatton and J. G. Williamson, 'What explains wage gaps between farm and city? Exploring the Todaro Model with American evidence, 1890–1941', *Economic Development and Cultural Change*, 40 (1992), 267–94.

27 G. R. Boyer, T. J. Hatton and K. O'Rourke, 'The impact of emigration on real wages in Ireland, 1850–1914', in T. J. Hatton and J. G. Williamson (eds), *Migration and the International Labour Market, 1850–1939* (Routledge: London, 1994), p. 221. Note that the authors of this chapter do not specifically analyse women's wage rates.

28 Mary Daly's review of training fees for nurses found a range from 10 guineas in Mercer Hospital to £100 in Jervis Street in the 1940s, although some hospitals had abolished training fees due to lack of applicants – these trainees would still not have been paid wages as in British hospitals. See M. E. Daly, *The Slow Failure: Population Decline and Independent Ireland, 1920–1971* (Wisconsin: University of Wisconsin Press, 2006), p. 172.

29 P. Schweitzer (ed.) *'Across the Irish Sea'* (London: Age Exchange Theatre Trust, 1989), pp. 19–21.

30 *The Irish Catholic*, 27 July 1944, p. 4, letter signed by F. D. Brereton.

31 N. Yeates, 'Migration and nursing in Ireland: an internationalist history', *Translocations: Migration and Social Change*, 5 (2009), 9.

32 P. Scanlan, *The Irish Nurse: A Study of Nursing in Ireland – History and Education 1718–1981* (Manor Hamilton, Leitrim: Drumlin Press, 1991), p. 361, footnote 144, quoting *The Irish Nurses Magazine*, July 1946.

33 *Ibid.*, information extracted from Figure 6, p. 148. This figure includes three men and does not specify what countries the nurses were trained in.

34 The Commission on Emigration and Other Population Problems (1948–1954) was established to investigate the causes of Ireland's dwindling population and to propose solutions to the government. The Irish Nurses Organisation was among a number who were interviewed by the Commissioners. Arnold Marsh was a Commissioner and the only one to have kept his papers of their proceedings, all of which are available at the Manuscript's Department, Trinity College Dublin.

35 Evidence submitted by Miss Healy (President), Miss Grogan (Secretary) and Mrs Nix (Member of the Executive) on behalf of the Irish Nurses' Organisation, Friday 14th January 1948, 8307–8/11 Arnold Marsh Papers, Trinity College Dublin Manuscripts Department.

36 *Ibid.*

37 *Ibid.*

38 A. Barr, 'Training of student nurses', *British Journal of Preventive and Social Medicine*, 13:3 (1959), 149.

39 See Arnold Marsh papers, 8300/12/1 and 8300/12/2, TCD Manuscripts Department, for further details of the correspondence and the memo.

40 L. Miskell, '"The heroic Irish doctor"? Irish immigrants in the medical profession in nineteenth century Wales', in O. Walsh (ed.), *Ireland Abroad: Politics and Professions in the Nineteenth Century* (Dublin: Four Courts Press, 2003), p. 82.

41 L. Kelly, *Irish Women in Medicine, c.1880s–1920s: Origins, Education and Careers* (Manchester University Press: Manchester, 2013).

42 G. Jones, '"Strike out boldly for the prizes that are available to you"', 55.

43 Greta Jones has made this assertion as regards the destination of Irish doctors in her article '"A mysterious discrimination"'. As Jones notes, the restrictions placed on Irish medical graduates in the US in the early 1950s prohibited migration for some years, which may have made Britain even more of a draw as a migration destination.

44 *Ibid.*, 140.

45 Jones, '"Strike out boldly for the prizes that are available to you"', 68.

46 O. Gish, 'Emigration and the supply and demand for medical manpower: the Irish case', *Minerva*, 7:4 (1969), 668.

47 *Ibid.*, 670.

48 Jones, '"Strike out boldly for the prizes that are available to you"', 70.

49 *Ibid.*

50 There was one more female applicant working as a doctor in the files but she was born in Scotland and appeared to be going to her husband's address. It is likely that she had previously lived in Ireland or had Irish parentage otherwise she would have been directed to obtain a British travel permit to come to Ireland. However, without definitive evidence she has been excluded from this analysis.

51 J. Welshman, *Churchill's Children: The Evacuee Experience in Wartime Britain* (Oxford University Press: Oxford, 2010), pp. 5–6.

52 *Ibid.*, p. 6.

53 Miskell, '"The heroic Irish doctor?"', p. 83.

54 For example, the statistical study conducted by Greenslade, Madden and Pearson points to the evidence for conceptualizing the Irish in Britain as a distinct ethnic group (from British people) in terms of health outcomes. See L. Greenslade, M. Madden and M. Pearson, 'From visible to invisible: the "problem" of the health of

Irish people in Britain', in L. Marks and M. Worboys (eds), *Migrants, Minorities, and Health: Historical and Contemporary Studies* (London: Routledge, 1997), pp. 147–78.

55 E. J. Yeo, 'Gender and homeland in the Irish and Jewish Diasporas', in Schrover and Yeo (eds), *Gender, Migration and the Public Sphere*, p. 17.

56 Interview by Christopher Maggs with Mrs Maden, Royal College of Nursing History Group Interviews, C545/21/01, British Library Sound Archive.

57 *Ibid*.

58 K. Paul, 'A case of mistaken identity: the Irish in postwar Britain', *International Labor and Working-Class History*, 49 (1996), 117.

59 J. Seale, 'Medical emigration from Great Britain and Ireland since 1962', *British Medical Journal*, 2:5513 (1966), 576.

60 Gish, 'Emigration and supply and demand for medical manpower', 676.

61 Yeates, 'Migration and nursing in Ireland', 2.

62 *Ibid.*, 1.

6

Reflecting on gender, generation and ethnicity in celebrating St Patrick's Day in London

Mary J. Hickman

Introduction

In this chapter I reflect on the significance of the categories of gender and generation, and their intersection with ethnicity in the context of the official London
St Patrick's Day Festival. St Patrick's Day celebrations have a particular resonance
within studies of the Irish diaspora as they are subject to a debate about their
relevance and meaning in relation to Irish identities. As identities are constructed
within, not outside, discourse we need to understand them as produced in
specific historical and institutional sites within specific discursive formations and
practices, by specific proclaiming strategies.[1] Historically St Patrick's Day parades
have been much more important outside than inside Ireland, reflecting the
need/desire to assert diasporic ethnic identities in however fleeting a manner. In
this chapter I examine some of these wider debates about St Patrick's Day as a
preamble to a discussion of the Mayor of London's St Patrick's Day Advisory
Forum (from herein referred to as the Advisory Forum) which was established
in 2002 to advise the then Mayor, Ken Livingstone, as he inaugurated an official
St Patrick's Day Festival, backed by City Hall. The Advisory Forum has remained
in existence ever since and now advises the current Mayor, Boris Johnson. At the
outset I should declare that I write as someone who is a member of the Advisory
Forum. This membership delivered me the opportunity to reflect on the experience as a participant observer, so the chapter represents a form of ethnography,
but also gave me the opportunity to survey the other members of the Advisory
Forum about the first six years of its operation, 2002–2008. My reflections on
the Festival are therefore both as a member of the Advisory Forum and as a
member of the heterogeneous diasporic formation we might refer to as 'the
London Irish'.

My working definition of diaspora is that it refers to a hybrid, historical social
formation in process produced by migration.[2] Diasporas are historical formations

in process because they change over time as part of the political, social and economic developments in and between various places of settlement (including 'the homeland'). Diasporas are constituted by hybridity, in that any migration from a particular country is heterogeneous (in terms of class, gender, religion, age, sexuality, ethno-national identifications) and migrations go to multi-locations in each place of settlement. If we retain a conception of diaspora as constituted by and through hybridity then it assists us in explaining how in specific contexts either the conflicts of interest or the points of communion amongst different social groupings or differently located groupings within a diaspora can be predominant and why at other times they are not.[3] This examination of the organisation of the St Patrick's Day Festival in London is a means in one institutional site at a particular conjunctural moment to explore what brought people together and what produced tensions.

In much social analysis we are trying to understand, in a grounded fashion, the intersections of a range of social divisions. These are the practices around which social relations are organised. Gender and ethnicity are recognised as two leading categories of social division. They are, as Nancy Fraser points out, 'bivalent categories', that is, categories indicative of potential marginality and disadvantage in that gender and ethnicity display simultaneous discriminations in areas of resource allocation but they are also important resources for socially acceptable identities and in this way they can be a source of bonding.[4] Generation, although recognised as an axis of social division, based on a cohort of individuals born within a certain time frame, is less frequently associated as a resource for identifications. However, there is a long sociological tradition of conceptualising generation in a broader manner. This approach also stresses age strata but places more emphasis on people living in a particular historical period and thus the formation of a generation is understood in terms of the emergence of the politics and culture of a particular generation.[5] I want to discuss the inter-section of these three axes of social division and social coalescence in order better to understand the Irish diaspora in London through a study of the contemporary St Patrick's Day Festival.

Celebrations of St Patrick's Day are important in the diaspora and have their own specificity rather than involving a straightforward adoption of the national practices of the 'homeland'. In the different ways the day is celebrated, commemorated, contested and responded to we can, for example, trace the tensions between or co-existence of 'homeland' and diaspora in different places of Irish settlement over time. These tensions are, for example, illustrated in many commentaries on the New York City parade. To take but one instance, there was a fierce disagreement in the *Irish Times* in March 1998 between the journalist and essayist Fintan O'Toole and the historian Marion Casey. O'Toole ridiculed the New York Irish parade in comparison with the one taking place in Dublin and castigated those who repeatedly took the decision in the 1990s to exclude the Irish Lesbian and Gay Organisation (ILGO) from the New York parade, in particular the Ancient Order of Hibernians (AOH), the principal organisers. He argued that the 'Irish State should start to push for a re-imagining of what is, after all, the world's largest display of Irish values and aspirations'.

Marion Casey, replying in a letter to the newspaper, described O'Toole's view as exclusive, intolerant and smug in advocating that Dublin should dictate a 'new' definition of being Irish. Possible tensions between 'homeland' and the diaspora perfectly framed! Having walked in the NYC parade myself in 1997, I think the experience and many of the people on it are different to the stereo-type. While I agreed with O'Toole's critique of the narrow exclusivity of its organisers, I also strongly agreed with Marion Casey that the specificity of the expression of Irishness in each diaspora space is not the business of the Irish state. O'Toole did more than most in 1990s Ireland to argue for a non-territorial definition of Irishness,[6] however, in this instance, the spectre of the AOH was sufficient for him to invoke the Irish state to protect 'Irishness'. The AOH do not represent everyone on the parade let alone the entirety of Irish America, but they do represent something concrete that sprang from the political, economic and social conditions that produced a significant element of the social relations that constitute 'Irish America'. Recognising this requires seeing the Irish diaspora for the heterogeneous formation it is.

The imaginings of Ireland or of what it is to be 'Irish', 'Irish American', 'Australian-Irish' and so on in people's heads, as they celebrate with others, will be varied and changing even if there can be many shared elements. Cronin and Adair in their diaspora-wide study of St Patrick's Day found that the vast majority of people who celebrate the day do so at their own behest and it is a means of invoking their personal/family history.[7] For some of their older correspondents the church service was a key part of marking the day; some remember it as a 'party day' at school and replicate aspects of that experience; for others it was inseparable from eating bacon and cabbage or corned beef and cabbage with soda bread after church or the parade; and for yet more St Patrick's Day is associated with conviviality and drinking and therefore the pub is a prime venue for celebrations. No one could surmise that this range of responses and activities from around the world could lead to any uniformity in the meanings that attach to celebrating St Patrick's Day, nevertheless, across continents millions of people engage on the same day in celebrations that identify them to one degree or another as 'Irish' or indicate that Irish identifica-tions are meaningful to them.

My focus here is to explore the basis of these commonalities and differences as they were manifest in organising the St Patrick's Day Festival in London. First I review some of the literature about the representations and meanings attached to St Patrick's Day, especially as they may be relevant to Britain. Next I examine the establishment of the Festival in London, thus covering the 'steering' of a major St Patrick's Day parade, planning liaison between local authorities and community organisations and representatives as well as the parade itself. Third I discuss the thoughts and reflections of the community members of the Mayor's St Patrick's Day Advisory Forum in London and consider some of the common goals and the tensions that were manifest in the Festival organisation through the lens of gender, generation and ethnicity.

Meanings and representations of St Patrick's Day

Cronin and Adair's (2002) view is that St Patrick's Day celebrations are sustained by the continued demographic and cultural renewal of Irish communities as a result of continued migration and by the expanding appeal (often a consequence of heavy marketing by commercial firms) of St Patrick's Day to non-Irish populations across the globe. They think St Patrick's Day celebrations appeal to people who are not Irish because the festivities have lost their assertive Irishness and have become 'self-congratulatory events that are both tolerated and actively embraced by non-Irish communities'.[8] Another perspective on what engenders this wider appeal sees the celebrations as offering participants an identifiable ethnicity that is unthreatening and familiar.[9] These sources of continuing support are thought crucial because there is an implicit assumption that people of Irish descent are likely to have a tenuous connection with their Irish heritage. Cronin and Adair, for example, appear to support as more generally applicable Reginald Byron's thesis that by the third-generation Irish absorption into American culture is complete and only 'small vestiges, such as celebrating St Patrick's Day' remain of a specific Irish identity. Byron bases this view on his study of Irish Americans in Albany, New York, where he found that while claiming that their sense of Irishness was important to them his respondents could not identify any family traditions that expressed this other than St Patrick's Day.[10]

Byron's is a classic articulation of the assimilation paradigm and while seeming to explain the reported phenomena can be subject to question. Instead of representing a 'small vestige' of cultural identity, participation in St Patrick's Day celebrations might be conceptualised as a significant moment in a hybridised life, one in which family history, memories and other experiences crystallise together in different ways over time and space. The assimilation paradigm cannot explain hybridity, the salient feature of diasporic space, nor that diasporic identities are simultaneously local and global.[11] Conceptualising participation in St Patrick's Day as representing trace elements of the strong identifications of previous generations, relies on depicting identity formation for immigrant groups as a historically inevitable passage along a continuum from the (assumed) strong national identifications of new immigrants through to the inevitable extinction of these meanings for subsequent generations. An alternative way of understanding identity formation is as a continual process of making and unmaking, expressed within and across different discourses and different contexts. So that 'at any given moment, we are positioned across multiple processes of identification which shift and configure into a specific pattern in a designated set of circumstances'.[12] Thus exploring the varied meanings that contemporary multi-generation participants attach to St Patrick's Day and its activities can be a means of understanding the complexity and contingency of diasporic and ethno-national formation in specific places.

In Britain there has been some attention to the contemporary meanings attached to St Patrick's Day by those of Irish descent. Cronin and Adair quote one of their second-generation Irish respondents from Birmingham (England) as saying that the parade gives her and other second-generation Irish people an opportunity to express and investigate how they feel about their roots and their own identities.[13] Bronwen Walter's analysis of interviews with adult second-generation Irish people in Britain demonstrates gender and regional differences and the saliency of particular institutional contexts for understanding the meanings attached to St Patrick's Day. She explores the disparate reactions of the second-generation Irish to the arrival in their homes, when they were children, of boxes and envelopes containing shamrock, medals, badges and cards. She detects a gender difference in response with boys more prominent amongst the reluctant recipients. Their reactions ranged from disinterest, to puzzlement, to fears of being different if they wore them. Girls shared those fears after 1968 and the escalation of the Troubles but many had been happy to be dressed up with green ribbons in their hair. Walter found that in Catholic state schools there was a mixed response to St Patrick's Day, reflecting the ambivalence of the Catholic Church towards the Irishness of the second generation and a general downplaying of Irish national and ethnic difference. In non-denominational state schools there was no evidence of St Patrick's Day being recognised or accepted but there were accounts of bullying of children for wearing shamrocks.[14] At the level of everyday lived experience therefore there is some evidence here of gender differences about modes of participation in St Patrick's Day.

Walter makes the important point that the arrival of shamrock and other items from Ireland was a clear message that second-generation children were part of the 'national Irish family' as far as their immediate families in Ireland were concerned. Their arrival also revealed a taken-for-granted assumption that these second-generation children would accept this identity and be prepared to proclaim it publicly in Britain. Prior to 1968 this might have been a reasonable expectation but even then it did not take account of the particular history of the Irish in Britain. In general the lack of public space for or recognition of, in particular, a working-class Irish-Catholic identity ensured local parades existed but were of different longevity and patchily distributed across the country.[15] Further, the enthusiasm for parades ebbed and flowed amongst Irish communities themselves. At the time that most of the current second generation were young, in the 1970s and 1980s, there were fewer parades than usual anyway because of the escalation of conflict in Northern Ireland. Additionally, there was no official acclamation of the diaspora in Ireland at that time as there was after Mary Robinson's presidency in 1990. But privately there was considerable contact across extended families and continents and the sending of shamrock was one symbol of the connections being reinforced. So we learnt about wearing shamrock in the privacy of our homes, or rejected wearing it with an eye on our other world at school, rather than through participating in or witnessing major public events. All the more momentous therefore was the arrival of an officially sponsored St Patrick's Day Festival and Parade in central London in 2002.

John Nagle, in a detailed ethnographic study of this first St Patrick's Day Festival argues that it 'dangerously flirted with the double play, wherein space claimed for cultural expression becomes a constricted and restrained space within a wider system of co-option'.[16] The Greater London Authority (GLA) he noted supports such festivities as part of its explicit advocation of multiculturalism and inclusivity. Ethnic celebrations were an expression of its commitment to anti-racist policies and instilling a shared sense of London identity. Nagle describes this as part of the 'double bind' of multiculturalism. In that:

> On the one hand, 'ethnic minority' groups are encouraged within the multicultural paradigm, to make their cultures inclusive and accessible in order to contribute towards a liberal-pluralist celebration of 'cosmopolitan' diversity; on the other, it is forbidden to threaten their particularism, as to do so would contradict their claim to resources as a distinctive group.[17]

However, Nagle found that:

> Events such as the London St Patrick's Day parade and festival are problematic because they are anomalous and conspicuously fail to be neatly categorised as either liminal and transcendent, or ceremonial and the negation of social critique. The parade and festival contained elements of both. On the one hand, there was no real themed structuring of the parade, and anybody could take part and represent a brand of Irishness they deemed fit. On the other hand, the route of the parade, the venue of the music, and the choice of acts taking part were all fixed.[18]

He concluded that the St Patrick's Day Festival was neither a site in which the potential visibility of Irishness is enclosed and fetishised, nor was it representative of a harmonious model of multiculturalism, and neither did he find evidence that it was contentious: 'There were different narratives of the Irish community present, but there was no attempt by the organisers to exclude any identity.'[19] Nagle concludes therefore that multicultural initiatives can provide scope for building coalitions across communities to foster discussion on progressive political strategies. Let me turn to the organisation of St Patrick's Day Festival in London, how it came to be established and how it was perceived by members of its Advisory Forum.

The establishment of the St Patrick's Day Festival in London

The emergence of the Festival in London was intertwined with both national (British) and local (London) politics. The New Labour government in the late 1990s as part of its devolution strategy implemented a manifesto promise to create a system of elected city mayors where there was electoral support for the policy. In London the popularity and effectiveness of this policy was expected to lie in its resolution of problems resulting from the power gap left in the capital city by the abolition of the Greater London Council (GLC) in 1986 by the Conservative government of Margaret Thatcher. The leader of the GLC had been Ken Livingstone. Frequently abhorred by the media and referred to as 'Red' Ken, one of his most controversial policies had been to invite Gerry Adams, President of Sinn Fein, to meet with him in London in 1983. This was a period when the Irish Republican Army's (IRA) bombing campaign was very active in London. Livingstone anticipated by a number of years what was eventually to be acknowledged as the only route to a peaceful resolution in Northern Ireland, and in particular the goal of the IRA laying down its arms, namely that it was necessary to talk with all parties to the conflict. Livingstone was, in taking this action, reflecting a widespread view about policy direction on Northern Ireland amongst the Irish in London that differentiated them from much of the rest of the population.[20]

Livingstone was unsuccessful in obtaining the nomination to be the Labour Party's candidate for Mayor of London and he decided to stand for election as an independent. He ran a populist campaign that revisited many of the community-orientated hallmark policies of his previous period in local government. Livingstone focused some policy commitments towards the Irish in London as the expectation was that they, along with other minority ethnic groups, might well provide a substantial share of his potential votes. One of his pre-election pledges was to do more for the Irish community, including support for a major St Patrick's Day parade in the city. After his electoral triumph and installation as Mayor Livingstone moved to make good on this promise. In August 2000 Irish organisations from across London met at the offices of the GLA. Well aware of existing events that annually celebrated St Patrick's Day in London the proposal was to bring 'together all the different events into one big festival and promote it to everyone'.[21] Cronin and Adair have documented the impact that the Troubles in the 1970s and 1980s had on St Patrick's Day celebrations. With the rise in anti-Irish feeling 'the Irish in Britain were observing 17 March only in the closed surroundings of their own sporting clubs and bars'.[22] Although this was broadly true, in London there had also been support from the GLC in the 1980s for various Irish events including on St Patrick's Day. Also throughout the period (except for 1972) the Council of Irish Counties Associations (CICA) held a parade usually ending in mass at a Catholic Church. So there was some localised, often constrained, visibility on St Patrick's Day even at the politically most sensitive times. Nevertheless the pledge to run a major festival and promote it to all in London was potentially a landmark event. The year 2000, in the wake of the Good Friday Agreement and amidst the fashion for a 'global Irishness' that developed under the spell cast by an accelerating 'Celtic Tiger', was considered an apposite moment in which to announce a major St Patrick's Day Festival.

The significance of this development was encapsulated in the aim to have the parade march to Trafalgar Square. The arrival of an officially supported Irish parade through central London to Trafalgar Square would be invested with significance. Trafalgar Square served throughout the twentieth century as Britain's most important space for political protest. Its use by Irish organisations was banned from the mid-1970s onwards. This was part of the response to events in Northern Ireland and to opposition expressed towards government policy in Britain, especially by the Troops Out Movement. There had been many protests over the years about the ban and so an intention to stage a large Irish event within its precinct was a political statement about the restoration and affirmation of the rights of Irish communities in London. The aim was to have the first Festival in 2002. A small team in the GLA was tasked to bring this about, in liaison with community representatives, and to place a high priority on gaining sponsorship for the event. A critical partnership was formally established between the GLA and the *Irish Post* newspaper, then part of the Smurfit Media Group. The Mayor had requested that the *Irish Post* assist him in seeking the views of the wider London Irish community on how the Festival might be developed. This alliance was important both because of the need to raise private funds and because of the paper's circulation, the largest proportion of which was based in London and the south-east of England.

One of the first issues to be grappled with was the relationship of the Festival to the existing St Patrick's Day events, especially the annual parade organised by CICA. A spokeswoman for CICA was quoted after the meeting in August 2000 as saying:

> I think all these people should get together and get behind the Council of Irish Counties Parade that has been in existence for so long … There's been enough division in our country for too long and we shouldn't divide any of the Irish over here. We should all be working for the same aim.[23]

This statement indicates both the measure of the task involved in gaining assent for a new festival and the strength of the sentiment that a high-profile event in London should not be divisive. It was not the recent history of the New York parade that provided the counter measure, in this respect, but that of Northern Ireland. Some groups also hoped that a new festival and parade organisation would secularise the event as some objected to the overt alignment of the CICA parade with the Catholic Church.

It was a priority to bring CICA on board and the decision was taken by the organisers to create two parallel sets of meetings in 2001 for the run-up to the

2002 Festival: a parade meeting and a community meeting to overview the Festival. GLA staff attended both meetings. A key organiser in the original Community Steering Group for the 2002 Festival and member of the Forum told me:

> It is very difficult now to imagine just how difficult it was to set the St Patrick's Day Festival up. Even with the Mayor's support there were significant difficulties in getting the various stakeholders and authorities on board … Getting all of the various factions of the community to come together and convincing (primarily) Irish businesses to help fund the costs. The CICA were naturally very nervous about the festival and what it would mean for them and all the years they had put in to running a parade in London – especially during the difficult years. It took time and patience on both sides to learn how to work together and I am really glad that we did make the effort to understand one another because the festival is all the better for having the CICA's invaluable input.

The parade group was primarily made up of CICA members. The same organiser commented 'We decided to keep the two separate to ensure that the parade received a strong community focus and built on the excellent work that CICA had begun all those years ago in running the parade in London'. Given that the other group meetings were also made up of community representatives the development of two separate sets of meetings in retrospect was an effective method of ensuring a continuing strategic influence for CICA in the formation and organisation of the parade. In this way CICA was brought on board as a significant stakeholder in the new parade.

The first parade, instead of ending at Westminster Cathedral as CICA's parade had done in recent years, commenced there and finished at Trafalgar Square where a programme of music ran throughout the afternoon. The acts on that first occasion ranged from Comhaltas Ceoltóiri Éireann, the Wexford Male Voice Choir, the Celtic Feet Dance Troupe, the Celtic Tenors, Mary Coughlan and Finbarr Furrey through to the headline act, the Dubliners. The finale was a special Evensong at St Martin-in-the-Fields dedicated to St Patrick. The sponsors included Irish companies with a market in Britain (Irish Beef, Murphy's Stout), Irish construction companies based in Britain (Murphy, McNicholas, Laing/O'Rourke), local London media outlets (BBC LDN, Metro), and companies interested in the Irish in Britain market (Stena Line). The Festival programme carried messages from the Mayor and Norah Casey, at the time CEO of Smurfit Media. The Mayor emphasised the contribution of the Irish over many generations and invited Londoners and visitors to celebrate all things Irish 'from literature to music and song, from dancing to oysters'. Norah Casey also gave prominence to the centrality of the Irish for London and stated that there had never been a better time to celebrate 'the rich tapestry of life in our multi-cultural capital'. Both mentioned the significance of the Good Friday Agreement for creating a new climate in which a high-profile St Patrick's Day Festival was possible in London. The efforts to encourage all Londoners to participate involved not only the wide distribution of leaflets and advertising on the underground train network and local radio but also an art competition for schools whose theme was 'Ireland – Through My Eyes'.

The Festival grew considerably after 2002. With the regular attendance of an Irish Minister and other politicians from London, Ireland and Northern Ireland the Festival came to represent a convergence of official London and official Ireland 'a space whose Irishness could be simultaneously performed as transnational in relation to the homeland and as a facet of the multicultural city'.[24] In 2003 and 2004 the police objected to the use of Trafalgar Square and in both years the Festival was held on a compressed site on the south bank of the Thames. As a result of pressure from the Forum and the hard work of the GLA team the event was repositioned in three prime sites from 2005 onwards: Trafalgar Square (rock bands), Leicester Square (Irish ceili music, arts and crafts fair and music workshops for children) and Covent Garden (traditional music and Irish food fair). Since March 2009 the Festival has had to be scaled back due to financial cuts and has mainly focused on the parade and activities in Trafalgar Square. The Mayor, Boris Johnson, who as the Conservative Party Candidate defeated Livingstone in the 2008 and 2012 Mayoral elections, committed continued, though reduced, support to the Festival from 2009 onwards. The decision to instigate a central London parade and festival was freighted with multi-layered politics. Despite this the organisation and running of the Festival between 2002–2008 was relatively harmonious. This does not mean there were no tensions or disagreements, rather it reflects that the harmony achieved was a politicised stance gestated by experiences of the Irish in Britain during the Northern Ireland Troubles.

The Mayor of London's St Patrick's Day Advisory Forum 2003–2008

The Forum was established in 2003 after two festivals had taken place and aimed to build on the work of the original Community Steering Group. The Forum is purely advisory and has no executive functions and membership is by appointment of the Mayor. The initial proposal suggested thirty-five members endeavouring to represent a wide cross-section of Irish organisations and prominent individuals. By 2005 the regular membership rarely exceeded twenty organisations/individuals (for example, Comhaltas, Bar Bia, the Federation of Irish Societies, the London Irish Women's Centre, the Irish Cultural Centre in Hammersmith, the London Irish Centre in Camden, the Aisling Project in Camden, the Irish Studies Centre, London Metropolitan University, the Irish Embassy, the two newspapers the *Irish Post* and the *Irish World*) and by 2008 it was regularly sixteen to eighteen. The membership varied most years as people dropped out and usually the Chair or someone else suggested replacements. In the event a changing core of about twelve to fourteen people regularly attended, plus the GLA staff involved in the organisation of the event. The first Chair of the Forum was Norah Casey. When she left in 2009 she was replaced by another woman, Catherina Casey, who was General Manager of the Hammersmith Irish Cultural Centre. In 2003, when a very large number of organisations were part of the Advisory Forum, women were in a small minority. However, when the Forum reduced in size women were often 40–50 per cent of the members, as many organisations sent women as their representatives. Indeed amongst regular attendees at the meetings the gender balance was often even or could sometimes produce a majority of women. As the majority of organisations sending representatives were NGOs (non-governmental organisations) and the GLA itself is part of the public sector this may reflect broader employment patterns. The overwhelming majority of the members were Irish migrants, however there was always a small number of second-generation Irish members.

I circulated the community members of the Advisory Forum (this therefore did not include the GLA officers sitting on the Forum) with a questionnaire that asked them to reflect on the first six years of the Festival. This was sent out in autumn 2008, a few months after Livingstone had failed to win a third term as Mayor. I was asking the Forum members therefore to reflect on the six years of an initiative that had stemmed from the previous Mayor's office. I asked them various questions about their view: of the most important aspect of the Festival; about its organisation and the role of the Advisory Forum; about what they enjoyed the most; of the Festival's significance for the place of the Irish in London; and the role of ethnic festivals in general. The questionnaires were sent and returned by email. This was a small, relatively informal survey of the views of individuals who had been involved for a number of years on the Advisory Forum. A large majority of the regular attenders of the Advisory Forum responded to my request, including the Chair. The exceptions were a couple of people who had left London by then. The survey was not anonymous so this may have constrained responses. On the other hand as a regular attender of the Advisory Forum myself I was trusted colleague and had guaranteed that no names or other means of individual identification would be used in reporting the results.

In the main their responses echoed the aims articulated by the Festival organisers back in 2002. Closely intertwined for many Forum members as the most important aspects of the Festival are the opportunity to express Irish culture and the recognition it gives of the Irish contribution to London. The Festival is valued for being an occasion when on the one hand the Irish of all generations can think about Ireland and their Irishness. On the other hand it is seen as a means by which Ireland and her culture are brought to a new audience. There was some emphasis on 'reminding' people both that 'we are a vital, happy and important part of the make-up of London' and reminding 'the English of how relations have developed in a short time'. The significance of a public display in central London was constantly alluded to and was summed up by one respondent as: 'After years of being a pariah nation, Irish are welcomed for their contribution to culture i.e. food, drink, music, dancing and, more recently, film.' A sub-theme expressed by a small number of respondents was that the bringing together of all 'sides' of the Irish community was an important aspect of the Festival and this was seen as in part embodied by the Advisory Forum. The most frequent comment about the composition of the Advisory Forum was that it represented a 'good cross section' although a couple of voices suggested its composition could be revisited and that it might usefully be combined with the parade committee (something that occurred in 2009).

The Advisory Forum members were asked about the value of ethnic/national festivals in general. Their views were positive, mixed with a shade of caution by a few. For example, many thought ethnic festivals signal ethnic diversity and are therefore to be seen as emblematic of London; it was viewed as exciting to celebrate each part of the mix. In the course of this process a number of respondents thought there was an inevitable educative effect that generates understanding of and respect for different cultures/nationalities. Caution was expressed by a couple of people that such festivals ran the risk of being exclusive and this would negate the aim of being informative and fun for all. There was some feeling that the festival should reach out further for participation with 'our English hosts'; and others thought the parade could include more middle-class participants and a 'younger voice throughout'. Some urged more inclusion of sport and an even greater focus on the arts. Generally it was felt that the Festival had surpassed the expectations originally held and that by 2007 and 2008 it was a credit to the Mayor's office and individuals were happy to have played some role on the Advisory Forum.

Over ten years on from the Good Friday Agreement there was still caution about associating the word Irish with anything viewed as political. The parade represents the London Irish putting their heads above the parapet in a way not viewed as possible in the previous few decades. Undoubtedly there was a shared vision on the Forum that the Festival was an opportunity, as one respondent put it, for 'putting to rest' the impact of Northern Ireland on representations and perceptions of 'Irishness' in Britain. As such most of those involved in organising the event were concerned not to fall out and were motivated to come to a consensus on difficult issues. Previous research has shown that there were few gender differences amongst the Irish in Britain in respect to the Northern Ireland conflict and its impact and resonance in the public sphere in Britain.[25] This was, in part, due to a general assessment that Northern Ireland was a 'sensitive' or 'taboo' subject in Britain. In the 2000s, after the Good Friday Agreement of 1998, participating in a politicised project of reclaiming public space for the celebration of St Patrick's Day seemed to generate significant levels of unanimity. Neither in the meetings nor in the questionnaires to which members responded were there any notable differences on gender lines. Previous research as noted above found that there were gender differences amongst the second generation in their response to St Patrick's Day when younger. There were too few second generation on the Advisory Forum to comment on this.

However, the question arises: does the fact that the Forum has had a fairly even balance of male and female members and a woman as Chair bear any relationship to the negotiation and mediation mode that has been its dominant form of conflict resolution? Many studies of the leadership styles of men and women conclude that they are different, with women being less hierarchical, more cooperative and collaborative; other studies find less difference, but with a balance of view that women leaders can be very useful when certain leadership styles are required.[26] In the context of organising the Festival and the great store that was set from the beginning in bringing a diverse range of voices from amongst the Irish in London on board I think the fairly even gender membership and the gender of the Chair may well have had the effect of ensuring a co-operative spirit. Ireland was on to its second successive female president by the time the Advisory Forum was established – did this play any subliminal role in the acceptance of her authority? The Chair also always had the authority of the Mayor (being his appointment) and the financial commitment given by City Hall. This combination of conditions seems to have ensured the elevation of points of communion, rather than dissonance, about the central goals of the St Patrick's Day Festival amongst those advising on its organisation.

Certain subtle tensions were however, evident on the Forum over the years and these were mostly underpinned by different generational positionings. These tensions were between different generations of migrants from Ireland and between the second generation and the more recent migrants from Ireland. Music dominates the Festival and the selection of bands can spark considerable debate about what constitutes an appropriate 'Irish band'. The gatekeepers of this still tend to be the Irish-born who are a clear majority on the Forum. People of the second and third generation, with strong Irish identifications, still often have looser, more hybridised definitions of what constitutes appropriate content. Even while they did not necessarily have strong objections to much of what is included in the Festival, some of the second-generation members have solidarities, often with other ethnicities, that they want to express, born of growing up in urban Britain. Some felt that these affinities had not always been fully represented by the content of the London Parade and Festival. One second-generation member of the Forum expressed the dilemma as follows:

> Can we find ways to showcase and be proud of Irish art traditions, music, dance and language in a way that highlights what the culture has brought to others? Many world musicians use the Irish/Celtic beat in ways that are a long way from the traditional reel – but are surely just as valid. I personally feel that being Irish is a lot more than liking the Sawdoctors. Can we use St Patrick's Day to share that experience better? Can we avoid the stereotypical and the banal and offer a richer diversity?

This is one example of the way in which the London St Patrick's Day Festival represents a 'contested territory' in Irish diasporic space.[27] Breda Gray argues that the second-generation Irish in England unsettle naturalised assumptions that link Irish culture to Ireland and to particular narratives of modernisation and change in Ireland. The encounter with the second generation, as a category of the Irish in England, tends to unsettle Irish migrants who came to Britain from 1980 onwards in particular.[28] Older migrants who came over in a previous era, the 1950s and 60s, who have made their adult lives in Britain and have second-generation children who are now young adults or approaching early middle age, tend to be cognisant of and supportive of the 'Irishness' of the second generation and its variety of forms of expression. It is also possible that some latent class divisions in the Forum, between more recent middle-class migrants from Ireland and the 1950s generation, were expressed through different generational solidarities.

Commercial sponsorship is vital to the staging of the Parade and Festival and this has the inevitable effect that the mainstream content is fairly safe and predictable. For some of the second generation on the Forum representing the diasporic space that is London, and the range of Irish positionings within it, did not always fit easily with the type of representations of the Celtic Tiger economy that were being sought by business groups on the Forum. Nevertheless, this rarely came to any strong disagreement because the reality of the need for sponsorship was apparent to all. Of more issue was a proposal in 2008 that the Festival fund the making of thirty-two banners to represent every county in Ireland on the parade, so that everyone could find themselves represented and have a place to walk. After some discussion it was agreed to produce thirty-three flags. The thirty-third flag was inscribed 'London Irish' in recognition that those of the second and third generations might prefer that designation. This decision was advocated by second-generation members of the Forum and strongly supported by some members who had come to London in the 1950s, the 'parental generation'. The final decision to have a 'London Irish' banner was further evidence of the dominant ethos of the Forum, and of its Chair, of deferring to specific interests represented in its membership. This practice ensured both a fair degree of harmony and a heterogeneous outcome in that the Festival did not install just one conception of Irishness. Many other varieties coexisted with a certain 'commercial Celticism'.[29]

Conclusion

Conceiving of St Patrick's Day celebrations as 'contested territories' informs us about different diaspora spaces. If we return to the New York City Parade, at one level there is no comparison with the St Patrick's Day Parade in London, in terms of longevity, size, profile or the history of how the two events came into being. They represent the specificity of these two national/diasporic spaces and their different histories in terms of relationship to Ireland and of incorporating immigrants. Cochrane forecasts the decline of the AOH in the context of dwindling numbers leaving Ireland for the USA (although this is now changing again) and those that continue to arrive are less interested in joining groups like the AOH with its elderly demographic.[30] These trends point to it losing its grip on the leadership of the New York St Patrick's Day Parade in due course. So St Patrick's Day will likely change, but it has always represented more than the AOH – it is a creation of the complex nexus that is Irish America in the greater New York area.

The St Patrick's Day Festival in London, on the other hand, is of recent origin, smaller in size and came into being as a result of an initiative of the Mayor, although the backdrop of community advice and the *Irish Post* newspaper was pivotal in its development. It represented the reclaiming of central London by the city's most sizeable minority ethnic population after three decades of public constraint as a result of the conflict in Northern Ireland. That claim was made insulated by the backing, financially and strategically, of City Hall. It is doubtful that the ILGO situation would occur in the London event because of the emphasis placed on representing all 'the community' (in agreed ways) and because the main sponsoring body, the GLA, under Livingstone's leadership was associated with progressive policies concerning sexual identities (the Conservative Mayor has not been at variance with this).

In his study of the London Carnival, which takes place every August bank holiday weekend in west London, and the manner in which it became an all-West Indian institution in the 1970s and 1980s, encompassing as it did the divisions between island of origin, age and neighbourhood, Abner Cohen analyses Carnival as a cultural form that became a political intervention, not just an expression of community.[31] I argue that the St Patrick's Day Festival was a political intervention that became an expression of community in a contested cultural form. Many critics of multiculturalism cite a 'double bind', whereby alliances are encouraged between different groups while their particularity is maintained, as its fundamental flaw. This is because multiculturalism is viewed as negating the possibility of dissolving ethnic differentiation. My view is that this inherent characteristic is not a flaw and it does not land multiculturalism in a 'double-bind'. It is more useful to conceptualise this characteristic as part of the embedded contradictions of any diasporic space (multicultural by *default*). And that a policy that aims at achieving cohesion by celebrating unity and difference, rather than dissolving difference, is one for our hybridised times.[32]

A heterogeneous mix of the Irish in London, some involved in previous St Patrick's Day events and others who had not been, recognised the moment and seized the opportunity to create a festival in central London. The dominant desire was to express an ethno-national identity in a public realm that both embraced immigration as a source of cohesion and vitality and to form a strong alliance with the local civic administration. It was the 1950s emigrants and their children who bore the brunt of the political and media fall-out from the IRA bombings in England and the implementation of counter-terrorism policies. These events also impacted on Irish immigrants who arrived in the 1980s, however, their more middle-class positioning may well have protected them from the worst effects.

I have examined what was shared by the members of the Advisory Forum as a social identity – in the sense of what brings them together as a group – in the context of the St Patrick's Day Festival. In any one situation, a particular social division may assume greater importance, but people do not exist in a social world where only class, or only gender or only ethnicity matters. All of us have multiple membership in a number of such groups, so that, depending on one's standpoint, people may be different in one context but similar in another. Personal links with people in one category may sometimes be at odds with one's differences from them owing to membership of some category or another social division.[33] The commonalities and shared identity that emerged strongly in the Advisory Forum revolved around two goals: reclaiming public space in central London for Irish communities after a ban lasting nearly thirty years; and presenting a different image of Ireland and the Irish in Britain compared with that which had been dominant from the 1970s through the 1990s. In other words the shared acknowledgement of the impact the Troubles had had on the Irish in Britain was sufficient to galvanise people who had other differences together to this common end and over-rode most conflicts of interest. Thus the identification of all involved, in one way or another, with 'Irishness' in the heavily freighted context of Britain, ensured that ethnic identity was the dominant basis of social coalescence.

The absence of gender differences where this occurs seems as important to note as their structuring of other contexts. Do we conclude that ethno-national solidarities suppressed gender differences on the Advisory Forum? If so, why were generational differences not submerged in the same way? In the interests of ensuring that the Festival be an enduring success even these latter differences, to the extent they occurred, were mediated in such a manner that ensured all interests on the Forum be represented in the celebration of St Patrick's Day. This was, arguably, the key way in which gender did impact on the proceedings of the Advisory Forum. The differences that did emerge in the Forum were over what constituted the appropriate 'Irish' content of the St Patrick's Day Festival; they were not about the political programme into which the Festival was inserted and which delivered funding and organisational capacity. Rather the differences centred on the relative importance to be given to showcasing particular representations of Ireland and the Irish in Britain. As already noted here (and by Nagle) the Festival was successful in giving a platform to a variety of representations, however, there were occasionally heated discussions about some aspects. The social divisions that surfaced on occasions exposed generational rather than gender divisions over the content and the power dynamics of the Festival.

When it comes to definitions of Irishness in the diaspora, and related questions of authenticity, differences are likely to be manifest along generational lines between the Irish-born and the second and third generations. In articulating the hybridised specificity of their positioning in relation to Irishness and place of settlement/birth the latter challenge the assumptions of the Irish-born to designate what constitutes Irishness. Echoes are here of the argument between Casey (second-generation, Irish American) and O'Toole (Irish-born) over the New York parade. What the debates on the Forum, largely between the small number of second generation and more recent emigrants also indicated was that generational differences are not necessarily about the withering away of Irish identities rather they point to the specificity of differently formed identifications. Also noteworthy was that the 'parental generation' of Irish-born, supported interventions by those espousing second-generation positionings, they too had differences with the more recent migrants and this was one of the 'safe' ways of expressing them without threatening the whole project. Nevertheless the views of other Irish in London, viewing the Festival, will not necessarily be in agreement on this.[34] Small though this study was, it focused on a key group of people in relation to St Patrick's Day in London and undoubtedly suggests that we need further research on the intersection of social divisions in the Irish diaspora, and specifically the role of gender and other social divisions in a variety of contexts.

Notes

1 S. Hall, 'Who needs identity?', in S. Hall and P. du Gay (eds), *Questions of Cultural Identity* (London: Sage, 1996), pp. 1–17.

2 M. J. Hickman, 'Diaspora space and national (re)formations', *Éire-Ireland*, 47:1 (2012), 19–44.

3 M. J. Hickman, '"Locating" the Irish diaspora', *Irish Journal of Sociology*, 11:2 (2002), 8–26.

4 N. Fraser, *Justice Interruptus: Critical Reflections on the "Postsocialist" Condition* (London: Routledge, 1997).

5 For example see J. Edmunds and B. Turner, *Generations, Culture and Society* (Milton Keynes: Open University Press, 2002).

6 F. O'Toole, *The Ex-Isle of Erin* (Dublin: New Island Books, 1996).

7 M. Cronin and D. Adair, *The Wearing of the Green: A History of St Patrick's Day* (London and New York: Routledge, 2002).

8 *Ibid.*, p. 231.

9 D. Negra, 'The Irish in us: Irishness, performativity, and popular culture', in D. Negra (ed.) *The Irish in Us: Irishness, Performativity, and Popular Culture* (London: Duke Press, 2006), pp. 1–19.

10 R. Byron, *Irish America* (Oxford: Clarendon Press, 1999).

11 A. Brah, *Cartographies of Diaspora: Contesting Identities* (London: Routledge, 1996).

12 A. Brah, 'Non-binarized identities of similarity and difference', in M. Wetherall, M. Laflèche and R. Berkeley (eds), *Identity, Ethnic Diversity and Community Cohesion* (London: Sage, 2007), p. 144.

13 Cronin and Adair, *The Wearing of the Green*, p. 238.

14 B. Walter, 'Celebrations of Irishness in Britain: second-generation experiences of St.

Patrick's Day', in M.C. Considère-Charon and P. LaPlace (eds), *Ireland: The Festive and the Tragic* (Cambridge: Cambridge Scholars Press, 2009), pp. 192–207.

15 See Chapter 4.

16 J. Nagle, '"Everybody is Irish on St Paddy's": ambivalence and alterity at London's St Patrick's Day 2002', *Identities: Global Studies in Culture and Power*, 12 (2005), 565.

17 J. Nagle, 'Multiculuralism's double bind: creating inclusivity, difference and cross community alliances with the London-Irish', *Ethnicities*, 8:2 (2008), 178.

18 Nagle, '"Everybody is Irish on St Paddy's day"', 571.

19 *Ibid.*, 579. For further analysis of the St Patrick's Day parade in London, see M. D. Scully, 'Discourses of Authenticity and National Identity among the Irish Diaspora in England', unpublished PhD thesis, (Department of Psychology in the Social Sciences, The Open University, 2010); M. Scully, 'Whose day is it anyway? St Patrick's Day as a contested performance of national and diasporic Irishness', *Studies in Ethnicity and Nationalism*, 12:1 (2012), 118–35.

20 For further development of this point see M. J. Hickman, 'A Study of the Incorporation of the Irish in Britain with Special Reference to Catholic State Education', PhD thesis, (Institute of Education, University of London, 1990), p. 399.

21 John McDonnell MP speaking at the meeting, quoted in the *Irish Post*, 12 August 2000.

22 Cronin and Adair, *The Wearing of the Green*, 196.

23 Quoted in the *Irish World*, 11 August 2000, 1.

24 Scully, 'Discourses of Authenticity and National Identity', p. 192.

25 Hickman, 'A Study of the Incorporation of the Irish in Britain', chapter 11.

26 See discussion in A. H. Eagly and M. C. Johannesen-Schmidt, 'The leadership styles of women and men', *Journal of Social Issues*, 57:4 (2001), 781–97.

27 A. Cohen, *Masquerade Politics. Explorations in the Structure of Urban Cultural Movements* (Berkeley: University of California Press, 1993).

28 B. Gray, 'Curious hybridities: transnational negotiations of migrancy through generation', *Irish Studies Review*, 14:2 (2006), 219.

29 Nagle, 'Multiculturalism's double bind'.

30 F. Cochrane, 'The end of the affair: Irish Migration, 9/11 and the evolution of Irish America', *Nationalism and Ethnic Politics*, 13 (2007), 335–66.

31 A. Cohen, *Masquerade Politics. Explorations in the Structure of Urban Cultural Movements* (Berkeley: University of California Press, 1993).

32 M. J. Hickman, N. Mai and H. Crowley, *Migration and Social Cohesion in the UK* (London: Palgrave Macmillan, 2012).

33 G. Payne, 'Introduction', in G. Payne (ed.), *Social Divisions* (London: Palgrave Macmillan, 2006), pp. 6–7.

34 Scully, 'Discourses of Authenticity and National Identity'.

PART III

Irish women and the diaspora in the British world

7

Placing Irish women within and beyond the British Empire: contexts and comparisons

Bronwen Walter

Women have been leaving Ireland to settle abroad over many centuries. Although their scattering has been on a global scale, including locations both with substantial numbers and with small pockets, there has been a particular emphasis on the English-speaking world, shadowing the colonial enterprise of the larger neighbour, Britain. This chapter aims to explore different contexts in which settlement has taken place, both geographically and socially. It will draw on existing secondary sources, which frequently document in detail women's experiences in particular national situations but could also be interrogated to raise new questions about Irish women's 'places' in different societies. In this way it may provide a more coherent framework for thinking about Irish women in the diaspora, as well as including Irish women in a larger global picture.[1]

The notion of 'placing' is central to this discussion. It references the specificity of particular named locations at many scales from household and family to neighbourhood, region and nation. It also denotes social positioning, linking with class and social mobility, ethnic mixing and a range of other identities which may be claimed and ascribed. Irish women are 'placed' by themselves, members of their own ethnic group and by others, as well as by writers and artists who represent their lives in print and visually. Placing, rather than the more usual association of diasporas with *dis*placement, indicates concern with new attachments and identifications for women and their descendants.

Such a broad project could take many directions. Three will be attempted here, each drawing on case studies. The first is an exploration of intersections between Irish women and members of other diasporic groups in Britain, examining similarities and differences in their lives. The second compares Irish women's experiences of different destinations within the British Empire and its Commonwealth successor.[2] Finally parallels are drawn with a diaspora outside the English-speaking world where social and political similarities point up important facets of women's diasporic experiences.

Each of these approaches relies on different modes of comparison – between ethnic groups, between nations of destination, between diasporas from different national origins. Perhaps surprisingly work of this kind appears to be rare. In setting out a new research agenda in 2008, John Solomos and Martin Bulmer, editors of *Ethnic and Racial Studies*, observed:

> We have been able to publish relatively little in the journal on comparative analysis of ethnic and racial relations. This is partly a reflection of the relative dearth of empirically grounded research that is comparative in focus, and perhaps the difficulty in getting such projects funded by nationally based bodies. It remains necessary, however, to develop comparative analyses of race and ethnic issues more fully and we would welcome the opportunity to consider such papers.[3]

These reflections echo opinions directly related to the Irish diaspora. Kevin Kenny noted that: 'Current conceptions of diaspora rarely contain an explicit comparative dimension.'[4] He advocated a new approach: 'What is needed is a migration history that combines the diasporic or transnational with the comparative or cross-national.'[5] In attempting to discern 'Where Irish studies is bound' Liam Harte also drew attention to opportunities offered by joint programmes of area study to challenge an ongoing deficit; 'Irish and Scottish studies ... have the added advantage of encouraging comparativist perspectives, of *which there is still a marked dearth*' (emphasis added).[6]

The problems which have impeded the embrace of comparative approaches, broadly identified by Solomos and Bulmer, were fleshed out by Kenny from the perspective of an historian. He listed four methodological issues, namely the need to master more than one national historiography, the tendency for projects to become unwieldy, the submergence of narrative history by schematic analysis and the absence of institutional and financial support. Whilst the third may be of less concern to social scientists whose approach is likely to be thematic, the issues of large size and lack of funding apply to most disciplines.

However, set against these obstacles are a number of important advantages which can enhance the more traditionally mono-ethnic studies of the Irish diaspora. At a group level, these include opportunities to broaden the impact of research on Irish women by focusing on their places in the multi-ethnic societies of which they are part. This is particularly important in the case of the Irish, whose identities are often conflated with the 'white mainstream', especially British populations.[7] Comparative studies may highlight shared positionings with other minority ethnic groups which are frequently overlooked because of the emphasis on 'whiteness' and native English language. Submerged identities, especially in second and subsequent generations, may be recognised when parallels become apparent.

At a national level, comparative studies of Irish women's experiences in different destinations within the English-speaking world give greater weight to political, social and economic contexts than will be obvious in single-nation cases. What is taken for granted by researchers studying their own societies will be 'made strange' when differences surface, perhaps in everyday occurrences not previously considered worthy of notice. Conversely similarities may take on added significance if they appear in contrasting situations. Finally comparisons between diasporas from different national and ethnic origins may locate Irish women as part of global processes outside the English-speaking world where the majority of research to date suggests they belong. In all these cases the dangers of the 'ghettoisation' – and sidelining – of Irish Studies are reduced and a more 'mainstream' acceptance of Irish ethnicity may benefit both academic and policy agendas.

Intersections: shared group spaces

Although Avtar Brah's concept of 'diaspora space' has been widely acclaimed as a valuable tool, few attempts have yet been made to operationalise some of its most creative possibilities. Amongst these is the intriguing observation that ethnic groups mix amongst themselves as well as with the majority ethnicity, and that the so-called 'mainstream' population itself is continuously constructed by these processes.

> In the diaspora space called 'England', for example, African-Caribbean, Irish, Asian, Jewish and other diaspora identities *intersect among themselves* as well as with the entity constructed as 'Englishness', thoroughly re-inscribing it in the process.[8] [Emphasis added]

As one of the oldest and longest established diasporas the Irish have intersected with all of these groups at different time periods and with different consequences. Often such contacts have been overlooked and the Irish have been treated as part of the 'white' majority, especially in later generations. Taking a comparative approach to minority ethnicities will challenge conventional research strategies which underplay or ignore altogether Irish difference, whilst acknowledging ways in which closeness to white English cultures may be evident.

Two case studies are introduced here. The first is a comparison between Irish and Jewish women settling in the East End of London from the later nineteenth century. Despite obvious similarities in the theoretical locations of Irish and Jewish ethnicities, there have been remarkably few studies which place them side by side, although this was their geographical experience in a number of British cities, including Manchester and Leeds.[9] Outside London there are only snippets of evidence about the social relationships of Jewish and Irish women. In Greater Manchester for example the Jewish Museum records Jewish and Irish nurses working together in the hospital on Cheetham Hill, the centre of settlement for both groups.[10] Strangely the website does not mention this link in its list of diasporas with which the Jews in Manchester overlapped and intersected, including those from Russia, the Austro-Hungarian Empire and in the post-World War Two period, Egyptians, Hungarians and Iranians. Perhaps this reflects a view that antagonism between the two groups was the most common experience.[11] This would accord with the account of 'Mary', interviewed in the 1990s. She reported the anti-Jewish attitudes of her Irish family in Bolton: 'I went for a job at Moses Gate [early 1940s], but they were Jews so my cousin's wife wouldn't let me take it because they were Jews.'[12]

One study interestingly makes direct comparisons between the two populations, Lara Marks's 1990 paper *Working Wives and Working Mothers*.[13] Marks identifies a number of parallels between Irish and Jewish women's lives but also some major contrasts. The differences included the nature of paid work: whereas both groups of women were engaged in street selling, Irish women also played a major role as domestic servants in private households and carried out home piece work. Jewish women on the other hand took in sewing and washing, but did not enter other households in a paid capacity. Popular images of women in each group contrasted: those of Irish women were more negative – they were considered neglectful, slovenly and prone to alcoholism, whereas Jewish women were respected for the high quality of childcare.

The two groups also intersected and co-operated at several spatial scales. At the closest level Irish women were frequently employed as domestic servants in Jewish households, both for wealthier families who could afford to employ additional help and by poorer families who could not manage daily tasks unaided. In part this indicated a hierarchy of ethnic acceptability in London, where both groups were close to the bottom. As Lynn Lees noted:

> Irish servants abounded in London. Allegedly saucy and incompetent, they seem to have taken up the less desirable posts in the metropolis. And many more Irish women wanted such jobs than could find them … One said in 1853 that positions were almost impossible to find. Girls usually had to accept work either in a pub or with an East End Jewish family, where they were paid only one or two shillings a week plus board.[14]

Later in the nineteenth century more prosperous Jewish families had come to rely on longstanding family servants, as Israel Zangwill's fictional character in *Children of the Ghetto* (1892) illustrated:

> Mary O'Reilly, as good a soul as she was a Catholic, had lived all her life with Jews, assisting while yet a girl in the kitchen of Henry Goldsmith's father, who was a pattern of ancient piety and a prop of the Great Synagogue. When the father died, Mary, with all the other household belongings, passed into the hands of the son, who also came up to London from a provincial town, and, with grateful recognition of

her motherliness, domiciled her in his own establishment. Mary knew all the ritual laws and ceremonies far better than her new mistress ...[15]

In this account Mary's qualities deriving from her Irish cultural background, which included religious observance, domestic skills, a caring approach to children and an awareness of the importance of ritual, meshed closely with the Jewish culture of the Goldsmith household and were highly valued.

At the same time shared poverty provided the setting for small paid services between neighbours. Jerry White recorded the memories of one tenant in his oral history of *Rothschild Buildings*:

> Susie, an Irish woman, lived in one of the lodging houses in Flower and Dean Street and she used to do work for my mother. She used to clean up the flat and go on little errands – mother was getting on. This was after I'd married and left the Buildings [about 1919]. Susie was very trustworthy, although she drank. And I'd go up to the lodging house to ask Susie if she'd come over and look after my eldest baby when we went out. It was a terrible place. It smelt awful, it was horrible. Her room, which she had to herself, was terrible; very dilapidated, really shocking.[16]

As a consequence of these intimate connections, not surprisingly mixed relationships developed, though the extent of these is hard to assess. Certainly there are references to children of Jewish/Irish parents. For example, Bill Fishman, the oral historian and vivid raconteur, speaking of the 1920s, recounted : 'And we used to have an odd *Jewish woman* come in, *of Irish descent*, and we always gave her a penny or tuppence' (emphasis added).[17] Similarly Gilda O'Neill describes her own mixed ancestry in her memoir *My East End* (1999): 'it is a history of which, with my mongrel, English, Irish, Scottish, Welsh, Jewish, East End background, I am very much part.'[18]

But not all interactions were positive and the balance of friendly co-operation and mutual antagonisms is clearly complex and needs to be further teased out. Evidence at present appears to be very mixed. Chaim Bermant, in *London's East End* cited a report in the *Eastern Post* in 1901 describing a situation 'when a Jewish family tried to move into a largely Irish dockland street, people poured out from every house, smashed up the van, and routed "the unfortunate foreigners"'.[19] Yet Bill Fishman, writing about a slightly later period, the 1930s, observed:

> between eleven and fifteen were the happiest days of my youth [1932–36]. There were other Jewish lads, brought up among Irish dockers' sons and daughters, and I must tell you, I could only say that there was a tremendous rapport between us.[20]

Referring elsewhere to a political event significant at the national scale, Fishman reinforced this view in his personal account of the so-called Battle of Cable Street on 4 October 1936, when the British Union of Fascists, led by Oswald

Mosley, planned to march through the East End. An estimated 300,000 members of anti-fascist groups erected roadblocks and although over 10,000 police attempted to clear the road for the march and 150 demonstrators were arrested, the march was abandoned.

> I heard this loudspeaker say 'They are going to Cable Street'. Suddenly a barricade was erected there and they put an old lorry in the middle of the road and old mattresses. The people up the top of the flats, *mainly Irish Catholic women*, were throwing rubbish on the police. We were all side by side. I was moved to tears to see bearded Jews and Irish Catholic dockers standing up to stop Mosley. I shall never forget that as long as I live, how working class people could get together to oppose the evil of racism.[21] [Emphasis added]

But again there is conflicting evidence. In an almost diametrically opposed account, Henry Srebrnik's research showed that:

> Despite strenuous recruiting efforts on the part of the STDL [Stepney Tenants' Defence League], *the number of Irish women* involved in left-wing political activities in Stepney remained low. Indeed, many more of them, like their male relatives, were attracted to Sir Oswald Mosley's British Union of Fascists (BUF), which in the 1930s built a base among London's East End Irish Catholics through anti-Semitic agitation, including denunciation of Jewish landlords.[22] [Emphasis added]

It is particularly striking that both these accounts reference Irish women, indicating their involvement outside the home in neighbourhood politics with wider national and international implications.

Sources are quite widely available for the period leading up to World War Two, including newspaper accounts, records of political movements and oral histories. However there is a sudden drop in commentary on the Irish presence in the East End of London in the 1950s. In part this reflects the relocation of longstanding families of Irish descent as result of bomb damage and 'slum clearance' to outer suburbs to Essex in the east, as well as the growth of major clusters of Irish neighbourhoods to the inner west London boroughs of Camden, Islington and Brent. But it also appears to signal the conflation of the so-called 'indigenous' working-class population into a 'white English' category.[23] For example the major sociological study of the East End, Peter Willmott and Michael Young's *Family and Kinship in East London* (1963), makes no reference to the ethnicity of the families it describes.[24] Interestingly it does place a very strong emphasis on the intergenerational importance of mothers which suggests that the very large number of Irish women known to be present in the 1930s are likely to figure amongst this now unattributed population.

The recent follow-up study, Geoff Dench, Kate Gavron and Michael Young's *The New East End* made similar assumptions when it noted the dispersal of Jewish populations in the 1950s and that 'others had assimilated into what was an unusually stable local community'.[25] However intriguingly they also suggest continuities, including the observation that a large proportion of the white population in Bethnal Green have Irish surnames.[26] This would of course exclude women of Irish descent who married into other ethnic groups so that the actual numbers with Irish ancestry may be much higher. They also offer the view that the yuppie/white working social class gap may be more significant than that between the Bangladeshi/old white working class, 'many of whom are the offspring of previous immigrants'.[27] However these traces of Irish roots are more usually overlooked and the 'white' Eastenders are implicitly 'English' in origin.[28]

The second case study focuses on the postwar period when a different set of intersections between Irish women and members of other diasporas in Britain was established. These relationships, involving 'mixed-race' partnerships, are quite frequently noted in research accounts, but often the Irish women are simply described as 'white' without further comment on their distinctive ethnicity. One example is Vicki Harman's report on the findings of her study of lone white mothers of mixed-parentage children.[29] One of the thirty in the sample described her children as 'Irish and North African', but there is no elaboration, and indeed other Irish women could have been included in the 'white' sample without mention. A clearer set of statements is made by Jayne Ifegwunigwe in her classic study *Scattered Belongings*, where two of the six detailed case studies relate to sisters with an Irish mother and African Caribbean father.[30] On the one hand Ifegwunigwe asserts that: 'the primary culture the women I spoke with is White English'[31] although she later elaborates:

> *Griottes* Sarah and Akousa grew up in an African Caribbean community in Liverpool with their White Irish mother and a certain degree of consistency about being métisse, Black but not White, and Caribbean.[32]

A much more direct recognition of the significance of shared racialised backgrounds was provided by Frances Twine's (2004) interview with Taisha, daughter of a 1950s Irish migrant mother and Barbadian father.

> Recalling her mother's practices when she was a child, she argued that her mother routinely discussed race and racism with her and thus provided her with a vocabulary for thinking about the political meaning of being black, Irish and British heritage. In her analysis of why she became strongly identified with the African Caribbean community and why she shifted has from self-identifying as 'mixed race' to a 'black' woman, Taisha cites the alternative history lessons that her mother provided at home.[33]

This clear awareness of the parallels between Irish and other racialised diasporic backgrounds in Britain was echoed by Tariq, a middle-class participant interviewed in London in 2001 for the *Irish 2 Project* which explored second-generation Irish identities. He said:

I guess for me my mum has never been white in the sense, not that she is not white in colour, but she is not British, she has never been white in any kind of way of identifying herself. For me I had a notion of what the implication was to be white on that form [the 2001 Census], there was almost this 'them' and 'us' feeling about it, 'inside' or 'outside' feeling about it. My mum is Irish she has the same attitude towards Britishness, more so than I do. English, no way.[34]

Although there is no space on the UK censuses to register mixed heritage identities other than by accepting the homogenising category 'White' as one of the cultural backgrounds, such identities are becoming more visible in everyday life.[35] One vivid representation is the film *East is East* which features Ella, a wife and mother of Irish background, who is married to George, a Pakistani man, in 1970s Manchester.[36] Once again reviewers of the film categorised Ella variously as British and English, but her Catholicism, fleeting images of shamrocks on St Patrick's Day and a map of Ireland in the home clearly indicate her Irish family origins. The growing size of the mixed heritage population in Britain, estimated to increase by 93 per cent between 2001 and 2020 to make up 2 per cent of the total population, means that disentangling the 'white' contribution will become increasingly significant in the recognition of cultural backgrounds.[37] Acknowledging the cultural specificity of 'white' heritages would add support to emerging debates around the concept of creolisation, which have flowed outwards from an earlier focus on global locations where 'race' is a major component of difference, to understandings that 'humankind is refashioning the basic building blocks of organised cultures and societies in a fundamental and wide-ranging way'.[38]

Comparative experiences of Irish women within the British Empire

Comparisons between the experiences of Irish women in different parts of the diaspora are rare. Attempts have been made to identify similarities and differences between the largest destinations, the USA and Britain,[39] but elsewhere research on Irish women is focused on studies of single societies.[40] A comparative approach reminds us of the importance of context. Women from very similar backgrounds in Ireland, and their descendants, may lead very diverse lives by moving to different parts of the world. It also highlights variations within migration flows – at different historical periods and from different places of origin, social classes and religions.

The case studies juxtaposed here, Newfoundland and New Zealand, share one important dimension – movement to parts of the former British Empire which have retained their postcolonial political ties with the United Kingdom.[41] They are both relatively small societies, but in other ways there are important contrasts. Newfoundland, which was a separate Dominion until a very closely contested referendum in 1949 brought it into confederation with Canada, was settled by fishery workers from England and Ireland from the mid-seventeenth century until the mid-nineteenth century.[42] New Zealand was colonised much later – in the second half of the nineteenth century – and settlement has continued on a smaller scale until the present day.[43] Indeed its popularity is growing in the recent explosion of new emigration from Ireland as it becomes 'an increasing home to a growing number of Irish migrants seeking a fresh start in the southern hemisphere'.[44]

Irish-born women and their descendants in Newfoundland have long ancestral timelines, many beginning in the eighteenth century. In contrast to most other locations in the diaspora, women's emigration to Newfoundland was actively discouraged in the earlier decades in an attempt to retain the pattern of male seasonal migration, rather than permanent settlement.[45] The British Government used the Newfoundland cod fishery to train seamen for the navy, whilst English merchants wanted to keep the cod trade in their own hands rather than allow small local boat owners to enter the trade. As a naval officer, Captain Francis Wheler, wrote in 1684: 'Soe longe as there comes noe women they are not fixed.'[46] However the tide could not be stemmed for long and permanent households were established in the early to middle years of the eighteenth century. Irish women were arriving as servants and quickly established households in partnerships with Irish and English fishermen.

Again in contrast to other areas of settlement in the diaspora where women were recruited primarily for reproductive purposes – both maintaining households and bearing children – Irish women in Newfoundland were an integral part of the dominant industry, the fishery. This distinctive economy, based almost exclusively on large-scale cod fisheries which supplied Europe, North America and the Caribbean, gave women specific roles in family-based enterprises. In some cases these involved direct employment in the shore-based aspects – splitting, drying, packing – and in others support functions including child-rearing, gardening, food production and medical care. Willeen Keough, author of *The Slender Thread*, a rich historical account of Irish women's lives in Newfoundland, offers her own maternal family tree as an illustration of the range of ways in which women were central to the economy and society over at least seven generations.[47] Her ability to document such an extensive timeline owes much to the striking continuity of place in the ancestries of Irish families. Fishery buildings – or 'rooms' – were passed down generations, in similar ways to small farms in Ireland where the 'name on the land' was preserved. Oral histories, again echoing traditions in Ireland, ensured that children were reminded of the precise trajectories of their family origins often over several hundred years, reinforcing the evidence of their own eyes in homes and localities.

My maternal roots are in the area, and I have encountered there a tradition of strong, resourceful Irish Newfoundland foremothers: *my great-great-great-great-grandmother Catherine*, who raised a large family in Ireland, often alone while her husband worked at the Newfoundland fishery, until she finally joined him on the southern Avalon in the 1790s; *my great-great-great-aunt Margaret*, who came out from Ireland, became mistress of a planter household, and inherited from her first husband land and fishing premises—property which she gave to her brothers upon her remarriage and which is still in the family today; *my great-great-aunt Sally*, who provided board and medical services to fishermen to earn extra income for her family; *my great-grandmother Bridget*, who nursed her family alone during a diphtheria epidemic, carrying the black waste of infection down to the sea in the early morning under the watchful eyes of the quarantine officer; *my great aunt Sarah*, who kept a gracious three-story home in Shore's Cove on the proceeds of a shebeen she ran on the side; *my grandmother Julianne*, her hands as large as oven mitts and work-roughened from making fish and hay and clothing and endless loaves of bread to feed her brood of twelve; *my own mother, Gertrude*, whom a priest warned my father not to marry because Southern Shore women had 'far too much to say for themselves'.[48] [Emphasis added]

Keough's story highlights the early origin of her family with a four-times great grandmother, Catherine, joining her husband, a single male fishery worker, to create a permanent household. Her three-times great aunt, Margaret, arrived as a single woman and married in Newfoundland, establishing fishing 'rooms' which are still owned by the family. In subsequent generations, women provided key services of medical care and board and lodging to members of the community as well as their own families. Sarah was upwardly mobile and able to move to a more substantial local house by successfully providing illicit liquor to the community. The unusual economic and social independence of this line of women is underlined by the final comment by the priest, strongly disapproving of such an aberration by local women from the model of a meek Mary traditionally demanded of Catholic women.

An interesting form of further comparison, which is not apparent in this case study, is that between the Irish population of Newfoundland and members of the English diaspora who lived alongside them. As already suggested intermarriage was quite common, especially in the early years when Catholic and Protestant institutions had not been rigidly established. Newfoundland offers an unusual example of English migrants 'becoming Irish' in religion and speech patterns through mixed marriages with Irish women, but retaining English surnames. Alongside such intersections, however, parallel lives also developed, strengthening over time as churches exercised their exclusive claims and geographical separation increased.[49]

A very different pattern of settlement by Irish women characterises New Zealand. The contrasts which may be drawn are evidence of the huge range of experiences which defy easy categorisation of the experiences of Irish women in the diaspora. Whilst these are also present at regional and local scales within nations, the larger picture exemplifies the impact of global political and economic contexts. Major features of Irish settlement in New Zealand include much later settlement than in Newfoundland, mainly after the 1870s. Many women arrived after living in other locations, including Australia and Britain.

There is a larger proportion of Protestants than in most other locations in the diaspora, except mainland Canada. Unlike Newfoundland where Irish identities remain very visible, in New Zealand these appear to be subsumed into an overarching 'British' identity. Indeed New Zealand has viewed itself overall as 'a better Britain'. Whereas estimates of the proportion of the present-day population of Newfoundland with a significantly Irish cultural background can be as high as 50 per cent, in New Zealand the ratio is 20 per cent at maximum.

There is a relatively small published historiography specifically relating to Irish women in New Zealand.[50] In 1990 Donald Akenson observed that the hidden histories of Irish women in New Zealand remained 'the largest single lacuna in the history of the Irish in New Zealand'.[51] Although the proportion of Irish settlers in New Zealand was quite high, at around 20 per cent overall, geographical patterns showed distinct clustering. The major period of settlement on the West Coast was 1864-1915, explored in a case study by Lyndon Fraser.[52] Key features of this settlement, in which Irish women comprised one-third of the female population from 1867 to 1896, included further important differences from Newfoundland. Many women came to New Zealand after a period of family formation in Australia and were older, bringing children with them. Numbers were also self-funded, from more prosperous farming and trade backgrounds. Whereas women travelling to Newfoundland originated from backgrounds in south-east Ireland, especially in and around Waterford, those migrating to New Zealand had roots in more prosperous parts of Ulster and the midland counties of Ireland.[53]

Unlike the Newfoundland Irish women in Willeen Keough's family whose timeline stretched back over seven generations, migrants to New Zealand had arrived within the living memory of surviving descendants. One consequence of this more recent settlement pattern, and their higher levels of wealth and education, is the existence of private correspondence from which details of everyday experiences and feelings can be gleaned. Angela McCarthy has analysed 253 personal letters, including those of 89 women.[54] Although there were slightly more letters from Protestants than Catholics, she did not find major differences in their concerns and preoccupations.[55] Lyndon Fraser also opens his account of Irish women's migration to the west coast of the South Island with quotations from a letter written by Ellen Piezzi to her brother-in-law in California, contrasting her difficulties of early widowhood and social isolation with his imagined comforts.[56] Fraser focuses on a few themes, including the role of personal networks, familial mutual support, marriage and religious affiliation 'to show that Irish women preserved and adapted certain Old World cultural resources in order to survive in a new environment'.[57]

Differences in Irish women's social, economic and demographic characteristics in the two diasporic locations illustrate the heterogeneity of experiences at different time periods and destinations. Attempts have been made to synthesise global patterns of Irish women's lives. For example Donald Akenson identified some key questions relating to Irish women's places in the diaspora, using selected evidence from a wide range of places and periods.[58] These are also illustrated vividly in the choice of personal stories told in Episode 3, 'A World Apart', of the video series *The Irish Empire,* which traced the lifestories of nine women who settled in Britain, USA, Zimbabwe and South Africa.[59] But there is scope to link as well as place these stories side by side since, as the New Zealand case study showed, Irish women have also been mobile on a global scale and cannot simply be categorised by settlement in a single destination. It raises the issue of return migration to Ireland as well as future moves by returners such as Mary Williams, whose story was examined in detail in the video. She moved to the USA for several years as a young woman in the 1930s, returned to Ireland but found it socially stifling, and moved on to England in the 1950s. In many ways she enjoyed a rich and varied life with far greater freedom and independence than her sisters in Ireland. But she also reflected sadly on the double loss of family – the parents and siblings left in Ireland who no longer fully accepted the 'returned Yank' and her own children whom she had lost to 'Englishness'. Her diasporic identity had cut her off from the mono-ethnic self-representations of those who remained, or became, 'settled'.

Parallels with global diasporas: the Irish in Britain and Koreans in Japan

The issue of 'Irish exceptionalism' is sometimes raised critically by academics, usually to question claims that the Irish experience of emigration is unique in its size and impact.[60] It is salutary therefore to find parallels in other parts of the world and in otherwise contrasting cultures. One such case is that of Korean settlement in Japan. Only one publication has explored this similarity, a book by a Japanese scholar not translated into English.[61] As Sonia Ryang points out, Koreans in Japan are a little-known minority in western discourse, reflecting 'the western domination of the business of constructing minorities'.[62]

The major features of the Korean diaspora in Japan which resonate with those of the Irish in Britain include the following: each was colonised by their larger imperial neighbour, Korea by Japan between 1910 and 1935 and the Irish by Britain over a much longer period.[63] In both cases the colonised populations were despised as backward in comparison with their 'civilised' conquerors, despite evidence of highly developed cultures in the past. In an almost exact parallel to the aphorism 'the Irish can never forget their history, the English can never remember it' is John Lie's observation that 'the Japanese are indifferent to history whereas the Koreans are obsessed with history'.[64]

Migrants from each colony were brought to, or recruited by, the larger centre to provide manual labour, women in domestic service and, in the case of Korea especially, for prostitution, and men for work in the construction industry. In each case the migrant ethnic group was indistinguishable from the majority society in physical appearance, identified only by name (though often this was changed) and family background.[65] This made it possible to 'pass', a strategy adopted by many Koreans to avoid punitive discrimination, but also by unknown numbers of the Irish in Britain. Koreans in Japan were labelled dirty, smelly, lazy, stupid and their children were bullied, again strongly echoing Irish stereotypes in Britain from the nineteenth century.[66] Moreover there is a striking similarity between signs displayed in English rented accommodation saying 'no blacks, no Irish, no dogs' and those in Japanese boarding houses declaring 'Not available for Koreans and Ryukyuans'[67] or even the almost identical 'No North Koreans. No blacks. No dogs'.[68] As a consequence in the postwar period of the 1950s–70s Korean identities were largely invisible and people were fearful of identification. This 'disrecognition' may have been more extreme in its impact than rejections experienced by the Irish, but specific incidents could be very similar.

However, like the Irish in England and Wales, though to a lesser extent in Scotland, where discrimination appears to have decreased since the Good Friday Agreement,[69] there has even been a positive welcome in certain situations for the respective minority ethnic groups.[70] At the same time members of the two diasporas have felt more confident in claiming their distinctive identities. In Japan more people of Korean descent, known as the *zainichi*, now feel entitled to claim 'Korean descent, Japanese livelihood', benefitting from the decline of the myth of mono-ethnicity.[71] In Britain the inclusion of Irish ethnic tick boxes in the 2001 and 2011 Censuses and a wide range of ethnic monitoring forms signalled a state willingness to recognise this identity.[72] Interestingly both the Irish in Britain and *zainichi* in Japan are strongly represented in the cultural field. This has long been true of Irish literary figures in Britain, often claimed as British, and more recently television presenters, actors and entertainers.[73] Similarly in Japan *zainichi* people play positive leads in soap operas and include admired literary figures.[74]

These changes have accompanied both the growing economic strength of each 'home' nation, the 'Celtic Tiger' in Ireland and IT-led industrial expansion in Korea. They also reflect greater acceptance of multicultural societies, evident in Britain from the 1970s and more recently in Japan from the 1990s.[75] Yet the process of acknowledging difference is uneven. By the early twenty-first century there are still significant barriers in terms of employment, marriage and civic participation for the *zainichi* although they are no longer seen as a uniformly inferior group. But pockets of extreme poverty, such as the village of Utoro in Kyoto where *zainichi* people live without running water or sewerage after sixty years, still remain.[76] Lower level, more hidden, discrimination also persists in everyday life. One woman, 'KY', with *chosen-seki* status from the pre-partition Korean peninsula, which continues to identify them with despised North Korea, described her experience in job applications:

> After knowing my 'nationality', some companies withdrew their expression of interest, saying 'it's our policy not to hire foreigners' ... One company made me

panic. It announced the hire of a person who had practical knowledge of foreign-trading and was fluent in Korean. I thought I was the right person, but the company refused to hire me, saying I was disqualified. I was not able to understand why I was disqualified ... I was completely dumbfounded.[77]

Similarly in Britain the issue of anti-Irish discrimination remains an unresolved issue in parts of the West of Scotland and continues to punctuate representations of the Irish in England.[78]

Another important similarity between the two diasporas is the experiences of the second and third generations in their relationships to both countries of family origin and settlement. The major period of family formation after immigration in both cases was the postwar period of the 1950s and 60s. The changes experienced by the second generation which shifted them closer to the majority society, especially in language and accent but also in clothing, tastes and attitudes, also meant that they were not always accepted as authentic members of their parents' homelands when they visited as children and later as adults. As one interviewee said: 'My mother says that it is more unbearable to be discriminated against by Koreans than by Japanese. In Korea we are looked down upon because we live in Japan.'[79] There are parallels then in the placings of the *zainichi*, who are not accepted either as authentic in Korea or as full Japanese citizens, and the Irish in Britain who can be labelled 'plastic paddies' by Irish-born people and may not see themselves as exclusively British.[80] This is not a universal experience of 'second generations' and points to similarities in the colonial backgrounds of the two ethnic groups which may lead postcolonised societies to refuse inclusion to the children of emigrants. In the case of the Irish in Britain, there is a contradiction between the legal position of full citizenship rights and the everyday experience of these rights being questioned[81] or discriminatory comments which pass unchallenged in the majority society.[82]

The specific positioning and experiences of women in these two diasporas needs further research but there are pointers to ways in which their lives have parallels. In addition to employment in manual labour, especially in the early years after arrival, in both cases women had to deal with unequal treatment within their own ethnic group as well as from the majority society.[83] In her study of ethnicity and class amongst *zainichi* Koreans, Bumsoo Kim reported interviews with women who complained about gender barriers in Korean-run workplaces in Japan, one asserting that 'patriarchy is prevalent among the *zainichi* Korean community'.[84] This echoes the aims of the London Irish Women's Conferences in the 1980s. In 1984 Sabina Sharkey introduced the first event, entitled *Irish Women: Our Experience of Emigration*, explaining: 'Our intention is not just to insist on our existence in English surroundings, but to insist on it within our own Irish community.'[85] Women have also been central to educating children about their cultural backgrounds, which took place in the home. Sonia Ryang describes the situation in the 1950s and 60s when 'colonial memories of the first generation penetrated every nook and cranny of social and family life'.[86]

This echoes Irish family experiences in many English towns and cities where cultural backgrounds were passed on within families, but often hidden from or ignored by English neighbours.[87] In both cases too, the cultural backgrounds were missing from school curricula.[88]

In other ways women of the Korean diaspora in Japan may have experienced even harsher treatment than Irish women in Britain. For example, the enforced prostitution of Korean women during World War Two has only recently been brought to light and is still unacknowledged officially. The Japanese government has refused to pay compensation or apologise.[89] More widely migrant women have criticised the Japanese feminist movement for their lack of attention to issues of discrimination and prejudice against minority ethnic women.[90] However again this echoes almost exactly concerns of Irish feminists that their issues and interests have been absent from British feminist agendas:

> More trenchant and more commonly heard criticisms of the exclusion of Irish women from the broader canvas of British feminist history suggest that a deeper ideological inquiry is necessary. This should involve questioning why feminist historians have followed the broad pattern of socialist historiography by concentrating on the commonality of interests, primarily class-based, and have filtered out difference, such as race, nationality, ethnicity and religion.[91]

Conclusion

Comparative approaches challenge ways of thinking about particular parts of the Irish diaspora which focus exclusively on national arenas and risk losing sight of the 'bigger picture'. They also bring to the fore relationships between those of Irish cultural background and other ethnicities, which may be lost if the focus is simply on Irish identities. By stressing multi-generational patterns, comparisons also draw attention to hybridisations which begin as soon as the Irish arrive in new destinations, and expand exponentially in each subsequent generation. Placing Irish women within 'diaspora spaces', such as England, highlights their roles in wider social processes of class and gender formation, as well as ethnic and racial constructions.

What is clear is that the specific context of settlement, both initially and in subsequent years, is extremely important. Newfoundland is a profoundly different place in which to claim Irish descent than New Zealand. Both are very different from England, although elements of Englishness are central to the construction of Irish identities in each. In Newfoundland there is ongoing tension between groups from Irish and English origins even after seven or eight generations, because of differences in political power within the Empire which have residues today.[92] In New Zealand Irish identities seem to have been submerged within a 'British' or perhaps now 'White European' identity.[93] But contrasting contexts can also produce parallels as in the case of the Korean diaspora in Japan, offering new ways to interpret such current issues as the sometimes uncomfortable fit of English-accented second-generation children in Irish 'home' localities.

These are very broad questions which allow us to make different and imaginative uses of existing research to devise projects which explore issues from new angles. The re-emergence of a large-scale outpouring of emigrants from present-day Ireland continues to give them contemporary relevance as Irish women shift their destinations to different locations as well as adding new generations in established places.

Notes

1 P. O'Sullivan (ed.), *Patterns of Migration, Volume 1, The Irish World Wide: History, Heritage, Identity* (Leicester: Leicester University Press, 1992), p. xx.

2 Preliminary findings from research project supported by British Academy Small Grant SG101221, 'Citizenship and genealogy: multi-generational Irish identities in New Zealand, Newfoundland and England'.

3 M. Bulmer and J. Solomos, 'Changing research agendas in ethnic and racial studies', *Ethnic and Racial Studies*, 31 (2008), 1192.

4 K. Kenny, 'Diaspora and comparison: the global Irish as a case study', *Journal of American History*, 13 (2003), 161.

5 *Ibid.*, 135.

6 L. Harte, 'Introduction: where is Irish Studies bound?', in L. Harte and Y. Whelan (eds), *Ireland Beyond Boundaries: Mapping Irish Studies in the Twenty-first Century* (London: Pluto Press, 2007), p.12.

7 See B. Walter, 'Whiteness and diasporic Irishness: nation, gender and class', *Journal of Ethnic and Migration Studies*, 37 (2011), 1295–312.

8 A. Brah, *Cartographies of Diaspora: Contesting Identities* (London: Routledge, 1996), p. 209.

9 For a comparative case study see B. Walter, 'Irish/Jewish diasporic intersections in the East End of London: paradoxes and shared locations', in M. Prum (ed.), *La Place de L'Autre* (Paris: L'Harmattan Press, 2011), pp. 53–67.

10 Manchester Jewish Museum, Cheetham Hill, available at www.manchesterjewish-museum.com/collection, accessed 10 May 2012.

11 Bill Williams, social historian, personal communication.

12 B. Walter, *Outsiders Inside: Whiteness, Place and Irish Women* (London: Routledge, 2001), p. 219.

13 L. Marks, *Working Wives and Working Mothers: A Comparative Study of Irish and East European Married Women's Work and Motherhood in East London 1870–1914* (London: University of North London Press, 1990).

14 L. H. Lees, *Exiles of Erin: Irish Migrants in Victorian London* (Manchester: Manchester University Press, 1979), p. 95.

15 I. Zangwill, *Children of the Ghetto* (London: Heinemann, 1892).

16 J. White, *Rothschild Buildings: Life in an East End Tenement Block 1887–1920* (London, Routledge and Kegan Paul, 1980), p.138.

17 Bill Fishman, Oral Archive, V&A Museum of Childhood, available at www.vam.ac.uk/moc/childrens lives/east end lives/Lifestories/bill fishman/index.html, accessed 1 April 2012.

18 G. O'Neill, *My East End: Memories of Life in Cockney London* (London: Penguin, 1999), pp. xxii–iii.

19 C. Bernant, *London's East End: Point of Arrival* (London: Eyre Methuen, 1975), p.147.
20 Bill Fishman, Oral Archive, V&A Museum of Childhood.
21 *Ibid.*
22 H. Srebrnik, 'Class, ethnicity and gender intertwined: Jewish women and the East London rent strikes, 1935–1940', *Women's History Review*, 4 (1995), 293.
23 Walter, 'Whiteness and diasporic Irishness', 1304–5.
24 P. Willmott and M. Young, *Family and Kinship in East London* (Harmondsworth: Penguin, 1963).
25 G. Dench, K. Gavron and M. Young, *The New East End: Kinship, Race and Conflict* (London: Profile Books, 2006), p. 18.
26 *Ibid.*, p. 15.
27 *Ibid.*, p. 24.
28 See for example G. Wemyss, *The Invisible Empire: White Discourse, Tolerance and Belonging* (Aldershot: Ashgate, 2009), p. 137.
29 V. Harman, 'Experiences of racism and the changing nature of white privilege among lone white mothers of mixed-parentage children', *Ethnic and Racial Studies*, 33 (2010), 176–94.
30 J. Ifegkunigwe, *Scattered Belongings: Cultural Paradoxes of 'Race', Nation and Gender* (London: Routledge, 1999).
31 *Ibid.*, p. 171.
32 *Ibid.*, p. 191.
33 F. Twine, 'A white side of black Britain: the concept of racial literacy', *Ethnic and Racial Studies*, 27 (2004), 885.
34 B. Walter, 'Exploring diaspora space: entangled Irish/English genealogies', in L. Harte, Y. Whelan and P. Crotty (eds), *Ireland: Space, Text, Time* (Dublin: Liffey Press, 2005), p. 174.
35 B. Walter, 'English/Irish hybridity: second-generation diasporic identities', *International Journal of Diversity in Organisations, Communities and Nations*, 5 (2005), 17–24.
36 *East is East*, dir. Damien O'Donnell (2002).
37 L. Smith, 'Lives More Ordinary', *The Guardian*, 5 October 2011, 36.
38 R. Cohen, 'Creolization and cultural globalization: the soft sounds of fugitive power', *Globalizations*, 4:3 (2007): 369–84.
39 See Walter, *Outsiders Inside*, Chapters 2 and 3.
40 For example, H. Diner, *Erin's Daughters in America* (Baltimore: Johns Hopkins University Press, 1983); M. Lennon, M. McAdam and J. O'Brien, *Across the Water: Irish Women's Lives in Britain* (London: Virago, 1988); S. Conway, *The Faraway Hills are Green: Voices of Irish Women in Canada* (Toronto: Women's Press, 1992); T. McLaughlin (ed.), *Irish Women in Colonial Australia* (St Leonards NSW: Allen and Unwin, 1998); L. Fraser, 'No one but black strangers to spake to God help me: Irish women's migration to the west coast, 1864–1915', in L. Fraser and K. Pickles (eds), *Shifting Centres: Women and Migration in New Zealand History* (Dunedin: University of Otago Press, 2002), pp. 45–62.
41 This section is based on initial findings of research funded by the British Academy Small Grant 2010–12 'Citizenship and genealogy: multi-generational Irish identities in New Zealand, Newfoundland and England'.
42 G. Handcock, *'Soe Longe As There Comes Noe Women': Origins of English Settlement in Newfoundland* (St Johns: Breakwater Books, 1989).
43 B. Patterson (ed.), *The Irish in New Zealand: Historical Contexts and Perspectives* (Wellington: Stout Research Centre for New Zealand Studies, 2002).
44 'New chances in New Zealand', *Irish Times*, 1 January 2011.

45 Handcock, *'Soe Longe As There Comes'*, pp. 23–5.

46 *Ibid.*, p. 32.

47 W. Keough, *The Slender Thread: Irish Women on the Southern Avalon, 1750–1860* (New York: Columbia University Press, 2008), available at www.gutenberg-e.org/keough, accessed 12 May 2012.

48 *Ibid.*, p. 1.

49 J. Mannion, 'Tracing the Irish: a geographical guide', *Newfoundland Ancestor*, 9 (1993), 4–18.

50 For example, Fraser, 'No one but black strangers'; C. Macdonald, *A Woman of Good Character: Single Women as Immigrant Settlers in Nineteenth-Century New Zealand* (Wellington: Allen and Unwin, 1990); A. McCarthy, '"In prospect of a happier future": private letters and Irish women's migration to New Zealand, 1840–1925', in L. Fraser (ed.), *A Distant Shore: Irish Migration and New Zealand Settlement* (Dunedin: University of Otago Press, 2000), pp. 105–16; S. McKimmey, '"A Thorough Irish Female": Aspects of the Lives of Single Irish Born Women in Auckland, 1850–1880', MA dissertation (University of Auckland, 1997); H. Mehaffy, 'A Matter of the Heart: Some Perspectives on the Cultural Identities of Female Irish Migrants in New Zealand from Vogellite Immigration to the Irish Free State', MA dissertation (University of Auckland, 2002).

51 D. H. Akenson, *Half the World from Home: Perspectives on the Irish in New Zealand, 1860–1950* (Wellington: Victoria University Press, 1990), p.197 cited in Fraser, 'No one but black strangers', p. 45.

52 Fraser, 'No one but black strangers'.

53 T. Hearn, 'The origins of New Zealand's Irish settlers, 1840–1945', in Patterson (ed.), *The Irish in New Zealand*, pp. 15–34.

54 A. McCarthy, *Irish Migrants in New Zealand, 1840–1937: 'The Desired Haven'* (Woodbridge: Boydell Press, 2005).

55 *Ibid.*, p. 7.

56 Fraser, 'No one but black strangers', pp. 45–6.

57 *Ibid.*, p. 46.

58 D. H. Akenson, *The Irish Diaspora: A Primer* (Belfast: Institute of Irish Studies, Queen's University Belfast, 1996), pp. 157–87.

59 *The Irish Empire* (2000), Clarence Pictures for RTE/BBC/SBS.

60 See for example D. Akenson, *Ireland, Sweden and the Great European Migration 1815–1914* (Montreal and Kingston: McGill-Queen's University Press, 2011), p. 7.

61 K. Sakuma, *Zainich-Korean to Zaiei-Airishu – Orudo-Kama to Tositeno Kenri: Korean in Japan and Irish in Britain – The Oldcomers and Citizenship* (Tokyo: Tokyo University Press, 2011).

62 S. Ryang (ed.), 'Introduction', in *Koreans in Japan: Critical Voices from the Margins* (London: Routledge, 2000), p. 10.

63 D. Chapman, *Zainichi Korean Identity and Ethnicity* (Abingdon, Oxon: Routledge, 2008), p. 84; J. J. Lee, *Ireland 1912–1985: Politics and Society* (Cambridge: Cambridge University Press, 1989).

64 J. Lie, *Multiethnic Japan* (Harvard: Harvard University Press, 2001), p. 51.

65 *Ibid.*, p. 2.

66 J. Lie, *Zainichi (Koreans in Japan): Diasporic Nationalism and Postcolonial Identity* (Berkeley: University of California Press, 2008), p. 81.

67 Lie, *Multiethnic Japan*, p. 111.

68 Jong-In Kim, 'In the course of mounting tension between North Korea and Japan: difficulties for zainichi Korean women who live in Japan', *Women's Asia 21 Voices from Japan*, 18 (2007), 44.

69   J. Nagle, *Multiculturalism's Double Bind* (Farnham: Ashgate, 2009) uses the term 'banal cosmopolitanism' to describe the experience of Irish difference in England.

70   Lie, *Multiethnic Japan*, p. 164.

71   K. Nagayoshi, 'Support of multiculturalism, but for whom? Effects of ethno-national identity on the endorsement of multiculturalism in Japan', *Journal of Ethnic and Migration Studies*, 37 (2011), 561–78.

72   Walter, 'English/Irish hybridity'.

73   A. M. Scanlon, 'Irish stereotypes left on the cutting room floor', *Irish Post*, 6 June 2009, 5.

74   Lie, *Multiethnic Japan*, p. 192; Ryang, *Koreans in Japan*, p. 164.

75   B. Kim, 'Bringing class back in: the changing basis of inequality and the Korean minority in Japan', *Ethnic and Racial Studies*, 31 (2008), 880.

76   Chapman, *Zainichi Korean Identity and Ethnicity*, p. 80.

77   Kim, 'Bringing class back in', 888.

78   See for example T. M. Devine (ed.), *Scotland's Shame? Bigotry and Sectarianism in Modern Scotland* (Edinburgh: Mainstream Publishing, 2000); B. Walter, 'Including the Irish: taken-for-granted characters in English films', *Irish Studies Review*, 19 (2011), 5–18.

79   Lie, *Multiethnic Japan*, p. 164.

80   M. J. Hickman, S. Morgan, B. Walter and J. Bradley, 'The limitations of whiteness and the boundaries of Englishness: second-generation Irish identifications and positionings in multi-ethnic Britain', *Ethnicities*, 5 (2005), 160–82.

81   M. J. Hickman and B. Walter, *Discrimination and the Irish Community in Britain* (London: Commission for Racial Equality, 1997), pp. 172–9.

82   Walter, 'Whiteness and diasporic Irishness', 1297.

83   Chapman, *Zainichi Korean Identity and Ethnicity*, p. 81.

84   Kim, 'Bringing class back', 872.

85   *Irish Women: Our Experience of Emigration* (London: Camden Irish Centre, 1984).

86   Ryang, 'Introduction', p. 5.

87   B. Walter, S. Morgan, M. J. Hickman and J. Bradley, 'Family stories, public silence: Irish identity construction among the second-generation in England', *Scottish Geographical Journal*, 118 (2002), 201–17.

88   Chapman, *Zainichi Korean Identity and Ethnicity*, p. 77; M. J. Hickman, 'Integration or segregation? The education of the Irish in Britain in Roman Catholic voluntary-aided schools', *British Journal of Sociology of Education*, 14 (1993), 285–301.

89   Chapman, *Zainichi Korean Identity and Ethnicity*, p. 106.

90   *Ibid.*, p. 112.

91   A. Rossiter, 'In search of Mary's past: placing nineteenth-century Irish immigrant women in British feminist history', in J. Grant (ed.) *Women, Migration and Empire* (Stoke on Trent: Trentham Books, 1996), pp. 1–30.

92   J. Devlin Trew, 'The forgotten Irish? Contested sites and narratives of nation in Newfoundland', *Ethnologies*, 27 (2005), 43–77; W. Keough, 'Creating the "Irish Loop"; cultural renaissance or commodification of ethnic identity in an imagined tourist landscape?', *Canadian Journal of Irish Studies*, 34 (2008), 12–22.

93   P. Farrell, 'On being New Zealand Irish', in Patterson (ed.), *The Irish in New Zealand*, p. 10.

8

Border crossings: *being* Irish in nineteenth-century Scotland and Canada[1]

S. Karly Kehoe

This chapter's role in a book about Irish women in the diaspora is twofold: to consider how those who entered religious communities functioned as migrants with distinct identities and to examine the extent to which their Irishness influenced the development of Catholic culture in different locations. In doing so, it presents a more nuanced understanding of the global diaspora by highlighting the extent to which national preoccupations informed the local experience. During the nineteenth century, French women entered the religious life in greater numbers than any other group, but the Irish were not far behind. Approximately 8,000 women entered Irish convents between 1800 and 1900 and by 1901 sisters and nuns represented 70 per cent of the nation's religious workforce.[2] This flood of women to the religious life extended throughout the diaspora and was a phenomenon that marked the Irish as committed Catholics who stood at the forefront of the Church's developing social welfare agenda. The extent to which their national identity was incorporated into this process depended on the priorities of the existing or indigenous Catholic churches and sharp contrasts come to light when comparing Scotland and Canada. Although each received significant numbers of Irish migrants during the nineteenth century, their relationship with the British state was fundamentally different. Both were engaged in processes of identity construction and nation-building that would have very different outcomes: Canada would evolve into a self-governing Dominion and then country in its own right and Scotland would remain as one of Britain's four constituent nations. Thus, in spite of the many similarities between the Irish and Scottish Catholics in Scotland and the Irish and French Catholics in Canada, particularly in Ontario and Quebec, it was the relationship that Catholicism had with each nation that ultimately determined the role that the Irish would play. Nation-building in Scotland and Canada would not and could not follow the same path.

In spite of Catholicism's image as a consolidated and global church with common methods of worship, clerical structures and parish or mission organisation, new research is showing that factors such as culture, ethnicity, language and gender complicate this picture.[3] Mass emigration from Ireland during the nineteenth century introduced a new dimension to Britain's imperial identity and facilitated the establishment and formation of new Catholic communities that would help to cement Britain's authority as a governing power.[4] The organisational and support networks that they established would become part of an evolving civil society that functioned as a conduit for extended citizenship. Examining the degree to which Irish ethnicity persisted within religious communities offers scholars an opportunity to understand more about the influence of local circumstances on Catholic culture as explored in the chapters by Louise Ryan and Charlotte Wildman in this volume. Religious communities spearheaded the Church's broader socio-cultural mission during the nineteenth century and created international networks in the process; their organisational structures provide useful examples of transnational institutions since a community of the Sisters of Mercy in Dublin, for example, possessed the same rule and constitutions as a community of the same name in Chicago. Differences within communities and between congregations were most noticeable (and contested) when it came to issues of ethnicity and class and so by understanding more about these distinctions scholars will be in a better position to consider the overall experience of Irish women in the diaspora.[5]

The communities highlighted here come from Edinburgh and Glasgow in Scotland and Toronto in Ontario, Canada. All three cities were strategically important to Britain's imperial programme and central to the prosperity of each nation. In Scotland, these include the French-founded Ursulines of Jesus (Edinburgh, 1834) and Franciscan Sisters of the Immaculate Conception (Glasgow, 1847), the Irish-originated Sisters of Mercy (Glasgow, 1849 and Edinburgh, 1858) and the Belgian-rooted but English-founded Sisters of Notre Dame de Namur (Glasgow, 1894).[6] In Ontario, the focus is on the Irish-founded Institute of the Blessed Virgin Mary (Toronto, 1847), also known as the Lorettos, and the Sisters of St Joseph (Toronto, 1851), founded from a French community in Philadelphia. What they all had in common was a primary focus on the education of girls and young women, despite undertaking other works of charity, such as nursing, dispensary provision and prison and poor house visitations when required. Teaching congregations like these were usually the first to be recruited into any mission and as a result played a more instructive role in the formation of religious culture. It is important to understand, however, that in addition to possessing spiritual conviction, the religious who formed these communities were also migrants, teachers, friends, relatives and women with national identities and cultural attachments.

Among women religious, like anyone else, an awareness of their sense of national belonging became acute when it was challenged or contested and to demonstrate how this was manifest in Scotland and central Canada, this chapter is divided into two parts: the first will deal with Scotland and the second will examine central Canada. Before moving on to these discussions, however, it is important to highlight some overarching points. The mass migration of Irish prompted indigenous Catholics in Scotland and French Catholics in Quebec to fear the effect that this movement would have on their religious culture and traditions. In Scotland, anti-Irish sentiment from within Scottish Catholic ranks was common and was connected to broader concerns about Scotland's identity within Britain and Catholicism's place in Scottish society. Scotland was a complex and inherently anti-Catholic nation and it was difficult for many recusants to see how the newcomers could be accommodated within its boundaries.[7] Nineteenth-century Scots defined themselves as equal and committed partners in the British union and many perceived the Irish as political and cultural subversives who threatened this image. In Canada it was a different story because its Catholic population was central to securing Britain's authority in North America. The political importance of Quebec, coupled with the security that the Catholic Church achieved through the Quebec Act of 1774 and, latterly, the British North America Act of 1867, meant that Catholicism played an active role in moulding the identity and character of the emerging nation. As a result, the authority that the Irish were able to acquire within the Church outside of Quebec during the middle decades of the nineteenth century meant that they were poised to make significant contributions to this process of nation-building.[8]

Scotland

The jump in Scotland's Catholic population from 30,000 in 1800 to 332,000 in 1880 was largely due to migration from Ireland.[9] This increase inflamed an already existing tension that had emerged in the post-Reformation period when Irish missionaries began crossing the Irish Sea to minister to Scotland's dispersed and isolated Catholics in the western Highlands and Islands.[10] In the nineteenth century, this friction became a more prominent feature of Scottish Catholicism and the indigenous clergy looked upon the newcomers with intense suspicion, believing them to possess radical agendas.[11] The vast majority of the migrants had no interest in radical politics, but there was sympathy among some Irish clergy and this put the Scottish bishops in a difficult position. As the number of Irish Catholics rose beyond the Scots clergy's ability to cope during the 1840s and 1850s, they had no choice but to draft in Irish religious personnel to help 'save' their fellow Catholics from Protestant proselytisers.[12] The ways in which indigenous or convert Catholics related to these Irish 'outsiders' was influenced by anxiety about Catholicism's precarious position in a nation dominated by hostility towards Catholicism and pervasive anti-Irish sentiment.[13] As a result, the Scots clergy tended to crack down on 'anything which smacked of a political or national feeling' among the Irish and this kind of reaction was to shape future relations between the two groups throughout the Church, including the religious communities.[14] The result was an attempt to exclude, where possible, the Irish from the governing structure of the Church and this extended into the realm of convent leadership – the ethnicity of the sisters and nuns was something that was closely scrutinised.

The first community to return to Scotland after the Reformation were the Ursulines of Jesus, who arrived from France in 1834 with two Scottish-born novices. Very much an upper-class community, they established themselves in Edinburgh and were, in many ways, removed from the ethnic tensions that plagued the Scottish mission. In Glasgow, a city with a stronger industrial base that attracted more Irish migrants, these tensions were particularly acute among those communities that drew their membership from the middling classes and divided their attention between tuition-based education for the daughters of wealthier Catholics and poor parish schools for the girls and young women destined for industrial work or cottage labour. The first of these communities, the Franciscan Sisters of the Immaculate Conception, arrived in Glasgow from France in 1847. They were followed two years later by the Sisters of Mercy who came from Limerick at the tail end of a cholera epidemic. Another Mercy foundation, also from Limerick, settled in Edinburgh in 1858. The last teaching community to arrive in Scotland's central belt were the Sisters of Notre Dame de Namur, who arrived in 1894. They moved into Glasgow's wealthy West End and established Dowanhill, Scotland's first Catholic teacher training college.

At this point, some basic demographic data about community membership is instructive. In total, 194 women entered the Franciscan community between 1851 and 1910 and the majority of sisters, 104, came from Scotland and 70 came from Ireland.[15] Glasgow's Sisters of Mercy were a diocesan community and so were naturally smaller than the Franciscan Sisters, and their records reveal that between 1849 and 1907, 19 of the 36 sisters who entered were Scottish-born (from recusant strongholds), 9 were of Irish birth, 7 were of English birth and 1 was French.[16] Interestingly, the Sisters of Notre Dame de Namur, an upper-middle-class community focused on the professionalisation of female education, had a very different composition in contrast to Glasgow's other two communities: 63 of its 110 sisters were English, 22 were Scottish (the majority were of Irish descent from Glasgow) and 20 were Irish.[17] In Edinburgh, the Ursulines saw a total of 68 women enter the community between 1832 and 1900 and of these 30 were Scottish, 16 were English and 18 were Irish. What is particularly noteworthy about these Irish-born sisters is that they only started joining in the late 1860s, more than thirty years after foundation, and were predominantly lay sisters.[18] This contrasted with Edinburgh's Sisters of Mercy where the Irish membership was comparatively small; among the 53 women who entered this community between 1858 and 1900, there were 22 Scottish sisters, 12 English sisters and 8 Irish sisters.[19] Sprinkled throughout all of the communities were women from other countries, but they were very much in the minority.

The profession lists, which provide the majority of the statistics noted above, also reveal the prevalence of sibling sets and while this is not in itself unusual, it does show how one ethnicity could dominate another by providing a block of support for a particular agenda. Almost one quarter, 22 per cent (23 women or 11 sibling sets), of the Scottish-born Franciscan Sisters were blood relatives with the majority coming from recusant pockets in the north-east and south-west as opposed to Glasgow, where there would have been a high level of Irish descent. In total, Irish siblings represented 30 per cent (21 women or 10 sibling sets) of the Irish-born membership.[20] In Glasgow's Mercy community, while there were just three Scottish sibling sets and no Irish ones, 58 per cent of all sisters came from two strands of one Kirkcudbrightshire family. During the first fifteen years of the community's foundation the Riggs and the Cavans, who were parachuted in to save the community from collapse after an acrimonious split between the founding Irish sisters and the Scottish bishops, dominated convent affairs. Representing 13 per cent of the community's total membership before 1907, these women played a critical role in securing a distinctively Scottish religious ethos among the Glasgow Sisters of Mercy.[21] Unfortunately, records of sibling sets are not available for the Sisters of Notre Dame or for the Edinburgh communities because parents' names were not recorded, but evidence of influential sibling sets exists nonetheless. One example, from Edinburgh's Mercy community, was Jane and Helen Grant who had been educated as children by the Ursulines of Jesus. They came from recusant stock and were expected to lead the Mercy community after their profession and while Jane died before she was professed, Helen did go on to become superior.[22]

Establishing a strong foundation relied as much upon ethnicity as it did upon finding women from the right social class and in this context Dundee is the exception that proves the rule. A community of the Sisters of Mercy was established there from Derry in 1859 and it was overwhelmingly Irish; only in 1870 did the first non Irish-born woman enter and only in 1888 did the first Scottish-born woman join (although she was of Irish descent). Two critical differences separate Dundee from the experience of the central belt communities and these were clerical leadership and the labour market. First, the town's senior priest, Fr Steven Keenan, was an Irishman who sought to recruit a religious community that could be filled with the 'best hearted Irish lasses' to help reform the culture of the town's Irish migrants and as a result, he was respected among Scotland's clerics.[23] Second, because Dundee was a town that relied heavily upon the labour of single women for its textile industry, Irish women congregated there. The result was an almost 100 per cent Irish-born convent membership before 1900, which makes Dundee an intriguing anomaly.

Outside of Dundee, there was a concerted effort to minimise the influence that Irish women were able to exert over convent affairs. Although convents were expected to be places where national attachments were set aside, a number of scholars show that this was not the case.[24] Ensuring the establishment of a community identity that was distinctively Scottish and, in the case of the Sisters of Notre Dame de Namur, British, meant that the community needed to be governed by women who were sympathetic to those ideas. The far-reaching influence that these women had, through their educational and social welfare activities, made them important players in the Church's efforts to consolidate Catholicism in Scotland. Often, this was accomplished by grooming Scottish women for positions of authority within the convents and these included superior, assistant superior and/or novice mistress. If possible Irish women were blocked from these positions, whereas some were discouraged from even applying for entry to a community or, if they did get in, were blackballed from progressing beyond the stage of postulant or novice. While there is no doubt that some had no vocation and instead looked to convent life as a means of achieving security, particularly in old age, others were rejected because they were Irish. Non-perseverance statistics can be particularly revealing in this respect. Deciding to leave a community could be caused by factors including wanting to transfer to a congregation with an alternative social welfare focus, illness or poor health, the lack of a suitable dowry or being broadly declared unfit for the religious life.[25] In the Franciscan Sisters' community 23 women left before profession: 12 Irish; 8 Scottish; 2 French; 1 English. The majority of the Irish (8) were declared unfit for the religious life, and in fact most were recorded as having been black-balled by failing to receive the votes needed from the community to remain, and 4 were sick. What is more, 5 of the 8 Scottish-born women rejected were of Irish descent. The convent leadership in place when the drop-outs happened is also interesting because between 1851 and 1855, when the community was led by its French foundress and plagued by clerical interference, 6 Irish women were dismissed, but only 1 Scot. Conversely, during a period of stable Irish leadership between 1857 and 1869, no Irish women were dismissed.[26]

In all the communities listed above, with the exception of Dundee, not one had a number of Irish superiors that was in proportion to their Irish member-ship and, given the small indigenous Catholic population, Scottish superiors were overrepresented. The ethnicity of the superiors is an important consideration when attempting to understand the development of a broader community ethos that would then be transferred through the day schools, evening schools and Sunday schools to children and young women. Among the Ursulines of Jesus, there were 7 superiors between 1834 and 1891 and 3 were French, 2 were English and 2 were Scottish. Edinburgh's Sisters of Mercy also had 7 superiors between 1858 and 1901 and while 1 was English and 1 was Irish, the rest were Scottish. In Glasgow, between 1849 and 1909, the Franciscan Sisters had 1 French (the foundress), 1 Scoto-Jamaican, 2 Irish and 3 Scottish superiors.[27] The Glasgow Mercies had 2 Irish, the first of which had been the original founding sister, 1 English and 4 Scottish superiors. The second Irish superior was only appointed after Charles Eyre, the English Ultramontane bishop, arrived to smooth out the city's ethnic tensions and had he not been there, it is unlikely that she would have held the post. The Sisters of Notre Dame, who arrived at the tail end of the century, had just one superior, Sr Mary of St Wilfred, between 1894 and 1910, and she was English. According to one scholar, Irish women in the Sisters of Notre Dame de Namur congregation tended to occupy the 'humble roles' which suggests an unofficial stratification despite the fact that this congregation did not have a division based on choir and lay sisters, the difference between which will be discussed in more depth in the following section.[28]

Sisters and nuns were widely recognised as assertive women whose access to international congregational networks could provide them with significant support, but individual communities were vulnerable, particularly during the early years, as they worked to establish an external base of local support. In cases where numbers were small, finances tight or foundations new, religious communities often fell prey to bishops' agendas. While some scholars have noted the departure of entire communities when confronted with a difficult priest, none of the Scottish communities were ever completely abandoned. When there was a risk of this, such as with the Glasgow Sisters of Mercy in the early 1850s, senior priests moved to fill the convent with Scottish-born women to ensure its survival. The amount of influence a bishop could exert over a community depended on whether it had a diocesan or pontifical structure. In pontifical communities, such as the Franciscan Sisters and the Sisters of Notre Dame de Namur, the positions of superior and assistant superior were elected by the community, whereas in diocesan ones like the Sisters of Mercy and Ursulines of Jesus these were appointed posts. Thus, in diocesan communities, priests could and did veto Irish choices, but in pontifical ones, where the ecclesiastical superior had no jurisdiction to remove an elected superior, his only recourse was to complain about it in his official reports.[29] On the whole, though, after 1880, as the Catholic Church began to settle into its role as a church with a defined place in Scottish society, and once the communities were comfortably established with strong educational portfolios, sufficient membership and a secure (enough) financial base, the intensity of the conflicts died down considerably. It was at this point, across the Atlantic in Canada and in stark contrast to Scotland, that an Anglo-Catholic Canadian Church, led by Irish immigrants and their descendants, was beginning to emerge in Ontario, the epicentre of the 'English' Church.

Canada

Throughout the eighteenth and early nineteenth centuries, the French had dominated Catholicism in what would become Canada. The majority lived in Quebec, albeit with a growing population in the Maritimes from the mid-1780s, and the strategic importance of this colony to the British Empire was obvious. After the Seven Year's War, Britain allowed the Catholics who lived there to build a strong and protected Church in the hope that they would provide a critical buffer against American incursions northwards. This was facilitated by the Quebec Act of 1774, an important piece of legislation that relaxed the penal laws in the colony and permitted freedom of worship.[30] Its timing, two years before the outbreak of the American Revolution, left no question as to Parliament's motives and Quebec and its population played a critical role in allowing Britain to retain a powerful foothold on the Continent after the American colonies were lost. In the nineteenth century, after the threat of American invasion subsided, Quebec's loyalty seemed to have been forgotten. After 1820 attention became focused on supplanting French cultural authority with something more Anglo-centric and the result would be the polarisation of French and English Canada. This division was replicated in the Catholic Church and the English-speaking Church was dominated by the Irish.[31] As late as 1930 Britain's Legation to the Holy See reported that the struggle between the French and Irish Canadians, which was based on 'language and orientation', remained a very serious issue.[32]

Prior to 1867 when Confederation confirmed Canada's national standing, Catholics represented approximately one half of the white population.[33] Throughout much of the century, they faced significant 'organised hostility', but as new immigrant groups arrived, language began to replace religion as the main source of tension.[34] Outnumbering all other British immigrant groups combined, the Irish emerged as the dominant force in Ontario, the province that borders Quebec to the west, because although still seen as problematic and subversive, their status as British citizens and English-speakers (by and large) made them an invaluable resource for establishing an Anglo-centric character in the emerging nation. The French, the majority of whom were Catholic, were understandably anxious about their status in an increasingly Anglophone country and feared the loss of a distinctive culture that was a blend of language, religion and tradition.[35] Representing approximately one-quarter of Quebec's urban population in 1861, the Irish were a sizeable minority there, but unlike in Ontario or in the Maritimes, they were unable to effect the same level of influence on Catholic culture. Part of the reason was that a significant number were transient people who stayed for a time in Quebec, the port of arrival, before moving on to join relatives or friends elsewhere in Canada or in the United States.[36] Ethnic tension was particularly acute along the Ontario/Quebec border and the first evidence of change came early in the nineteenth century when new, non-French Catholics began to settle there. Limited human and financial resources meant that it was becoming increasingly difficult for the Diocese of Quebec to cope with the needs of a rapidly expanding and geographically dispersed population. Alexander MacDonnel, a priest from the Highlands of Scotland, helped to bring former soldiers and their families to Glengarry County and played a leading role in having the ecclesiastical jurisdiction of Ontario transferred from Quebec to the newly created Bishopric of Kingston. Serving as Kingston's first Bishop from 1826 until his death in 1840, MacDonnel oversaw the break from Quebec's ecclesiastical authority. He had been inspired by Edmund Burke, an early Irish Catholic missionary in Ontario who had been convinced of the necessity of securing ecclesiastical independence for the English-speaking Catholics of Nova Scotia.[37] While the dominant Catholic groups at this time were French, Irish and Scottish, in Ontario the Scots faded into the background, lacking the numbers and traditional authority needed to challenge the Irish. The Irish were dominant from an early stage in Toronto and the surrounding areas and by 1867 their authority was firmly entrenched within the Church's governing structure.

Ontario's Irish population was a healthy mix of Protestants and Catholics since the immigration of both had been happening long before the Famine.[38] Numerically strong in a colony with no established or deeply entrenched religious tradition and despite intense anti-Catholicism fuelled largely by immigrants from Ulster, Irish Catholics seized the opportunity to build up and influence Catholicism in English Canada – Toronto would be its hub.[39] It was a city that had expanded rapidly after 1830 and in 1841 it became the second diocese to be created outside of Quebec. Led by Michael Power, the son of Irish immigrants in Nova Scotia, nineteen priests had served a population of approximately 50,000; 3,000 of them, representing roughly one-quarter of Toronto's population, lived within the city's limits.[40] By 1845 a cathedral was under construction (it was completed in 1848) and in 1847 the first community of women religious arrived from Rathfarnham, Ireland.[41]

The succession of Bishops reveals something of the pattern of ethnic influence and tensions in Upper Canada and the dominance of the Irish in Church governance and politics. Archbishop John Joseph Lynch, originally from Co. Monaghan, was installed after Michael Power's French successor, Armand Francios-Marie de Charbonnel, who was more suited to the contemplative life, resigned in 1860. Lynch was a pivotal figure in the development of an Anglo-Catholic identity in nineteenth-century Ontario. He prioritised the transformation of religious culture and promoted the English language thereby drawing a clear line between himself and the Francophone hierarchy in Quebec.[42] It is important to note, however, that Catholicism's cultural transformation was well underway before Lynch took up his post since the growing number of women religious had already begun to implement an extensive programme of educational and social welfare strategies with that in mind. Consolidating the Catholic community was achieved through the collective authority of those women religious who had successfully modified some of their own traditions and religious culture to 'make things work' in this new, North American mission. In sharp contrast to Scotland, even though they were spearheading a process of dramatic cultural change and adjusting to a new society, they were not under pressure to abandon or suppress their Irishness. On the contrary, it became, for the Sisters of St Joseph and the Institute of the Blessed Virgin Mary (the Lorettos), a defining feature and source of pride.

The Irish influence over the Lorettos was striking, particularly in terms of the Irish-born and descended sisters between 1847 and 1907. Over this period approximately 380 women entered the community; 72 were born in Ireland and 162 were of Irish descent.[43] The Sisters of St Joseph had a total of 308 women enter between 1851 and 1894 and of these 83 were Irish-born, and while there is no information about the parents' birthplace and so no way to accurately gauge Irish descent, a scan of surnames suggests that it was high.[44] As with the communities in Scotland, there is useful information about the prevalence of relatives within these congregations which helps to place Ontario within the broader context of religious life trends.[45] As noted above, sibling and cousin sets offered women the cooperative and collective authority needed to influence the development of Catholic culture. In total there were 6 Irish-born and 23 Irish-descended sibling sets in the Loretto congregation, with the largest set numbering 5. The Maganns, Frances, Lucy, Mary Josephine and Grace, who joined as choir sisters and were originally from Dublin, had been inspired by their older sister, Elizabeth, who went on to become superior and was widely regarded as a 'very successful teacher'.[46] Among the Irish-descended women, the largest set was the O'Connors from Pickering, Ontario. Agnes, Julia, Margaret and Mary Ann's father had come from Co. Cork and between 1846 and 1865 they all joined the Lorettos as choir sisters. Overall, there were ten sibling sets (13 women) among the Irish-born Sisters of St Joseph. Ann and Margaret Flemming were twins who had immigrated to Ontario with their family from Co. Kilkenny and had entered the congregation within three days of each other in 1854. Tragically, they died a little over a year later, one month apart, at the age of twenty-five.[47] As choir sisters, all of these women would have been destined to become teachers.

Lay sisters differed from choir sisters in that they took responsibility for the domestic work of a convent and while only two of the Scottish communities officially had lay sisters (the Ursulines of Jesus and the Franciscan Sisters), both of the Toronto congregations did, which suggests that more opportunities existed for women of limited means to enter convents there. It also shows that the religious communities emerging in Ontario, and across North America more generally were engaged in larger and much more extensive programmes of religious development and community building since no established churches or deeply-rooted religious traditions existed to prevent this growth. Lay sisters were critical to this expansion because they provided the practical support a congregation needed to enable its choir sisters to increase their influence through external works of charity. The presence of lay sisters can also help to demonstrate the extent to which Irish religious culture was influencing the development of religiosity in the new missions. Lay sisters were the direct result of the broader strategy of religio-cultural transformation that had been taking place in Ireland since the mid-eighteenth century and this process, which Mary Peckham Magray discusses in relation to Ireland, accompanied the Irish overseas.[48] Not only did entry to a convent as a lay sister offer poorer women much-needed financial and domestic security, but it enhanced their social standing and the respectability of their families.[49] One family, the Meehans from Co. Leitrim, illustrates this phenomenon and the Catholic Church's growing reach. Three of the siblings, Ellen, Margaret and Mary, entered the Lorettos as lay sisters, another is said to have joined the Sisters of St Joseph and a brother served as a chaplain in the American Civil War.[50] The networks that were forged through women's increased access to religious communities cemented the Church's foundation in North America. The significant movement of religious personnel across the Canada/United States border, as the two nations developed, is an important part of the story that needs development through more concentrated research.

There is no question that Irish women dominated many of North America's congregations and there is significant evidence to suggest that their religious identity was ethnically charged. In Toronto, much more so than in Glasgow or Edinburgh, national sympathies permeated the social welfare work that women religious undertook and this was particularly noticeable in education. Proof of this can be seen in a variety of examples, but one, the *Address of Welcome* that Sr M. Regina McLean, CSJ, wrote on behalf of the pupils of St Joseph's School in honour of the visit of O'Connor Power, an MP from Co. Mayo, in the spring of 1877, is particularly revealing. Invoking memories of the penal laws and of the Famine, the following excerpt gives a flavour of the poem's sentiment:

> The heavy cross and the thorny crown,
> Hush memory! Hush, Nor Breath again,
> That story of Famine, and woe and pain,
> And Sorrows the crowd and countless host
> – God loves the land he chastises most[51]

McLean is not listed as being of Irish birth, but she was probably of Irish descent. The invitation of an Irish politician to a Toronto elementary school is in itself significant and testifies to the Irish influence over Catholic education in the city and in Ontario more generally.[52] A visit from an Irish MP to Scotland's Catholic schools, for example, would never have been permitted. This poem was a public display of nationalist sentiment; it was an expression that was as much for McLean and her pupils as it was for the MP. Other women expressed their views privately, recording them in diaries and scrapbooks. Sr Mary O'Sullivan had entered the religious life in 1865 after attending a Loretto convent school in Ireland, probably at Rathfarnham, and had kept a scrapbook When writing about the death of Michael Power, Toronto's first bishop, from the typhus epidemic that hit the city in 1847, she wrote that her predecessors exclaimed: "'Oh my God, what crimes England has to answer for". The Bishop is dead, terrible was the blow to the nuns.'[53] This scrapbook, which remains in the congregation's Toronto archives, reveals an intimate and private connection to an imagined Ireland that was so important to the identity of North America's Irish diaspora. No similar expressions of nationalist sentiment have been discovered in any of the records viewed in the Scottish convents.

The transformation of Catholic culture, which included a reinvention of the image of the Irish abroad, meant that the Church participated in the process of nation-building by negotiating a space for itself on the urban and rural landscape that was rapidly becoming Canada.[54] Mark McGowan, whose work concentrates on the Irish in nineteenth- and early twentieth-century Toronto, explains that 90 per cent of Toronto's Catholic teaching staff came from the ranks of the religious and that from the late 1880s they were focused on producing pious and patriotic young *Canadian* Catholics.

> From 1887 to 1922, English-speaking Catholics in Toronto submerged their overt ties to Ireland, embraced many of the values of Canadian society, and allowed their faith life to make some needed adjustments to the North American environment.[55]

The research highlighted in the second section of this chapter supports this claim, but it also qualifies it. By the last decade of the nineteenth century an Anglo-Catholic culture, designed and dominated by the Irish diaspora, had been firmly established in Ontario which meant that they were secure in their position and thus free to get on with the joint responsibility of nation-building.[56]

Conclusion

This chapter has considered how the Irish female migrants, who entered religious communities, functioned as immigrants with distinct identities and it has examined the extent to which their Irishness influenced the development of Catholic culture in Scotland and Canada. Whilst both nations attracted significant numbers of Irish during the nineteenth century, each had a fundamentally different relationship with the British state and its empire and it was these relationships that shaped the responses to the Irish migrants. Scotland's inherently Presbyterian character, coupled with its deep commitment to the British union, meant that its relationship with Ireland, a nation whose population was predominantly Catholic, was complex. Although political radicalism was not on the agenda of most migrants, the fear that this 'alien' people would disrupt the indigenous Catholic tradition and inflame anti-Catholic anxiety provoked a concerted effort to limit Irish Catholic cultural influence in Scotland. In Canada, as this chapter has demonstrated, it was a different situation. Desperate to assert its authority over post-1783 British North America, Britain extended significant religious tolerance to the region's predominantly French Catholic population. During the nineteenth century, when it sought to undermine Francophone culture, Irish Catholics, who had been immigrating in significant numbers since the century's early decades, became important partners in Britain's imperial programme by securing, for the emerging Canadian nation, an English-speaking Catholic Church.

In many ways, this chapter has considered the process of nation-building and identity construction, and it has used local examples to illuminate broader trends. By comparing the experience of women religious in Scotland and Canada, it has been possible to see just how different the migrant experience could be, even within those institutions that were, for all intents and purposes, transnational. The evidence presented for Edinburgh, Glasgow and Toronto has demonstrated that concerns about ethnicity were core to the congregational and community ethos that were designed to complement perceptions of national identity. Thus, it was the case that religious communities, especially those that concentrated on education, were spaces where ethnicity was hotly contested and in both Scotland and Canada, women religious showed themselves to be active participants in the process of transforming both religious and national culture.

Notes

1 I am grateful to Terry Murphy for his helpful comments on an earlier version of this chapter.
2 M. P. Magray, *The Transforming Power of the Nuns: Women, Religion and Cultural Change in Ireland, 1750–1900* (New York: Oxford University Press, 1998).
3 P. C. Manuel, L. C. Reardon and C. Wilcox (eds), *The Catholic Church and the Nation-State: Comparative Perspectives* (Washington: Georgetown University Press, 2006). This book reveals the diversity that existed within Catholicism and the ways in which it was perceived in different countries.
4 S. K. Kehoe, 'Accessing empire: Irish surgeons and the Royal Navy, 1840–1880', *Social History of Medicine,* 63 (2013), 204–24.
5 The extent to which class was a more important consideration than ethnicity depended on local circumstances. My opinion is somewhat different to those expressed by Carmen Mangion and Susan O'Brien. See Mangion, *Contested Identities: Catholic Women Religious in Nineteenth-Century England and Wales* (Manchester: Manchester University Press, 2008) and S. O'Brien, 'French nuns in nineteenth-century England', *Past & Present,* 54 (1997), 142–80.
6 S. K. Kehoe, *Creating a Scottish Church: Catholicism, Gender and Ethnicity in Nineteenth-Century Scotland* (Manchester: Manchester University Press, 2010); S. K. Kehoe, 'Irish migrants and the recruitment of Catholic Sisters to Glasgow, 1847–1878', in F. Ferguson and J. McConnel (eds), *Ireland and Scotland in the Nineteenth Century* (Dublin: Four Courts, 2009), pp. 35–47; J. A. Watts, *A Canticle of Love: The Story of the Franciscan Sisters of the Immaculate Conception* (Edinburgh: John Donald, 2006); F. J. O'Hagan, *The Contribution of the Religious Orders to Education in Glasgow During the Period 1847–1918* (Lewiston, NY: Edwin Mellen Press, 2006); M. Dilworth, 'Religious Orders in Scotland, 1878–1978', *Innes Review,* 29 (1978), 92–109.
7 For more on the Irish in Scotland, see M. Mitchell, *The Irish in the West of Scotland, 1797–1848: Trade Unions, Strikes and Political Movements* (Edinburgh: John Donald, 1998); M. Mitchell (ed.), *New Perspectives on the Irish in Scotland* (Edinburgh: John Donald, 2008); J. F. McCaffrey, 'Irish immigrants and radical movements in the west of Scotland in the early nineteenth century', *Innes Review,* 39 (1998), 46–60; J. F. McCaffrey, 'Reactions in Scotland to the Irish famine', in S. J. Brown (ed.), *Scottish*

Christianity in the Modern World (Edinburgh: T. & T. Clark, 2000), pp. 155–75; T. M. Devine (ed.), *Irish Immigrants and Scottish Society in the Nineteenth and Twentieth Centuries* (Edinburgh: John Donald, 1991); B. Aspinwall, 'A long journey: the Irish in Scotland', in P. O'Sullivan (ed.) *The Irish World Wide: History, Heritage, Identity, Volume 5: Religion and Identity* (Leicester: Leicester University Press, 1996), pp. 146–82; Ferguson and McConnel (eds), *Ireland and Scotland.*

8 For more on the Irish outside of Quebec, see T. Murphy, 'Trusteeism in Atlantic Canada: the struggle for leadership among Irish Catholics in Halifax, St. John's and Saint John, 1780–1850', in T. Murphy and G. Stortz (eds), *Creed and Culture: The Place of English-Speaking Catholics in Canadian Society, 1750–1930* (Montreal and Kingston: MacGill-Queen's University Press, 1993), pp. 126–51; T. Murphy and C. Byrne, *Religion and Identity: The Experience of Irish and Scottish Catholics in Atlantic Canada* (St. John's: Jesperson Press, 1987); T. Punch, *Irish Halifax: The Immigrant Generation, 1815–1859* (Halifax: Saint Mary's University, 1981).

9 Kehoe, *Creating a Scottish Church*, p. 1.

10 F. MacDonald, *Missions to the Gaels: Reformation and Counter-Reformation in Ulster and the Highlands and Islands of Scotland* (Edinburgh: John Donald Publishers, 2006).

11 An obstacle to Church development, this tension cemented deep divisions that lasted well into the twentieth century. See David Ritchie, 'The Civil Magistrate: the Scottish Office and the anti-Irish campaign, 1922–1928', *Innes Review*, 68 (2012), 48–76. Works on the nineteenth century include A. Ross, 'The development of the Scottish Catholic community, 1878–1978', *Innes Review*, 29 (1978), 30–55; McCaffrey, 'Irish immigrants'; B. Aspinwall, 'Anyone for Glasgow: the strange nomination of the Rt. Rev. Charles Eyre in 1868', *Recusant History*, 23 (1996–97), 589–601; Kehoe, 'Irish migrants'.

12 D. McRoberts, 'The restoration of the Scottish Catholic hierarchy in 1878', *Innes Review*, 24 (1978), 11; B. Aspinwall, 'Catholic devotion in Victorian Scotland', manuscript of a paper delivered in May 2003 at the University of Aberdeen.

13 S. K. Kehoe, 'Unionism, Nationalism and the Scottish Catholic periphery, 1850–1930', *Britain and the World*, 4 (2011), 65–83.

14 McCaffrey, 'Reactions in Scotland to the Irish famine', p. 161; B. Aspinwall, 'The formation of a British identity within Scottish Catholicism', in R. Pope (ed.), *Religion and National Identity: Wales and Scotland c. 1700–2000* (Cardiff: University of Wales Press, 2005), p. 271.

15 Franciscan Sisters of the Immaculate Conception Archives. Obituary List and Sisters Professions & Receptions list. Although Irish migration to Scotland was strongest from Ulster, the majority had actually come from Munster (22), with Leinster being a close second (20), followed by Ulster (18) and Connaught (10).

16 It should also be noted that even though 36 women joined in Glasgow, 17 of the professed sisters (and four not professed) died as a result of the illnesses they contracted 'on the job'; typhus, consumption and cholera were the main culprits.

17 Sisters of Notre Dame Archives. This information was provided by the congregation's archivist from their central database.

18 Scottish Catholic Archives, Ursulines of Jesus Profession Book.

19 Sisters of Mercy Archives, Birmingham. List of Edinburgh Sisters.

20 FSICA, Obituary List and Sisters Professions & Receptions list.

21 There were no professions between 1907 and 1910. The Rigg family came from tenant farmer stock and their brother, George, was an influential and headstrong priest who once remarked that his family was remarkable only for 'clinging to the old faith'. SCA, FA/68/35/2. Letter from George Rigg to Grissel, autumn 1878.

22 A. X. Trail, *History of St Margaret's Convent, Edinburgh, the First Religious House Founded*

in Scotland since the So-called Reformation; and the Autobiography of the First Religious, Sister Agnes Xavier Trail (Edinburgh: John Chisholm, 1885), pp. 150–1.

23 SMA, Dundee. Letter from Stephen Keenan to M. Francis Locke, 30 March 1859.

24 O'Brien, 'French nuns', 159. C. K. Coburn and M. Smith, *Spirited Lives: How Nuns Shaped Catholic Culture and American Life* (Chapel Hill: University of North Carolina Press, 1999), p. 87.

25 All communities, bar none, would reject a woman in poor health because of the strain this would put on limited human and financial resources.

26 FSICA, Sister Professions & Receptions. This was a pontifical congregation and so elected superiors could not be removed, regardless of the bishop's wishes.

27 The three Scottish superiors came from old recusant families and ran the congregation from 1869 until 1901. They were elected after two Irish superiors had been in charge for much of the previous decade.

28 B. Walsh, *Roman Catholic Nuns in England and Wales, 1800–1937: A Social History* (Dublin: Irish Academic Press, 2002), p. 143.

29 Glasgow's Bishop Alexander Smith complained that whilst nothing was actually wrong with the Franciscan Sisters, he felt that the superior was too Irish. Kehoe, 'Irish migrants', p. 46.

30 http://avalon.law.yale.edu/18th_century/quebec_act_1774.asp,   accessed   8 November 2011. 'Sixty-five thousand persons professing the Religion of the Church of Rome' were estimated to have been living in Quebec at the time of the Act's passing.

31 T. Gallagher, 'The Catholic Irish in Scotland: in search of identity', in Devine (ed.), *Irish Immigrants and Scottish Society*, p. 33.

32 T. E. Hachey, 'Annual Report, 1930', in *Anglo-Vatican Relations 1914–1939: Confidential Annual Reports of the British Ministers to the Holy See* (Boston: G. K. Hall, 1972), p. 180.

33 There is no way to identify how many of the First Nations peoples converted to Catholicism.

34 J. R. Miller, 'Anti-Catholic thought in Canada: from the British conquest to the Great War', in Murphy and Stortz (eds), *Creed and Culture*, pp. 25–48.

35 J. A. Raftis, 'Changing characteristics of the Catholic Church', in J. W. Grant (ed.), *The Churches and the Canadian Experience* (Toronto: The Ryerson Press, 1963), p. 92.

36 R. J. Grace, 'Irish immigration and settlement in a Catholic City: Quebec, 1842–61', *Canadian Historical Review*, 84 (2003), 224–7.

37 T. Murphy, 'The emergence of Maritime Catholicism, 1781–1830', *Acadensis*, 13 (1984), 45–7.

38 B. P. Clarke, 'Lay nationalism in Victorian Toronto', in M. G. McGowan and B. P. Clarke (eds), *Catholics at the 'Gathering Place': Historical Essays on the Archdiocese of Toronto, 1841–1991* (Toronto: Canadian Catholic Historical Association, 1993), p. 41.

39 G. S. Kealey, *Toronto Workers Respond to Industrial Capitalism, 1867–1892* (Toronto: University of Toronto Press, 1980), p. 99; Grace, 'Irish immigration', 234, discusses growing Irish population in Hamilton, a city just south of Toronto; C. J. Houston and W. J. Smyth, *The Sash Canada Wore: A Historical Geography of the Orange Order in Canada* (Toronto: University of Toronto Press, 1980), p. 20, J. W. McAuley, 'Under an Orange banner: reflections on the northern Protestant experiences of emigration', in O'Sullivan (ed.), *Religion and Identity*, p. 47 and, finally, H. Senior, *Orangeism: The Canadian Phase* (Toronto: McGraw-Hill Ryerson, 1972), p. 47. Newfoundland is an exception as Orangeism was dominated by English immigrants. See W. G. Keough, 'Contested terrains: ethnic and gendered spaces in the Harbour Grace Affray', *Canadian Historical Review*, 90 (2009), 29–70.

40 C. J. Houston and W. J. Smyth, *Irish Emigration and Canadian Settlement: Patterns, Links and Letters* (Toronto: University of Toronto Press, 1990), p. 8. The Diocese of Halifax in Nova Scotia, the third established outside of Quebec, was established in 1842.

41 Entry for Michael Power in *Dictionary of Canadian Biography*, http://www.biographi.ca/009004-119.01-e.php?&id_nbr=3612, accessed 4 June 2010.

42 R. Choquette, 'The Archdiocese of Toronto and its metropolitan influence in Ontario', in McGowan and Clarke (eds), *Catholics at the 'Gathering Place'*, p. 302.

43 M. Kerr, *Dictionary of Biography of the Blessed Virgin Mary in North America* (Toronto: Mission Press, 1984). This number includes Guelph entries and is likely to be an underestimate because only the father's place of birth was recorded. Many more had Irish surnames.

44 Sisters of St Joseph Archives, Toronto, Sisters of St Joseph Reception Book (typed version) and Sisters of St Joseph Printed Obituary List. Both are held by the community's archivist.

45 In Quebec, 35 per cent of women in two congregations, the Congregation de Notre Dame and the Sisters of Misericorde, were related. M. Danylewycz, *Taking the Veil: An Alternative to Marriage, Motherhood and Spinsterhood in Quebec, 1840–1920* (Toronto: McClelland and Stewart, 1987), pp. 112–20.

46 Kerr, *Dictionary of Biography*, pp. 57–8.

47 SCSJA, Toronto, Sisters of St Joseph Reception Book. Anne died of consumption, but Margaret's cause of death was not recorded. It may have been from a broken heart for her sister.

48 Magray, *The Transforming Power of the Nuns*.

49 S. Hoy, 'The journey out: the recruitment and emigration of Irish religious women to the United States, 1812–1914', *Journal of Women's History*, 6 (1995), 70–1.

50 Kerr, *Dictionary of Biography*, pp. 123–4.

51 SCSJA, Community Annals, p. 63. Poem by Sr M. Regina McLean, 28 March 1877.

52 See for example B. Curtis, *Building the Educational State: Canada West, 1836–1871* (London, Ontario: The Althouse Press, 1988) and J. H. Love, 'Cultural survival and social control: the development of a curriculum for Upper Canada's common schools in 1846', *Social History* 15 (1982), 357–82.

53 Institute of the Blessed Virgin Mary Archives, Mary Evangelista's Black Scribbler.

54 M. G. McGowan, *The Waning of the Green: Catholics, the Irish and Identity in Toronto, 1887–1922* (Montreal: McGill-Queen's University Press, 1999), p. 58.

55 *Ibid.*, p. 7.

56 *Ibid.*, p. 132.

9

Irish Protestant women and diaspora: Orangewomen in Canada, *c.* 1890–1930

D. A. J. MacPherson

Far away across the ocean
Is the green land of my birth;
There my thoughts are turning ever
To the dearest place on earth.
Are the fields as green, I wonder,
As they were in days of yore
When I played in happy childhood
By the Blue Atlantic shore?[1]

Writing in the pages of the Toronto *Sentinel*, the self-styled 'voice' of Orangeism in Canada, Mrs Charles E. Potter from Saskatoon, articulated the complex relationship with Ireland experienced by many Orange men and women in Canada at the beginning of the twentieth century. As the threat of Home Rule loomed large, Potter felt the pull of 'old Ireland' as she called for Orange 'brothers and sisters' to fight the 'hateful yoke of Rome'. While Irish politics and identity were clearly important to Potter and the many thousands of women who were members of Canada's Ladies' Orange Benevolent Association (LOBA), by the 1920s the ethnic identification of the LOBA had become more complex, reflecting changing migration streams and the political turbulence in Ireland following the establishment of the Free State. During the interwar period, Orangewomen in Canada came from a diverse set of backgrounds, encompassing both recent migrants from Ireland, Scotland, England and elsewhere in the British world with those who were from more long-standing Canadian families. While a Scottish identity and an interest in Canadian politics came to the fore in the LOBA during the 1920s, this chapter argues that an Irish Protestant ethnicity remained central to these women's sense of identity. These Orangewomen embraced the multiple identities of the LOBA across Canada, reflecting the importance of migration and diaspora to the organisation's growth during the twentieth century. From the foundation of the LOBA in 1891 up until the 1930s, this chapter focuses in particular on the position of the organisation within the migration process and how this was part of the wider role of the Orange Order in creating a diasporic identity within the British Empire.[2] Although this sense of belonging to a global Orange world did include elements of Scottish and English identities, Orangewomen in this period appear to have continued to most closely identify with an Irish Protestantism, fed by the continuing physical process of migration and return visits to the 'old country', but also by the imaginative connections to Ireland fostered by networks of communication, most notably through the pages of the Toronto *Sentinel*.

While the Orange Order in Canada has received renewed attention from historians in recent years,[3] few have examined the experience of women in the LOBA. In their foundational study of the Orange Order in Canada, Cecil Houston and William Smyth recognise that women were members of the organisation. Despite commenting on the foundation of the LOBA in the late 1880s and how 'the sorority was to become in the twentieth century an extremely important element of Orangeism', Houston and Smyth restrict their analysis of female Canadian Orangeism to a couple of references in their overall study.[4] More recently, the work of Eric Kaufmann has been instrumental in establishing just how numerically significant the LOBA became during the twentieth century, yet his research does little to explore the activism and ideology of Canadian Orangewomen.[5] This chapter demonstrates not only that tens of thousands of women participated in the Orange Order, but also that women played a significant role in the construction of a diasporic Orange identity, connecting women in Canada with their Orange sisters in Scotland, England, Ireland and other locations throughout the British world. Equally, while the Orange Order's diasporic function and mentality has become the focus of a number of recent studies of the organisation, this analysis has been done largely from the perspective of Orangemen in Britain. For example, through institutions such as the Order's international Triennial Conference (established in 1865), the pages of the *Belfast Weekly News*, and the migration process itself, Orangemen in northern England developed a 'diaspora consciousness' from the mid-nineteenth century onwards.[6] This Orange diaspora stretched across the Atlantic world, connecting men 'institutionally, ideologically, and even emotionally, to a community that spanned the vast ocean'.[7]

This chapter builds on this debate about the Orange Order and diaspora by demonstrating that the many *women* who were members of the LOBA in Canada also thought diasporically. Moreover, it demonstrates the persistence of an Irish Protestant ethnic identification far later than historians have allowed. While Houston and Smyth rightly pin-point the Irish origins of the Orange Order in Canada during the early part of the nineteenth century, they argue that, largely due to changing migration patterns, the organisation lost much of its distinctive ethnic identity, becoming more of a pan-Protestant group. However, this analysis is based on a narrow definition of identity, rooted in place of birth, which downplays the continued traction that Irish politics and identity had in early-twentieth-century Canadian Orangeism. Furthermore, this chapter demonstrates that Orangewomen in Canada were just as diasporic in their thinking as the men. Members of the LOBA identified with Canada, England and Scotland, but overarching this was a connection to a British Protestant and Imperial world that remained focused on Ireland well into the twentieth century. Drawing on Avtar Brah's concept of 'diaspora space', this chapter considers the imagined space of the Toronto *Sentinel*. Here, Orangewomen would read about the Irish backgrounds of members of the LOBA, their visits 'back home' to Ireland and Scotland and the continuing importance of Irish politics to a sense of Orange identity in Canada.[8] Through the pages of the Orange press, Orangewomen in Canada experienced a networked sense of empire and Irish Protestant diaspora.[9]

This chapter also has important implications for broader studies of women's ethnic associational culture and their engagement with public life. It demonstrates the diversity of Canadian women's associational culture, indicating how public life was not just the preserve of women connected to feminist or socialist political organisations.[10] Furthermore, it problematises recent research on women's participation in migrant associations, which has suggested that women have been largely excluded from formal ethnic organisations.[11] I argue, therefore, that women's participation in the Orange Order not only demonstrates the diversity of women's public activism in early-twentieth century Canada, it also indicates how women were active agents in shaping the nature of the Irish Protestant ethnic community, as first, second and subsequent generation migrants. Through their work raising money for child welfare, campaigning politically against Irish Home Rule and for 'one language, one flag, one nation' in Canada, Orangewomen in Canada played an important role in the public life of the Orange community and beyond.

Female Orangeism in Britain and Canada

Women's participation in the Orange Order has been little studied by historians.[12] Not long after the foundation of the Orange Order in 1795, however, the very first female lodges had been formed in Dublin.[13] Beyond Ireland, women's Orangeism was more successful. A number of female lodges were formed in the north-west of England during the mid-nineteenth century and the organisation grew successfully, with Liverpool emerging as a particular stronghold of female Orangeism.[14] Although most historians identify 1909 as the inaugural year for the women's Order in Scotland,[15] some female lodges were formed there as early as the 1870s. Following their re-organisation in November 1909, women's lodges spread rapidly across the west central belt of Scotland and by the early 1930s, the female Order in Scotland could boast more members than their male counterparts.[16]

The female Orange Order in Canada, while not matching their Scottish counterparts in terms of numerical superiority over men, grew from its origins in the late 1880s to become an organisation of tens of thousands of women. The first ladies' Orange association in Canada was formed in December 1888 in Hamilton, Ontario. Mary Tulk, the wife of a wheel moulder and local leading Orangeman, sent letters to the members of Loyal Orange Lodge (LOL) No. 286 in Hamilton, requesting 'that they have their wives and daughters attend a meeting ... for the purposes of organising in the interests of Protestantism'.[17] The meeting was held on 12 December, drawing together 'a large number of ladies desirous of forming a society of a benevolent character, based on the principles of the Loyal Orange association', along with many Orangemen, who 'heartily endorsed' the scheme.[18] Echoing broader Victorian concern for the welfare of young women in the urban environment, the impetus for the meeting came from the influx of 'many girls coming into the city from their country homes who had no friends in the city'. This focus on public activism that was deemed appropriate for women, with its emphasis on benevolence and charity, would come to define women's Orangeism in Canada and provide it with a coherence arguably lacking in the English or Scottish female Order. However, at this first meeting, the women of Hamilton were faced with an immediate problem, raised by the County Master of the Orange Order, who 'informed the ladies that they could not organise a Ladies' Orange Lodge until authorised by the Grand Orange Lodge of British America', advising them to go ahead without 'Orange' in their title.[19]

The first meeting of the women's new organisation, to be called the 'Ladies' Protestant Benevolent Association' was held in Hamilton on 9 January 1889, drawing together over forty local women, including Miss Mary Cullum, who was voted President of the new organisation.[20] Cullum became a leading figure in the nascent women's Orange movement in Canada, spear-heading efforts to gain recognition from the men's Grand Lodge, the governing body of the organisation. The Hamilton Ladies' Protestant Benevolent Association immediately drew up a petition to be sent to that year's Grand Lodge, asking permission to call themselves the 'Ladies' Orange Benevolent Association'. Cullum and Turk, emphasising the gendered public role they expected women to play, argued in this petition that women could help the Order uphold the 'true Protestant religion', assist members 'in times of sickness and distress' and give 'aid to the orphans of deceased members'. According to Cullum and Turk, women would ensure that 'Popish doctrines' would be resisted by educating the children of Canada 'thoroughly in the Protestant Christian religion', but their petition was defeated by 'a large majority'.[21] A year later, a resolution was put to the Grand Lodge meeting in St John, New Brunswick and a committee was appointed to consider the advisability of allowing female Orange lodges in Canada.[22] The committee met the ladies in Hamilton and unanimously recommended that they be allowed to form 'Lady Orange Lodges', allowing 'our Association to perform a work of benevolence and charity hitherto performed in a very imperfect manner'.[23] In the meantime, women in London, Ontario decided not to wait for the approval of the Canadian men and, instead, became a lodge under a charter from the Ladies' Loyal Orange Association of the United States, a similar tactic to that adopted by women in Scotland who subverted their own country's Orange hierarchy by seeking warrants for female lodges through the English Grand Lodge.[24]

Having gained official Orange recognition, the LOBA grew steadily in the first twenty years or so of its existence. In 1892, it was reported at the Grand Lodge meeting of Ontario West that five lodges had been founded, in Hamilton, London and Toronto, attracting a membership of around 200 women.[25] A year later, the LOBA had grown to eleven lodges, and had been granted its own Grand Lodge, a signal achievement given that no other women's Orange organisation has achieved such official recognition of its independence from the male Order.[26] At a meeting of 'Mary Princess of Orange' LOBA No. 6 in Toronto in 1895, Mary Cullum (who was now the first Grand Mistress of the LOBA's Grand Lodge) could boast that there were over 800 members in lodges 'from New Brunswick on the east, to British Columbia in the west'.[27] Progress under the leadership of Cullum was, however, slow. In a letter to the *Sentinel*, Cullum recognised that they had been 'working slowly and steadily' since their inception, and it had required considerable effort in the organisation's early years in gaining official Grand Lodge recognition and in devising the ladies' Ritual (the set of procedures which governed Orange meetings).[28] By the time Cullum had retired as Grand Mistress in 1912, a total of 110 LOBA lodges had been formed, comprising 1,907 members.[29] Growth in the following two decades was exceptional, reflecting the dynamism of the new Grand Mistress, Mary Tulk, the increase in migration during the 1920s, and the impetus given to Orange organisation by both the First World War and the prolonged crisis over self-government in Ireland. By 1927, the LOBA could boast of 23,665 members across every province in Canada, comparing favourably to approximately 70,000 Orangemen in the Dominion.[30] However, the heartland and birthplace of the LOBA, Ontario, continued to have the greatest membership, comprising over a third of the total number of lodges (see Table 9.1).

Echoing the findings of Charlotte Wildman in her chapter in this volume on Irish-Catholic women in interwar Liverpool, the work carried out by members of the LOBA was often highly gendered, reflecting the emphasis placed upon Orangewomen's role in bringing up and educating children as good, patriotic Protestants. Within the private functioning of the Orange Order, rare minute books and reports of lodge proceedings from the Toronto *Sentinel* tell us much about the everyday activities of the LOBA, who, much like the men offered a strong mutualist benefit function, as well as providing considerable emotional support. The LOBA's engagement with more public aspects of Orange life was, however, contested, leading to heated debate at the foundation of female lodges

Table 9.1   LOBA lodges by province, 1927

Province	No. of LOBA lodges
British Columbia	34
Alberta	32
Saskatchewan	74
Manitoba	52
Ontario West	201
Ontario East	121
New Brunswick	41
Nova Scotia	24
Prince Edward Island	8
Quebec	19
Newfoundland	26
Total	632

Source: 'Remarkable Progress of the Ladies' Order', *Sentinel*, 14 July 1927.

in Canada about the presence of women at Orange events such as the 'glorious Twelfth'. Conforming to gender norms in a more obvious way, Orangewomen in Canada were enthusiastic in their philanthropic work. For many LOBA lodges, raising money for charitable causes became their principal goal, reflecting the emphasis placed upon this at the foundation of the organisation and reaching its height in the LOBA's war work and its care for orphaned children.

Migration and return visits: creating trans-Atlantic bonds

In addition to their considerable benevolent work and public activism, the LOBA also played a key role in the migration process, creating important transnational bonds across the Atlantic. The background of many LOBA members indicates the importance of Irish, Scottish and English migration to the women's Orange Order in Canada. The Irish background of Orangewomen in Canada remained prominent well into the twentieth century, indicating the continued traction of the Irish 'homeland' in the Orange world. Moreover, the membership of the LOBA continued to be shaped by migration well into the 1920s, reflecting the heightened levels of immigration to Canada during the interwar period, especially from Scotland.[31] In turn, visits to the 'old country', across the Atlantic back to Ireland, Scotland and England had, I will argue, a profound effect on the diasporic identities constructed by Orangewomen in Canada, discussed below. Through the process of migration and return visits, Orangewomen in Canada maintained important physical and imaginative connections back to the 'Motherland', creating a 'diasporic imagination'[32] not just for those who travelled but also for those who remained in Canada to hear of these trans–Atlantic adventures at lodge meetings or through the pages of the *Sentinel*.

Whereas the female Orange Order in Scotland and northern England was, like the men, the cultural product of Irish Protestant migration, in Canada, the Irish ethnicity of the organisation was, from a relatively early stage, subsumed within a 'pan–Protestant' identification.[33] However, the Irishness of many members of the Orange Order remained important to both male and female lodges in Canada well into the twentieth century. While Houston and Smyth acknowledge the importance of Irish immigration to the establishment and growth of the Orange Order in Canada, they argue that this Irish element declined in importance as the nineteenth century progressed.[34] The growth of the Orange Order in Canada was closely connected to the 'emergence and consolidation of the Second British Empire', attracting Scottish and English migrants to its ranks under the organisation's pan–Protestant British umbrella.[35] Houston and Smyth do, however, recognise that most members were of 'Irish stock', without exploring this facet of twentieth–century Canadian Orangeism in any great depth.[36]

The Irish background of a number of members of the LOBA was given prominence by the coverage of Orange affairs in the Toronto *Sentinel*. One of the founders of the LOBA, Mary Cullum, was frequently noted as coming from a good Irish family. Cullum was born in the village of Alma in Wellington County, Ontario. Her father, David Cullum, had come to Canada in 1834, leaving his boyhood home in Co. Longford, Ireland, to settle in Guelph, Ontario and soon after he joined the Orange Order in Canada.[37] Other members of the LOBA had a closer connection to Ireland, having only emigrated recently to Canada. In Ottawa, Sister Dawson, the Worshipful Mistress of LOBA No. 12, had emigrated from Coalisland, Co. Tyrone, sometime in the 1880s. Described as a 'true-bred Orangewoman', her Orange credentials were deemed to be first-rate, having escaped from the clutches of a 'Roman Catholic mob' who attempted to drown her on a Sunday school outing.[38] Sister Weir had moved to Saskatoon, Saskatchewan, in 1906, emigrating with her husband and family from Belfast to take up farming as one of the pioneers in the district. Weir was a Past Mistress of the local 'Maple Leaf' LOBA who, according to her obituary, did good work for Orange causes, raising money for the orphanage at Indian Head and speaking proudly of her loyalty to the British crown and her Irish Protestant heritage:

> With the proud strain of the "Dalardic chiefs of Ulster in her veins," a liberal education, and a clear foresight, she did much to cement loyalty in Canada to the British Crown. She was ever ready to help a good cause, more especially if it was in support of Protestantism. Veneration for the land of her birth, love for her adopted country, and the welfare of mankind was her motto. A worthy Daughter of Ulster.[39]

Such thoughts demonstrate how the era of dual identifications functioned in the early part of the twentieth century, long predating the current phrase of globalisation. The 'Ladysmith' lodge in Toronto, in particular, attracted a large number of Irish-born migrants, reflecting the city's status as the Irish-Protestant-dominated 'Belfast of Canada'.[40] At an entertainment held following a meeting of the 'Ladysmith' lodge, a rendition of 'Where the River Shannon Flows' was given by one of the members, a Sister Poole, described as 'a lady Unionist, formerly of Belfast'.[41] A Worshipful Mistress of the 'Ladysmith' lodge, Mrs Bruce, had come to Toronto in 1912, together with her daughter Elizabeth. Described by the *Sentinel* as 'Born Orange and in Ulster', Elizabeth, now Mrs Kennedy, had risen through the ranks of the LOBA to become Grand Mistress, the highest office in the organisation.[42]

While the Ladysmith lodge and others appeared to attract many Irish-born migrants, a number of LOBA lodges had members from a Scottish background. One of the founders of the LOBA, Mary Tulk, was born in Ontario, but had an Irish mother and a Scottish father.[43] One of the leading figures in the LOBA in Toronto, Jeanie Gordon, had been born in Glasgow in 1865 and emigrated to London, Ontario with her parents. On moving to Hamilton after her marriage, Jeanie became one of the founder members of the LOBA in the city, before rising to become Grand Mistress of the organisation.[44] During the 1920s, a period of intense emigration from Scotland, a number of recently arrived migrants were noted as having joined LOBA lodges in Canada. In Toronto a new lodge, 'Lady Wilson' No. 718, was founded in May 1926 with a Miss M. Miller as Worshipful Mistress. Miller, together with her mother and her sister, had recently arrived from Scotland, where they were members of FLOL No. 10 in St Rollox, Glasgow.[45] A year later, the 'Canada' lodge reported having 'two affil-iations of sisters from Scotland'.[46] Clearly, a number of Scottish women became members of the LOBA during this period. Many of these would have been from an Irish background, but the paucity of evidence makes tracing this connection back to Ireland hard to establish. However, it is possible to argue that the LOBA lodges in Canada had a role to play in the migration process, not just as 'a club at the end of the road' but also as a means of maintaining what for many of these women was a heartfelt connection back to their Orange roots in the 'old homeland' of Ireland or Scotland.[47]

Members of the LOBA in Canada also made visits back to England, Scotland and Ireland, indicating how a diasporic consciousness could also be forged through return visits to the 'old country'. Recent research has demonstrated that such return visits were by no means unusual, especially during the interwar period, and indicates that at least one of the strategies for maintaining a sense of connection with their 'homeland' was to visit Orange lodges in Britain and Ireland.[48] Discussed in further depth below, an English diasporic identity was maintained by a number of Canadian Orangewomen who made return visits to England.[49] In May 1919, the women of the 'Britannia' Lodge in Cabri, Saskatchewan, bid a fond farewell to Sister Baldwin, who was leaving Canada 'on a visit to friends in England'.[50] Other Orangewomen made journeys to the 'motherland' to visit women's Orange lodges. Ethel Easton, for example, travelled to London in the spring of 1924 from her lodge in Winnipeg to visit 'Lady Carson's' women's lodge in the 'World's Metropolis'.[51] In the 'capital of the Empire', Easton was welcomed enthusiastically by the London Orangewomen and was granted membership of the Westminster lodge.[52] Easton's visit was framed by the *Sentinel* very much in imperial terms, stressing the bonds created by the Orange Order throughout the British Empire by visiting members from across the globe:

> The widespread extension of the Orange Order throughout the Empire was further emphasised by the presence of Sister Miss Prangnell, a visitor from LOL No. 2, New Zealand. Her lucid and interesting address on the activities of Orangeism in the Antipodes was listened to with close attention, after which a profitable few minutes were spent in question and answer respecting the work of the Order in England, Canada and New Zealand.[53]

While visits to England were often presented in terms of a return to the Imperial 'motherland', visits to Ireland emphasised the Irish Protestant character of the LOBA in Canada. Travelling to Dublin in 1923, Sister Williams from the 'No Surrender' lodge in Vancouver was presented with an 'emblem LOBA pin' and a letter of introduction, to 'enable her to visit some of the lady lodges in her "Homeland"'.[54] Sailing back across the Atlantic could also take place in the context of the Orange Order's Triennial Conference. Established in 1865, this event drew Orangemen and, on occasion, women from across the Orange world to key sites of Orangeism, such as Belfast, Toronto, Glasgow and other locations.[55] The Triennial Council held in London during 1926 attracted a number of senior members of the LOBA (see Figure 9.1). At a meeting of the 'Daughters of Portadown' lodge in Toronto, the Grand Mistress, Sister Kennedy, spoke fondly of her visit to the 'Old Country' for the Triennial, where she visited lodges in England, Scotland and Ireland and went to the Twelfth July parade in Belfast.[56] Kennedy was accompanied by her successor as Grand Mistress, Mrs Stewart Adrian, from Craik, Saskatchewan, who spoke of her official role in representing the LOBA at the London Triennial.[57] After the Triennial meeting, Adrian joined her 'Scotch brothers and sisters' for a parade on 10th July and the Twelfth celebrations in Belfast two days later.[58] The Triennial Council meeting was, then, one of the most visible expressions of the Orange Order's diasporic nature and it is important to recognise that Canadian women took part during the 1920s and felt connected to their Orange sisters across the globe through such an event.

Orangewomen and diasporic identity

Demonstrating their commitment to the promotion of Orange politics and affairs in public life, members of the LOBA did engage with Irish politics and identity during the first half of the twentieth century. Centring on the Home

THE SENTINEL, JULY 27, 1926

"ORANGE DAY" CELEBRATION AT BELFAST.

Figure 9.1   Members of the LOBA at the Twelfth July Celebrations in Belfast, 1926
Source: *Sentinel*, 27 July 1926.

Rule crisis of 1912–14 and concern during the 1920s over the future of Protestant-dominated Ulster within a partitioned Ireland, Orangewomen in Canada promoted a strong diasporic Irish Protestant identity through their public, political activism. However, promoting an Irish Protestant ethnicity was only one part of Orangewomen's 'diasporic imagination' and, increasingly, we find members of the LOBA articulating English or Scottish identities through their participation in the Orange Order. In particular, the multiple and shifting sets of identities embraced by the LOBA became more complex during the 1920s, when many Canadian Orangewomen began to celebrate their Scottishness in more obvious and visible ways, reflecting the heightened levels of migration from Scotland.[59]

The crisis in Irish and British politics over the introduction of the third Home Rule Bill in 1912 provided a significant focal point for the expression of the LOBA members' diasporic Irish Protestant identity, emphasising the enduring, transnational links that bound Orange members across the Atlantic. In Ireland, women mobilised in significant numbers to demonstrate their opposition to Home Rule. The Ulster Women's Unionist Council had been formed in

January 1911, attracting a mass membership estimated at up to 200,000 women from across all classes in the province.[60] While the response of Orangewomen in Scotland to the Ulster crisis was relatively muted, the LOBA were rather more vocal in their support for their Protestant sisters in Ireland.[61] Speaking at a meeting of the 'No Surrender' lodge in Vancouver, Mary Tulk discussed her recent visit to the 'Old Land' of Ireland.[62] Tulk had taken part in the Twelfth July celebrations in Belfast, addressing a crowd of 'eleven thousand good Protestants'.[63] Demonstrating her commitment to the anti-Home Rule cause, Tulk had joined the Ulster Women's Unionist Council, whom she praised for their 'grim determination … never to accept Home Rule'.[64] Other LOBA lodges across Canada echoed Tulk's commitment to Ulster. To commemorate the signing of the Ulster Covenant on 28 September, the women of 'Boyne Jubilee' lodge in Montreal decided to hold an 'Ulster Day' church service.[65] As the Ulster crisis intensified, a number of lodges used their meetings to pass resolutions against Home Rule and suggest practical ways of helping their Orange sisters in Ireland. In Winninpeg, for example, the women of 'Rising Star' LOBA No. 62 declared their support for 'the male members of the Orange Association in the fight against the ascendancy of the Home Rule party in Ireland', adding that they were prepared to supply a nurse 'in the event of a regiment or regiments being sent from Winnipeg to Ireland'.[66] At the end of 1913, the *Sentinel* carried an extensive article by Irene Clare, a member of the LOBA, exhorting Orangewomen to fight for the Protestant cause against the threat of Home Rule and undergo medical training 'in case her nursing services and ministrations should be needed at home or abroad'.[67]

When the question of Ulster's status within Ireland arose again in the early 1920s, Orangewomen in Canada once more demonstrated their commitment to Irish Protestant politics. As the newly founded Free State plunged into Civil War in 1922, Unionists in the equally novel Northern Ireland feared that partition was merely a temporary precursor to being subsumed within a Catholic Irish state.[68] In Canada, members of the LOBA raised funds to provide for potential refugees from any conflict that might break out in Northern Ireland. At a meeting of the 'Britannia' lodge in Winnipeg, Sister McKee presented a 'plea for the assistance on behalf of distressed Loyalists in the Emerald Isle', to which the sisters responded by raising $10.[69] A number of other LOBA lodges also raised funds to support their Orange brethren and sisters in Ulster, such as the 'McCormack' lodge in Toronto collecting money 'to add to the fund being sent for the orphans in Ireland'.[70] While members of the Beeton LOBA donated $20 to the Ulster Relief Fund, this figure is relatively insignificant compared with the lodge's raising over $225 for the Orange Orphans Home in Richmond Hill.[71] This suggests that, while Irish political issues continued to have traction among many members of the LOBA during the 1920s, their priority lay with benevolent work and fundraising for charitable causes. The relative unimportance of Irish issues among the LOBA echoed the experience of other Orange associations outside of Ireland, where politics was less red in tooth and claw and less of an everyday issue.[72]

Identification with an *Irish* Protestantism was also becoming more problematic, given both the emergence of a firmly Ulster Unionist identity and the growing strength of Scottish identity within the Canadian Orangewomen during the 1920s.[73] The contested nature of an Irish Protestant identity was made clear at a meeting of the 'Daughters of Portadown' lodge in 1922 where, during an evening's entertainment, the Worthy Mistress was praised for making everyone feel at home 'in her usual Irish (I mean Ulster) style'.[74] As an Ulster identity gained greater prominence, so too did a sense of Scottishness within the LOBA. The 'Liberty' LOBA lodge in Winnipeg took the lead in holding Burns' nights, being the first women's lodge in Canada to organise an event that symbolised Scottishness for many Scots abroad. Aptly taking place in Scott Memorial Hall, over 300 people sat down for 'a menu entirely Scottish in which the Haggis played a prominent part'.

This event was, though, far more than simply a straightforward expression of the Scottishness of the LOBA in Winnipeg. After feasting and music, various Orangemen and women delivered 'anecdotes on the Scotch and Irish', while one speaker recognised the multi-ethnic nature of their entertainment and the LOBA in Winnipeg: 'Although this is Burns' Night, I gather there are a good many Irish present, but we Irish are generous sometimes, and honor the Scotch.'[75] Other expressions of Scottish identity by the LOBA took on a similarly cultural imprint. At an evening's 'whist drive and dance', the 'Ulster' lodge in Vancouver, the Orange sisters were entertained by 'a selection of Highland dance in costume' given by one of the ladies.[76] At a meeting of the 'Ladysmith' lodge in Toronto, the Scottish entertainment was connected directly to the activities of Orangewomen in Scotland. Inspired by 'the Highland dancing of the lassie, Miss Marion Smith', Jeanie Gordon talked at length about the success of the women's Order in Scotland, where 'in Glasgow alone there are sixty Orange lodges'.[77]

While Irish and Scottish ethnicities were clearly prominent within the LOBA and informed a strong sense of diasporic identity, some Orangewomen in Canada also articulated an attachment to a sense of Englishness. Some members of the LOBA combined their Orange commitments with involvement in the associational culture of the English diaspora in Canada. In Toronto, for example, Lillian Collins was not only Mistress of the 'Lady Russell' LOBA lodge, she was also an active member of the Maids of England and the Daughters of England, two groups dedicated to the maintenance of an English diasporic culture in Canada.[78] Moreover, the 'Imperial' LOBA lodge held an 'English Night' in March 1927, the members enjoying 'a programme of a strictly English character'.[79]

For members of the LOBA in Canada, then, their Irish Protestant diasporic consciousness was tempered by both Scottish and English identities. However, the Orange Order gave these women an institutional framework within which to reconcile their individual, multiple identities. The Orange Order across the globe articulated a deep commitment to the British Empire that was also entirely compatible with an Irish or Scottish identity in Canada.[80] The women of the LOBA certainly identified their Orangeism with the aims of the British Empire, frequently using the rhetoric of working under an Imperial flag to make sense of their activities in Canada. In the midst of the First World War (in itself, inter-preted as an imperial war by many in Canada and elsewhere in the Empire), Mary Tulk spoke about the women of Princeton, British Columbia, who wrote to her requesting to set-up an LOBA lodge 'to rally under the banner of Orangeism and stand together for our Flag and Empire'.[81] Furthermore, as we have already seen, at the 'No Surrender' LOBA lodge in Vancouver, the women framed their considerable public activism, on municipal authority committees and the like, in imperial terms.[82]

By the 1930s, the LOBA in Canada had, then, become a more multi-ethnic organisation, encompassing a pan-Protestant identity. Canadian Orangewomen, however, still retained a strong sense of Irish identity, reflecting the Irish background of many of its members and the continuing importance of migration, if not at the levels of the nineteenth century. The LOBA maintained an Irish Protestant identity that was diasporic, engaging in efforts to support their Orange sisters and brethren during the Home Rule crisis and the debate about the status of Ulster following partition in 1922. Moreover, return visits to the Orange 'homeland' were vital in creating a sense of 'diasporic consciousness', not just to those who physically travelled but also to Orangewomen who remained in Canada to hear about these events through the pages of the *Sentinel*. Orange jamborees such as the 1926 Triennial Conference in London and Twelfth July parades in Glasgow and Belfast were at the heart of this Orange diaspora. Here, the notion of 'diaspora space' can help us to understand how these women felt themselves to be part of an Orange diaspora. While Avtar Brah uses the term to denote how Britain has become a 'diaspora space', bringing together different migrant and non-migrant populations to create hybrid identities, in this chapter we can see how an imagined 'diaspora space' was created in the pages of the Toronto *Sentinel*, linking its readers with their Orange sisters across the globe and fostering a sense of diasporic connection to the 'old country'. While a Scottish identity became increasingly important during the 1920s, reflecting renewed migration streams from Scotland, Canadian Orangewomen's diasporic thinking continued to be shaped by the Irish Protestant background of many LOBA members. The Orange diaspora, focused on an Irish Protestant identity, retained its traction in Canadian society well into the twentieth century and, as the LOBA demonstrate, it had a strong gender dimension, in which women connected with their Orange sisters 'back home' in Ireland and Scotland.

Notes

1 Mrs Charles L. E. Potter, 'What we have, we hold', *Sentinel*, 3 October 1912.
2 The idea of an 'Orange diaspora' has been most clearly explored in the work of Don MacRaild. See, for a recent example, *The Irish Diaspora in Britain, 1750–1939* (Basingstoke: Palgrave Macmillan, 2010), especially pp. 209–12.
3 See, for example, D. A. Wilson (ed.), *The Orange Order in Canada* (Dublin: Four Courts Press, 2007) and D. M. MacRaild, 'Wherever Orange is worn: Orangeism and Irish migration in the nineteenth and early twentieth centuries', *Canadian Journal of Irish Studies*, 28/29 (2002–2003), 98–117.
4 C. J. Houston and W. J. Smyth, *The Sash Canada Wore: A Historical Geography of the Orange Order in Canada* (Toronto: University of Toronto Press, 1980), pp. 90–1, 133.
5 E. Kaufmann, 'The Orange Order in Ontario, Newfoundland, Scotland and Northern Ireland: a macro-social analysis', in Wilson (ed.), *The Orange Order in Canada*, pp. 42–68. In the same volume, Mark McGowan rightly identifies the need for further scholarly study of the LOBA in Canada. See M. G. McGowan, 'Where goes the parade? Some directions for the study of the Orange Lodge in Canada', in Wilson (ed.), *The Orange Order in Canada*, pp. 198–9.
6 D. M. MacRaild, *Faith, Fraternity and Fighting: The Orange Order and Irish Migrants in Northern England, c. 1850–1920* (Liverpool: Liverpool University Press, 2005), p. 296. The *Belfast Weekly News* was the weekly edition of the *Belfast News-letter* and contained reports of meetings in Orange outposts throughout the world. MacRaild describes how the paper functioned as 'some kind of chatroom' for Orangemen overseas during the Victorian and Edwardian periods, providing 'a vital conduit of communication between diasporic lodges and the homeland of Ireland'. See MacRaild, *Faith, Fraternity and Fighting*, p. 308 and D. M. MacRaild, '"Diaspora" and "transnationalism": theory and evidence in explanation of the Irish world-wide', *Irish Economic and Social History*, 33 (2006), 57.
7 J. Harland-Jacobs, '"Maintaining the connexion": Orangeism in the British North Atlantic World, 1795–1844', *Atlantic Studies*, 5 (2008), 28, 41.
8 Brah argues that the concept of 'diaspora space foregrounds the entanglement of genealogies of dispersion with those of "staying put".' A. Brah, *Cartographies of Diaspora: Contesting Identities* (London: Routledge, 1996), p. 16. For a useful discussion of the different social spaces and networks inhabited physically and imaginatively by Irish migrants in Buffalo and Toronto, see W. Jenkins, 'Deconstructing diasporas: networks and identities among the Irish in Buffalo and Toronto, 1870–1910', *Immigrants and Minorities*, 23 (2005), 359–98.
9 G. B. Magee and A. Thompson, *Empire and Globalisation: Networks of People, Goods and Capital in the British World, c. 1850–1914* (Cambridge: Cambridge University Press, 2010), p. 15.
10 For recent work on non-radical Canadian women's public activism, see M. Kechnie, *Organising Rural Women: The Federated Women's Institutes of Ontario, 1897–1919* (Montreal and Kingston: McGill-Queen's University Press, 2003); C. J. Dennison, 'Housekeepers of the community: the British Columbia Women's Institutes, 1909–1946', in M. R. Welton (ed.), *Knowledge for the People: The Struggle for Adult Learning in English-Speaking Canada, 1828–1973* (Toronto: OISE Press, 1987); L. M. Ambrose and M. Kechnie, 'Social control or social feminism? Two views of the Ontario Women's Institutes', *Agricultural History*, 73 (1999), 222–37; J. Fingard and J. Guildford (eds), *Mothers of the Municipality: Women, Work, and Social Policy in Post-1945 Halifax* (Toronto: University of Toronto Press, 2005); L. M. Ambrose, 'Our last frontier: imperialism and northern Canadian rural women's organisations', *Canadian Historical Review*, 82 (2005), 257–84; P. G. Mackintosh, 'Scrutiny in the city: the

domestic public culture and the Toronto Local Council of Women at the turn of the twentieth century', *Gender, Place and Culture*, 12 (2005), 29–48.

11 M. Schrover and F. Vermeulen, 'Immigrant organisations', *Journal of Ethnic and Migration Studies*, 31 (2005), 827.

12 For brief discussions of female Orangeism, see MacRaild, *Faith, Fraternity and Fighting*, p. 109, pp. 130–41; D. Fitzpatrick, 'Exporting brotherhood: Orangeism in South Australia', *Immigrants and Minorities*, 23 (2005), 277–310; W. Jenkins, 'Views from "the hub of Empire": Loyal Orange Lodges in early-twentieth-century Toronto', in Wilson (ed.), *The Orange Order in Canada*, pp. 128–45. For recent studies of women in the Orange Order see D. A. J. MacPherson and D. M. MacRaild, 'Sisters of the brotherhood: female Orangeism on Tyneside in the late nineteenth and early twentieth centuries', *Irish Historical Studies*, 35 (2006), 40–60; D. A. J. MacPherson, 'Migration and the female Orange Order: Irish Protestant identity, diaspora and empire in Scotland, 1909–40', *Journal of Imperial and Commonwealth History*, 40 (2012), 619–24.

13 'An Ulsterman's Letter', *Belfast Weekly News* (hereafter *BWN*), 5 January 1933. In 1801 there were at least eight female Orange lodges in Dublin. The warrant for Lodge No. 8 is held at the headquarters of the Orange Order in Ireland, Schomberg House, Belfast.

14 See MacRaild, *The Irish Diaspora in Britain*, pp. 106–8. The early success of female Orangeism in northern England was recognised by members of LOBA No. 714, in Creemore, Ontario at a meeting in May 1927. One of the members, Sister Best, had returned from a trip to England, where she had visited the first women's lodge to be formed in Preston and received a 'beautiful cup'. See 'Creemore, Ont., Ladies are highly honored', *Sentinel*, 19 May 1927.

15 E. McFarland, *Protestants First: Orangeism in Nineteenth-Century Scotland* (Edinburgh: Edinburgh University Press, 1990), p. 112; G. Walker, 'The Orange Order in Scotland between the wars', *International Review of Social History*, 37 (1992), 203.

16 E. Kaufmann, *Orange Order Membership Data with a Focus on Ireland, Canada and Scotland, 1852–2002* SN: 4916 (Colchester: UK Data Archive, 2002).

17 'Ladies Orange Benevolent Association', *Sentinel*, 3 July 1923; RG31, Census of Canada, 1891, District 72, Hamilton, Ontario, p. 29.

18 'The Orange Order', *Hamilton Spectator*, 14 December 1898.

19 'Ladies Orange Benevolent Association', *Sentinel*, 3 July 1923. For similar work performed by other women's organisations in Canada, see the account of the Girls' Friendly Society (formed in Canada in 1882) in L. Chilton, *Agents of Empire: British Female Migration to Canada and Australia, 1860–1930* (Toronto: University of Toronto Press, 2007) and M. Kohli, *The Golden Bridge: Young Immigrants to Canada, 1833–1939* (Toronto: Natural Heritage, 2003), p. 335.

20 'A new society', *Hamilton Spectator*, 11 January 1889.

21 *Report of the Proceedings of the Thirtieth Annual Meeting of the Right Worshipful and Provincial Grand Orange Lodge of Ontario West 1889* (Toronto, 1889), p. 27; 'Ladies Orange Benevolent Association', *Sentinel*, 3 July 1923.

22 *Report of the Most Worshipful Grand Orange Lodge of British America 1890* (Toronto, 1890), p. 33.

23 *Report of the Sixty-Second Meeting of the Most Worshipful Grand Orange Lodge of British America 1891* (Toronto, 1891), p. 61.

24 Mrs Thomas Davidson, 'The Ladies heaven bless them', *Sentinel*, 30 June 1892. For the foundation of female Orange lodges in Scotland under warrants from England, see D. A. J. MacPherson, 'The emergence of women's Orange lodges in Scotland:

gender, ethnicity and women's activism, 1909–1940', *Women's History Review*, 22 (2013), 51–74.

25 *Report of the Proceedings of the Thirty-Second Annual Meeting of the Right Worshipful the Provincial Grand Orange Lodge of Ontario West 1892* (Toronto, 1892), p. 39.

26 'Ladies' Orange Benevolent Association', *Sentinel*, 3 July 1923.

27 'Ladies' Orange Association', *Sentinel*, 21 March 1895.

28 'Ladies' Orange Association', *Sentinel*, 28 March 1895.

29 'Grand Lodge Meeting', *Sentinel*, 6 June 1912; 'Remarkable progress of the Ladies' Order', *Sentinel*, 14 July 1927.

30 'Remarkable progress of the Ladies' Order', *Sentinel*, 14 July 1927. Based on membership subscription data for 1929, Eric Kaufmann estimates there were 68,904 active Orangemen in Canada, comprising almost 50 per cent of the world's entire Orange membership. See Kaufmann, *Orange Order Membership Data*.

31 For the extensive migration from Scotland to Canada during the interwar period, see A. McCarthy, *Personal Narratives of Irish and Scottish Migration, 1921–65: 'For Spirit and Adventure'* (Manchester: Manchester University Press, 2007), p. 227; M. Harper and N. J. Evans, 'Socio-economic dislocation and inter-war emigration to Canada and the United States: a Scottish snapshot', *Journal of Imperial and Commonwealth History*, 34 (2006), 529–52; M. Harper, *Emigration from Scotland Between the Wars: Opportunity or Exile?* (Manchester: Manchester University Press, 1998).

32 M. F. Jacobsen, *Special Sorrows: The Diasporic Imagination of Irish, Polish, and Jewish Immigrants in the United States* (Cambridge, Mass.: Harvard University Press, 1995).

33 MacRaild, *Faith, Fraternity and Fighting*, pp. 14, 293. For the Irish background of the Orange Order in Scotland, see McFarland, *Protestants First*, pp. 103–6 and Kaufmann, 'The Orange Order in Ontario, Newfoundland, Scotland and Northern Ireland', p. 56. Kaufmann uses census data from 1881 to determine that 72 per cent of Scottish Orange lodge secretaries were Irish-born.

34 Houston and Smyth, *The Sash Canada Wore*, p. 91.

35 C. J. Houston and W. J. Smyth, 'The faded sash: the decline of the Orange Order in Canada, 1920–2005', in Wilson (ed.), *The Orange Order in Canada*, p. 171, 175.

36 *Ibid.*, p. 175.

37 *Ibid.*, p. 171; C. J. Houston and W. J. Smyth, *Irish Emigration and Canadian Settlement* (Toronto: University of Toronto Press, 1990).

38 'A successful Ladies' Lodge', *Sentinel*, 10 January 1895.

39 'Worthy Daughter of Ulster Passes', *Sentinel*, 23 February 1926.

40 For a critical discussion of Toronto's nickname 'Belfast of Canada', see W. M. Jenkins, 'Social and Geographical Mobility Among the Irish in Canada and the United States: A Comparative Study of Toronto, Ontario, and Buffalo, New York, 1880–1910', PhD dissertation (University of Toronto, 2001) and W. Jenkins, 'Identity, place, and the political mobilisation of urban minorities: comparative perspectives on Irish Catholics in Buffalo and Toronto 1880–1910', *Environment and Planning D: Society and Space*, 25 (2007), 170.

41 'Ladysmith', *Sentinel*, 25 September 1913.

42 'Honors and a birthday', *Sentinel*, 8 December 1925.

43 RG31, Census of Canada, 1891, District 72, Hamilton, Ontario.

44 'Thousands mourn for Grand Mistress LOBA', *Sentinel*, 16 October 1923.

45 'Another new Ladies' Lodge', *Sentinel*, 18 May 1926.

46 'Canada Lodge Ladies paid a visit to Oshawa', *Sentinel*, 2 June 1927.

47 MacRaild, *Faith, Fraternity and Fighting*, p. 148.

48 See the section on 'homecoming as tourism' in M. Harper and S. Constantine,

Migration and Empire (Oxford: Oxford University Press, 2010), pp. 333–6. See also McCarthy, *Personal Narratives*, pp. 204–8.

49 For recent research on the 'English Diaspora', see T. Bueltmann and D. M. MacRaild, 'Globalising St George: English associations in the Anglo-World to the 1930s', *Journal of Global History*, 7 (2012), 79–105.

50 'Farewell to Sister Baldwin', *Sentinel*, 29 May 1919.

51 'Miss Ethel Easton given reception', *Sentinel*, 29 April 1924.

52 'Miss Ethel Easton honored in London', *Sentinel*, 4 March 1924.

53 *Ibid.*

54 'No Surrender, Vancouver', *Sentinel*, 3 July 1923.

55 For the functioning of the Triennial Council, see D. M. MacRaild, 'Networks, communication and the Irish Protestant diaspora in northern England, c. 1860–1914', *Immigrants and Minorities*, 23 (2005), 317–18.

56 'Daughters of Portadown observe 11th Anniversary', *Sentinel*, 30 September 1926.

57 'Saskatchewan Ladies elect Mrs J. L. Spence R. W. Grand Mistress', *Sentinel*, 17 March 1927.

58 'M. W. Grand Mistress is honored by Toronto Past Mistresses', *Sentinel*, 21 July 1927.

59 For the multiple and overlapping sets of ethnic identities held by Orangewomen during the twentieth century, see D. A. J. MacPherson, 'Personal narratives of family and ethnic identity: Orangewomen in Scotland and England, c. 1940–2010', *Immigrants and Minorities* (2013). For an important article on how ethnic identities can shift and 'mutate', see A. O'Day, 'A conundrum of Irish diasporic identity: mutative ethnicity', *Immigrants and Minorities*, 27 (2009), 317–39.

60 D. Urquhart, *Women in Ulster Politics 1890–1940: A History Not Yet Told* (Dublin: Irish Academic Press, 2000), p. 57, 61.

61 For the limited response to the Home Rule crisis by female members of the Orange Order in Scotland, see MacPherson, 'The emergence of female Orange lodges in Scotland'. Orangewomen in Scotland did, however, give considerable sums of money to the Carson Defence Fund, established to raise funds for the nascent Ulster Volunteer Force.

62 'No Surrender Lodge, Vancouver', *Sentinel*, 28 November 1912.

63 'British Columbia', *Sentinel*, 23 January 1913.

64 'No Surrender Lodge, Vancouver', *Sentinel*, 28 November 1912.

65 'Boyne Jubilee Lodge, No. 26', *Sentinel*, 31 July 1913. Over half a million people signed the Ulster Covenant (for men) or the Ulster Declaration (for women). Most of these were in Ulster and, according to the Public Record Office Northern Ireland's database of signatories, only 56 people signed the document in Canada. See PRONI, 'The Ulster Covenant', available at www.proni.gov.uk/index/search_the_archives/ulster_covenant.htm, accessed 19 February 2012. For the limited success of the Ulster Volunteer Force in Canada, see MacRaild, *Faith, Fraternity and Fighting*, p. 317.

66 'LOBA urges a strong public school policy', *Sentinel*, 23 October 1913.

67 Irene Clare, 'A stirring call to Protestant women', *Sentinel*, 25 December 1913.

68 For Northern Ireland Unionist fears over partition, especially concerning the Craig-Collins pact in 1922, see P. Bew, *Ireland: The Politics of Enmity 1789–2006* (Oxford: Oxford University Press, 2007), p. 426.

69 'Britannia Lodge, Winnipeg', *Sentinel*, 28 March 1922.

70 'McCormack No. 191', *Sentinel*, 10 October 1922.

71 'Beeton Ladies gave over $225 to orphanage in year', *Sentinel*, 15 January 1924.

72 For a discussion of the lesser importance of Irish politics for Orangemen in the north of England, see MacRaild, *Faith, Fraternity and Fighting*, chapter 7.

73 For the growing strength of an Ulster Unionist identity during the early part of the twentieth century, see I. McBride, 'Ulster and the British problem', in R. English and G. Walker (eds), *Unionism in Modern Ireland: New Perspectives on Politics and Culture* (Basingstoke: Macmillan, 1996), pp. 7–11 and J. Loughlin, 'Creating "a social and geographical fact": regional identity and the Ulster question, 1880–1920', *Past and Present*, 195 (2007), 159–96.

74 'Daughters of Portadown, 212', *Sentinel*, 17 October 1922.

75 'Honor Scotland's Immortal Bard', *Sentinel*, 4 March 1924. For the importance of Burns' nights to diasporic Scottish identity, see T. Bueltmann, '"The image of Scotland which we cherish in our hearts": Burns anniversary celebrations in colonial Otago', *Immigrants and Minorities*, 30 (2012), 79–97.

76 'Ulster LOBA No. 121', *Sentinel*, 14 December 1920.

77 'Ladysmith No. 8 Had a Great Night', *Sentinel*, 5 October 1920.

78 'Youngest Orange Mistress married', *Sentinel*, 19 July 1921. For the activities of an English diaspora in Canada, see B. S. Elliott, 'Community life', in *Multicultural Canada*, available at http://multiculturalcanada.ca/Encyclopedia/A-Z/e3/11, accessed 19 February 2012. For the utility of the concept of 'diaspora' to English-speaking Canada, see D. H. Akenson, 'The historiography of English-speaking Canada and the concept of diaspora: a sceptical appreciation', *Canadian Historical Review*, 76 (1995), 377–409.

79 'Imperial LOBA No. 3 hold an English night', *Sentinel*, 24 March 1927.

80 For the significance of the British Empire to Orangeism during the nineteenth and early twentieth century, see G. Walker, 'Empire, religion and nationalism in Scotland and Ulster before the First World War', in I. Wood (ed.), *Scotland and Ulster* (Edinburgh: Mercat Press, 1994), p. 97. For the proliferation of multiple identities in Canada within an imperial context, see P. Buckner, *Canada and the British Empire* (Oxford: Oxford University Press, 2008), pp. 82–4.

81 'Mrs G. O. Akerly, St John, Grand Mistress, LOBA', *Sentinel*, 5 August 1915.

82 'No Surrender, Vancouver, a Flourishing LOBA Lodge', *Sentinel*, 20 April 1926. For the operation of pan-British Protestant identity in the context of nineteenth-century Newfoundland, see W. G. Keough, 'Contested terrains: ethnic and gendered spaces in the Harbour Grace affair', *Canadian Historical Review*, 90 (2009), 53. The LOBA's belief in and support of the British Empire also enabled them to engage in a number of aspects of Canadian politics, raising the possibility that women's participation in the Orange Order also fostered a Canadian identity.

Index